PUBLISHED

Jane Austen: *Emma* DAVID LODGE

Jane Austen: *'Northanger Abbey' & 'Persuasion'* B.C. SOUTH

Jane Austen: *'Sense and Sensibility', 'Pride and Prejudice' &*
  B.C. SOUTHAM

Beckett: *Waiting for Godot* RUBY COHN

William Blake: *Songs of Innocence and Experience* MARGARET B

Charlotte Brontë: *'Jane Eyre' & 'Villette'* MIRIAM ALLOTT

Emily Brontë: *Wuthering Heights* MIRIAM ALLOTT

Browning: *'Men and Women' & Other Poems* J.R. WATSON

Bunyan: *The Pilgrim's Progress* ROGER SHARROCK

Chaucer: *Canterbury Tales* J.J. ANDERSON

Coleridge: *'The Ancient Mariner' & Other Poems* ALUN R. JONES & WILLIAM TYDEMAN

Congreve: *Comedies* PATRICK LYONS

Conrad: *'Heart of Darkness', 'Nostromo' & 'Under Western Eyes'* C.B. COX

Conrad: *The Secret Agent* IAN WATT

Dickens: *Bleak House* A.E. DYSON

Dickens: *'Hard Times', 'Great Expectations' & 'Our Mutual Friend'* NORMAN PAGE

Dickens: *'Dombey and Son' & 'Little Dorrit'* ALAN SHELSTON

Donne: *Songs and Sonets* JULIAN LOVELOCK

George Eliot: *Middlemarch* PATRICK SWINDEN

George Eliot: *'The Mill on the Floss' & 'Silas Marner'* R.P. DRAPER

T.S. Eliot: *Four Quartets* BERNARD BERGONZI

T.S. Eliot: *'Prufrock', 'Gerontion', 'Ash Wednesday' & Other Shorter Poems*
  B.C. SOUTHAM

T.S. Eliot: *The Waste Land* C.B. COX & ARNOLD P. HINCHLIFFE

T.S. Eliot: *Plays* ARNOLD P. HINCHLIFFE

Henry Fielding: *Tom Jones* NEIL COMPTON

E.M. Forster: *A Passage to India* MALCOLM BRADBURY

William Golding: *Novels 1954-64* NORMAN PAGE

Hardy: *The Tragic Novels* R.P. DRAPER

Hardy: *Poems* JAMES GIBSON & TREVOR JOHNSON

Hardy: *Three Pastoral Novels* R.P. DRAPER

Gerard Manley Hopkins: *Poems* MARGARET BOTTRALL

Henry James: *'Washington Square' & 'The Portrait of a Lady'* ALAN SHELSTON

Jonson: *Volpone* JONAS A. BARISH

Jonson: *'Every Man in his Humour' & 'The Alchemist'* R.V. HOLDSWORTH

James Joyce: *'Dubliners' & 'A Portrait of the Artist as a Young Man'* MORRIS BEJA

Keats: *Odes* G.S. FRASER

Keats: *Narrative Poems* JOHN SPENCER HILL

D.H. Lawrence: *Sons and Lovers* GAMINI SALGADO

D.H. Lawrence: *'The Rainbow' & 'Women in Love'* COLIN CLARKE

Lowry: *Under the Volcano* GORDON BOWKER

Marlowe: *Doctor Faustus* JOHN JUMP

Marlowe: *'Tamburlaine the Great', 'Edward the Second' & 'The Jew of Malta'*
  JOHN RUSSELL BROWN

Marvell: *Poems* ARTHUR POLLARD

Milton: *Paradise Lost* A.E. DYSON & JULIAN LOVELOCK

O'Casey: *'Juno and the Paycock', 'The Plough and the Stars' & 'The Shadow of a Gunman'* RONALD AYLING

Eugene O'Neill: *Three Plays* NORMAND BERLIN

John Osborne: *Look Back in Anger* JOHN RUSSELL TAYLOR

Three Jacobean Revenge Tragedies

The Revenger's Tragedy

Women Beware Women

The Changeling

A CASEBOOK

EDITED BY

R. V. HOLDSWORTH

MACMILLAN

First published 1990
Reprinted 1991

BRN 67155
162348

Published by
MACMILLAN EDUCATION LTD
Houndmills, Basingstoke, Hampshire RG21 2XS
and London
Companies and representatives
throughout the world

822·308   HOL

Typeset by Wessex Typesetters
(Division of The Eastern Press Ltd)
Frome, Somerset

Printed in Singapore

British Library Cataloguing in Publication Data
Three Jacobean revenge tragedies: a casebook. – (Casebook
series).
1. Drama in English. Tragedies, 1558–1625 – Anthologies
I. Holdsworth, R. V. II. Series
822'.0512'08
ISBN 0–333–38337–0
ISBN 0–333–38338–9 pbk

CONTENTS

Part Two: *Women Beware Women* and *The Changeling*

1 Critical Comment, 1657–1935

2 Modern Studies

System of Titling: here and in the Selection, exterior quotemarks are used for editorially devised captions. In other cases, the caption employs the original title of the writer's book, chapter or section of a book, article or essay (in some instances abbreviated from that), and it is displayed without exterior quotemarks.

GENERAL EDITOR'S PREFACE

The Casebook series, launched in 1968, has become a well-regarded library of critical studies. The central concern of the series remains the 'single-author' volume, but suggestions from the academic community have led to an extension of the original plan, to include occasional volumes on such general themes as literary 'schools' and genres.

Each volume in the central category deals either with one well-known and influential work by an individual author, or with closely related works by one writer. The main section consists of critical readings, mostly modern, collected from books and journals. A selection of reviews and comments by the author's contemporaries is also included, and sometimes comment from the author himself. The Editor's Introduction charts the reputation of the work or works from the first appearance to the present time.

Volumes in the 'general themes' category are variable in structure but follow the basic purpose of the series in presenting an integrated selection of readings, with an Introduction which explores the theme and discusses the literary and critical issues involved.

A single volume can represent no more than a small selection of critical opinions. Some critics are excluded for reasons of space, and it is hoped that readers will pursue the suggestions for further reading in the Select Bibliography. Other contributions are severed from their original context, to which some readers may wish to turn. Indeed, if they take a hint from the critics represented here, they certainly will.

A. E. DYSON

NOTE ON TEXTS

Throughout this volume quotations from and references to the three plays have been made to conform to the editions of them in the Revels Plays series (Manchester University Press). These are *The Revenger's Tragedy*, edited by R. A. Foakes (1966); *Women Beware Women*, edited by J. R. Mulryne (1975); and *The Changeling*, edited by N. W. Bawcutt (1958). The text used for other Middleton works is, where possible, that of the 'complete' edition of A. H. Bullen, 8 vols (1885–86); the texts used for works by Middleton which have joined the canon since Bullen's edition appeared are identified as the need arises. Shakespeare references and quotations follow *The Riverside Shakespeare*, edited by G. Blakemore Evans (Boston, 1974).

Editorial additions, in the footnotes of the essays and elsewhere, are placed between square brackets. As noted in the Contents page, essay titles printed within quotation marks have been supplied by the Editor.

INTRODUCTION

The Revenger's Tragedy

Thomas Middleton, and not Cyril Tourneur or anyone else, wrote *The Revenger's Tragedy*. After its composition in 1605–6, the play remained anonymous for fifty years. Its publisher, George Eld, entered the play in the Stationers' Register in 1607, along with a Middleton comedy, *A Trick to Catch the Old One*, but without saying who wrote them; and he at first gave no clue on their printed title-pages. In the case of *A Trick*, however, which he printed second, Eld stopped the press and added 'Composed by T.M.' to later copies in the run, some of which have survived. *The Revenger's Tragedy* stayed unclaimed until 1656, when the bookseller Edward Archer published 'An exact and perfect catalogue of all the plays that ever were printed, together with all the authors' names'. Included is a play called 'Revenger', which is classed as a tragedy and ascribed to 'Tournour'. Faced with scores of other anonymous plays in his list, Archer was wrong in his attributions twice as often as he was right: lacking 'T.M.' on his copy of *A Trick*, for example, he assigned it to Shakespeare. Nevertheless, most modern editors and critics of *The Revenger's Tragedy* have accepted Archer's ascription.

It, too, is wrong, however. In 1926 E. H. C. Oliphant published an article in which he noted detailed resemblances, of phrasing, vocabulary, and versification, between *The Revenger's Tragedy* and Middleton's plays.[1] Since the links were widely dispersed through the Middleton canon, occurring in work which was earlier than *The Revenger's Tragedy* as well as later, he rejected plagiarism as an explanation, and concluded that Middleton must have written this play too. Oliphant's methods were vulnerable to the charge that he accumulated his evidence haphazardly, and did not test its distinctiveness by checking it against a body of plays by other Jacobean playwrights. Recent research has, however, put his finding beyond reasonable doubt. In particular, we have to thank the painstaking labours of David J. Lake and MacDonald P. Jackson, who, working independently of one another, applying different tests, and using a largely different sample of non-Middleton plays as a control, are united in their certainty that Middleton wrote *The Revenger's Tragedy*.[2]

Of the diverse kinds of evidence Lake and Jackson adduce, that of linguistic forms is the most powerful. Linguistically, Middleton was a highly colloquial and idiosyncratic writer, who cultivated a wide range of verbal and contractional forms, such as *I'm, I've, I'd, h'as, sh'as 'tas, 'em, on't, ne'er*, and *e'en*, which other dramatists either never or rarely used, and who consistently avoided others, such as *hath, doth*, and *them*, which they employed frequently. From this point of view the quarto of *The Revenger's Tragedy* is a typical Middletonian text: its linguistic pattern agrees with that of every single one of Middleton's acknowledged plays much more closely than it does with those of some 150 plays by other Jacobean authors to which Lake and Jackson compare it. Supporters of Tourneur object that scribes and printers' compositors, who sometimes tinkered with word-forms, may have accidentally created this exact linguistic match, but this is simply not credible. Many different copyists, widely separated in time and space, are involved, and the effect of their alterations would be quite random in direction. The odds against them shifting the linguistic details of these, and only these, texts so concertedly as to make them reduplicate one another, and reduplicate simultaneously Middleton's own practices as evidenced by his autograph manuscript of *A Game at Chess*, are many millions to one.

On top of this, *The Revenger's Tragedy* contains coinages, such as 'luxur' (I i 9) and 'sasarara' (IV ii 65), phrases, such as 'my study's ornament' (I i 15), and character-names, such as Lussurioso and Castiza, which appear nowhere else but in Middleton (who was, it should be added, a highly self-imitative writer). Its verse-style displays Middleton's peculiar habit of mingling blank verse, rhyme, and prose within single speeches; and it employs oaths and exclamations which are very rare outside his work. Take the case of 'push!'. There are six examples in *The Revenger's Tragedy*, six in *A Mad World*, six in *Your Five Gallants*, five in *No Wit, No Help*, five in *The Changeling*, and a further twenty-five elsewhere in Middleton. In 200 non-Middleton plays which Lake, Jackson, and I have checked between us, 'push' occurs just seven times, and never more than once per play. The evidence involved, of which the foregoing is merely a tiny sample, is different in kind, yet it all converges upon the same result.

Why, if Middleton is not the play's author, should this be so?

It is now clear that only tradition, abetted by an irrational distrust of 'internal' (that is, textually derived) evidence, has kept the Tourneur attribution alive. Its persistence has had remarkable consequences. For four centuries Middleton has been denied one of his best plays; Tourneur's name has become as familiar as those of Middleton and Webster; and Tourneur's one genuine play, *The Atheist's Tragedy*, instead of being as well known as *The Two Maids of Moreclack* or *The Duchess of Suffolk*, is widely studied and is currently in print in several paperback editions.

Criticism of the play has also been affected. Late Victorian critics, unhampered by the check on their imaginations that an awareness of Middleton's authorship would have imposed, were free to convert the obscure Tourneur into a late Victorian poet, a morbid and stricken visionary in the mould of Baudelaire's *poète maudit*. In this reading *The Revenger's Tragedy* becomes a neurotic and involuntary effusion, of mainly autobiographical interest; it provides, according to Churton Collins, a window into the author's 'diseased and perverted consciousness', and a revelation of his 'suffering, cynicism, and despair'. The subjectivity and tendentiousness of this response would have been more rapidly apparent had not T. S. Eliot re-endorsed it in his essay of 1930. But Eliot, too, was concocting an author who reflected his private preoccupations. Eliot's Tourneur, racked by life-hatred and 'some horror beyond words', is really Eliot – the poet who wrote *The Hollow Men* and who prefixed 'The horror! the horror!' to the first version of *The Waste Land*.

Later critics, while retaining Tourneur as the play's author, have been less ready to view it as the outpouring of a disordered life-hater. Robert Ornstein argues that the playwright's 'ironic intellect is always in control',[3] and Una Ellis-Fermor that 'his detachment from his characters is nearly as complete as Middleton's'.[4] M. C. Bradbrook notes the calculation which has gone into the play's construction: she counts 'a list of twenty-two ironic reversals' connecting the action, which is 'an enlarged series of peripeteia'.[5] These reversals, Peter Lisca shows, serve a coherent moral point: they dramatise 'the intestinal division of evil itself, a division which while seeming to lead to multiplication ironically ends in cross-cancellation'.[6]

Other studies demonstrate that the play achieves a deliberate and complex blending of diverse traditions, both dramatic and non-dramatic. As a revenge tragedy it adapts the formula established in Kyd's *The Spanish Tragedy* and continued in Shakespeare's *Hamlet*, displaying specific debts to both. Gloriana's skull, for example, aids Vindice's mortuary meditations as Yorick's skull does for Hamlet, but it is also the equivalent of the napkin dyed in his son's blood which Hieronimo vows to keep with him in Kyd's play, as an incitement to revenge. Jonson's and Marston's satiric comedies, in which a parade of grotesques is ridiculed and exposed by a wittily acerbic commentator, are also drawn upon, along with the perspectives and conventions of the earlier Morality plays. A major non-dramatic influence is the medieval homily, a formal exhortation on life's vanity and death's imminence. With Vindice's skull-assisted harangues, compare G. R. Owst's summary of the standard tactics of the medieval preacher, who would

point his audience to the skulls and bones of the departed, bidding them reflect how through the mouth once so delectable to kiss, so delicate in its eating and drinking, through eyes but a short while before so fair to see, worms now crawl in and out. The body or the head, once so richly attired, so proudly displayed, now boasts no covering but the soil, no bed of softness, no proud retinue save worms for the flesh, and, if its life was evil, demons for the soul.[7]

Finally, iconographical as well as literary traditions are utilised. Many critics note the pervasive suggestion of the Danse Macabre. In addition, Vindice pressing Gloriana's skull against the lips of the Duke recalls illustrations of the devil drawing together the heads of a man and a woman as they kiss,[8] and when he and his brother stamp on their dying victim they resemble the demons of medieval woodcuts who tread down the damned into hell.[9]

Recognition of the author's sophisticated control of his material has encouraged critics to separate him from his protagonist, so that whatever morbidity and cynicism they find in the play are now seen as a product of Vindice's distorted psyche rather than his creator's. Interpretations of Vindice differ significantly, however. Some critics detect a latent corruption, a pre-existing moral affinity with his enemies which it is the business of the play to make plain; others view him as initially virtuous but gradually contaminated by the depravity of the court, and by the violence he has to espouse in order to purge it; and a few; while conceding that 'Vindice's vengeance does at last unsettle his moral balance',[10] find him essentially noble and requiring our sympathy right to the end.

The first of these readings is surely the one which Middleton intends. Quite apart from Vindice's escalating sadism and his morally bankrupt celebration of the 'wit' of his deeds, his first speech gives evidence of perverted values. He prizes Gloriana's memory not for her virtue but for her beauty, and specifically for its power to lure 'the uprightest man' into the sin of lust (the pun on 'uprightest' smartly making moral excellence a matter of sexual prowess). He admires, too, her ability to provoke the very extravagance he elsewhere professes to deplore: 'she was able to ha' made a usurer's son / Melt all his patrimony in a kiss, / And what his father fifty years told, / To have consum'd' (i i 26–8). It is instructive that a later Middleton character, Horsus in *Hengist, King of Kent*, argues similarly when praising his love Roxena: 'A treasure 'tis, able to make more thieves / Than cabinets open to entice; / Which learn them theft that never knew the vice' (ii iii 151–3). Horsus is an unambiguous villain, and his attempt at praise is meant as further proof of his baseness.

Vindice's villainy is masked by his disguise as the malevolent Piato, but it is also embodied by it. As J. L. Simmons notes, comparing Jonson's identical strategy in *Volpone*, 'the hero's role-playing metaphorically projects his spiritual disease, and, in turn, exacerbates it'.[11] Vindice believes that his assumed identity is wholly distinct and false: he will merely 'put on that knave for once', 'turn into another', and be 'far enough from myself' (i i 93, 134; i iii 1). Later, when he puts off his disguise, his brother remarks with relief, 'So, so, all's as it should be, y'are yourself . . . now thou art thyself' (iv ii 1–4). But this asserts a truth which neither of them perceives. Vindice is now indeed fully himself, for Piato has brought his murderous nature to the surface; the disguise was all along the reality. Middleton repeats the irony in *Women Beware Women*, when Livia, allaying the suspicions of her intended victims after threatening them, pretends to have calmed down, and declares, 'I am now myself' (iv ii 172). This again carries a deeper truth, for Livia's real moral identity now stands fully revealed, in the fact that she is planning to murder her kinsfolk.

Accepting that Vindice is essentially corrupt, and even that the play is 'a nightmare of the Calvinist sense of sin',[12] does not, however, compel us to view the author's attitude as unrelievedly pessimistic. This will depend on our response to Antonio's succession, and the moralising finale he supplies. Some critics see Antonio as 'pious', and his condemnation of Vindice as signalling a final 'reversal of Evil to Good'.[13] A majority find him hypocritical and self-serving, and thus the play's ending as dark as its beginning.[14] A case against Antonio, who appears only twice, can certainly be made. A stage-direction introduces him as '*the discontented Lord* Antonio' (I iv 1), a worrying description, since we learn elsewhere that 'discontent' is 'the nobleman's consumption' (I i 127), and that 'discontent and want / Is the best clay to mould a villain of' (IV iv 47–8). In the ensuing scene, he accepts the prospect of non-legal revenge for the rape of his wife, thanking the lords who swear to exact it (I iv 65). Assuming the dukedom, he orders the death of the 'Fourth Noble' for a crime he has not committed (v iii 71–3), and his sentence on Vindice and Hippolito, 'Bear 'em to speedy execution' (v iii 102), disconcertingly echoes Lussurioso's 'bear him straight / To execution' of two scenes before (v i 127–8), pronounced on an innocent man.

A stronger case can, however, be made for Antonio's integrity. He is kept apart from all the play's revenges, not joining in the lords' oath in I iv (which will, he is assured, only come into force if legal remedies fail), and not appearing among Vindice's followers in v ii who plan to attack the ducal family. The Fourth Noble whom he condemns may not have killed Lussurioso, but he has formed part of the '*masque of intended murderers*' (v iii 48), and he has killed Spurio. A more pressing question is what we make of Antonio's lines explaining his condemnation of Vindice for killing the old Duke: 'Such an old man as he; / You that would murder him would murder me' (v iii 104–5). T. W. Craik thinks this 'pointedly selfish',[15] but it is readily defended. There is nothing in the text to show that Antonio is aware of the old Duke's villainy (or for that matter of Lussurioso's), so his death would really seem to him to be murder. Moreover, Vindice clearly has become an unguided missile, liable to launch himself at anyone, rulers included, in the future. As Lussurioso has pointed out (but failed to spot how it might apply to him), Vindice 'has wit enough / To murder any man' (IV ii 106–7).

Seeing Antonio as well-intentioned does not, however, remove all ambiguity from the play's conclusion. His verdict, which Vindice cheerfully endorses, that the killings Vindice has perpetrated are 'murder' rather than justifiable acts is merely asserted rather than argued for, and the repetition of the word 'murder' eight times in the last thirty lines only serves to beg the question more loudly. There is also the effect of the closing line, 'Pray heaven their blood may wash away all treason', which sows a further doubt with its insecure subjunctive.

Women Beware Women and The Changeling

'You may see, widow', the Mother of Women Beware Women tells Livia over their chess-game, 'How all things draw to an end' (ii ii 410–11). A journey to an end is what Middleton's last two tragedies are all about. Bringing to bear a far more unrelenting determinism than he attempted in The Revenger's Tragedy, they concentrate on the logic of a situation working itself out, and on the inexorable connection between choice and consequence. At the start of The Changeling Alsemero confesses, 'I do not know the end / (Which needs I must do) of an affair in hand', but adds, 'But I must on, for back I cannot go' (i i 52–3, 224). Later, as 'in order . . . one accident / Gives way unto another' (iv i 111–13), he comes to know the end which the linkage of events has made inevitable, and to understand it. 'It could not choose but follow', he observes, on learning that his wife has progressed from murder to adultery (v iii 108).

Matching the ending to the beginning, and measuring the distance between them, becomes accordingly very important in both plays. Bianca's first words in Women Beware Women are those of the virtuous and contented wife that she thinks that she is: 'there is nothing can be wanting / To her that does enjoy all her desires' (i i 125–6). It is a different self, now requiring not love but the obliterating penetration of death, that recalls these lines: 'So my desires are satisfied, / I feel death's power within me' (v ii 200–1). The Changeling begins with Beatrice veering from Alonzo towards Alsemero: 'I shall change my saint, I fear me' (i i 155). She does indeed, but the chain of events she instigates inflicts another change upon her, so that in the finale De Flores is revealed as her 'lip's saint' (v iii 53). At the same time, this play finds room for a more optimistic coupling. It opens with an instance of false seeing ('''Twas in the temple where I first beheld her') as Alsemero is taken in by Beatrice's modest and beautiful exterior, and from then on harps continually on the eye's capacity to mislead. But it ends with a moment of clearsightedness, as Alibius perceives Isabella's genuine virtue: 'I see all apparent, wife' (v iii 213).

Macbeth, which was not available to Middleton when he wrote *The Revenger's Tragedy*, seems to have focused his interest in protagonists who lock themselves into an irreversible process of moral decline, and who travel step-by-step towards an appalled awareness of what they have become. Having done 'the deed' (a heavily charged word in Shakespeare's play, as in *The Changeling*), Macbeth learns that 'What's done cannot be undone' (v i 68). For Beatrice, too, 'The deed shall find its time' (v i 54), through which her true identity will be thrust to the surface, and she will become 'what the act has made you . . . the deed's creature', *creature* meaning 'base hireling' as well as 'creation' (III iv 135–7). Specific echoes underline Middleton's indebtedness. ' 'Tis but want of use' is Livia's way of explaining Bianca's self-revulsion after her encounter with the Duke (*Women Beware Women*, II ii 470). Macbeth, too, declares that he 'wants hard use' when accounting for his guilty fears after Duncan's murder (III iv 142). In *The Changeling*, De Flores recoils from Tomazo because 'I smell his brother's blood when I come near him' (IV i 41). Lady Macbeth is similarly afflicted when reliving the killing of Duncan: 'Here's the smell of the blood still' (v i 50).

Middleton's Calvinism, however, as John Stachniewski demonstrates below, is the ultimate source of his fascination with the irreversible sequences to which his characters are subject. Pitched towards heaven or hell by the spiritual identity conferred on him by God before time began, the Calvinist's only recourse was a ceaseless monitoring of his innermost self in order to learn what awaited him. Perseverance in this, rather than in the 'forgetfulness' to which Middleton's characters are prone, might itself be a sign of election to heaven, but on the other hand a discovery of reprobate impulses did not mean that one could avert their implications through repentance. 'Return to the communion of Christ', Calvin warned, 'is not open to those who knowingly and willingly have rejected it' (*Institutes*, 3.3.23). Livia endorses this in a comment during the chess-game: 'Your pawn cannot come back to relieve itself' (*Women Beware Women*, II ii 302), a line which hangs equally oppressively over both plays. Calvinists stressed, naturally enough, God's sovereignty, and the immutability of his decrees, rather than his goodness. 'God is no changeling' was a contemporary proverb, taken from Calvin.[16]

As Middleton's protagonists journey towards a discovery of their reprobate selves, a wholly misplaced reliance on their self-sufficiency, and on the efficacy of human wisdom, spurs them on. 'The wisest men are blinded by their own pride', Calvin noted, joining in a widespread Protestant denigration of the intellect; 'human reason is utterly undiscerning, and human acuteness stupid, in the mysteries of God'.[17] Middleton's comic characters eventually accept that 'we're not ordained to thrive by wisdom' (*A Trick to Catch the Old One*, IV iii 41), but in the tragedies this realisation comes too late. 'Times are grown wiser . . . Therefore be wise', Vindice urges Gratiana, when, as Piato, he tries to corrupt her (*The Revenger's Tragedy*, II i 76, 186); but he nails his colours to the same mast, aiming to 'crown our wit', and boasting ''twas somewhat witty carried' when confessing his killing of the Duke (v i 170, v iii 97). In *Women Beware Women*, Leantio prides himself on his conviction that it would be 'more wise' to leave his new wife and pursue business (I iii 28). This rebounds against him when, in his absence, the Duke urges Bianca to 'play the wise wench and provide for ever' (II ii 382), and she later declares that the maids of Florence are 'wiser of themselves . . . And can take gifts when goodness offers 'em'. 'Damnation has taught you that wisdom', her husband retorts (III iii 132–4). Beatrice trusts to the same faculty. 'So wisdom by degrees works out her freedom', she announces, as she works herself into the clutches of De Flores (III iv 13). Throughout both plays related terms, such as *wit*, *judgement*, and *reason*, undergo parallel demolition.

The characters of *The Revenger's Tragedy* have been called 'laboratory specimens' whom their author subjects to 'scientific exposition'.[18] Middleton's approach in the later tragedies is comparable: there is a detachment (some critics would say, a coldness) of attitude more usually associated with satiric comedy. It seems odd on the face of it that the characters do not attract more sympathy or emotional engagement than they do, for they are often well-intentioned. Isabella in *Women Beware Women* is genuine in her claim that she is 'a woman / That means to keep her days true to her husband, / And know no other man' (I ii 160–2), and the description fits Bianca and Beatrice equally well. There is no doubting that Leantio, however complacent or mercenary, has love for Bianca, that the Duke has too, however brutally he begins, or that Bianca loves both of them. It is 'pity' for Hippolito which impels Livia to assist him in obtaining Isabella (II i 41), and 'love' for Livia which prompts Hippolito to kill Leantio (IV ii 17). The Duke arranges Leantio's death not so that he can marry his mistress (the Cardinal only subsequently puts that into his head), but because he believes her life is threatened (IV i 121–3). In *The Changeling* Beatrice recruits De Flores because she fears Alsemero's death in a duel, and it is Alsemero who first suggests to her the killing of Alonzo as a solution. Even De Flores in his pathological devotion offers a glimpse of the romantic hero who sacrifices all for love.

What prevents the kind of emotional involvement that such motives might have inspired (and would have been allowed to inspire in Shakespeare or Webster) is not simply the way they constantly misfire and propel the characters into vicious or self-serving actions which they never anticipated. More important is a relentless play of irony in the dialogue, unperceived by the speakers but perceived by us, which pulls us apart from them by insisting on the blinkered partiality of their point of view, and inducing us to laugh at their expense. Sometimes the irony is retrospective, as when Leantio congratulates himself on his marriage by exclaiming, 'I find no wish in me bent sinfully / To this man's sister' (I i 28–9) – this is before he has met Livia – or when Beatrice tells her father that Alsemero has 'left his own way to keep me company' (I i 158), the full truth of which will only become clear later. More often the irony is immediate, and immediately distancing, as when Beatrice is struck by De Flores' eagerness to serve her, and muses, 'Belike his wants are greedy' (II ii 125). We know that they are, but not for the money she offers him.

These tactics are maintained in the plays' finales, where emotional intensities would otherwise congregate. The masque in *Women Beware Women* is an extended ironic commentary on the characters who are both watching it and acting in it. In *The Changeling* Beatrice perseveres in her failure to see how her comments apply to herself. 'This strumpet serves her own ends . . . This whore forgets herself', she complains about Diaphanta (v i 2, 23), but this is true of *this* whore too, the one now speaking. Dying, she explains to Alsemero that 'your bed was cozen'd on the nuptial night, / For which your false bride died' (v iii 160–1). Again she means Diaphanta, yet she is also accurately describing herself.

In view of these ironic manoeuvres it is not surprising that it was to his comedies that Middleton frequently turned for verbal material. Two examples in *Women Beware Women* must suffice. 'As a man loves his wife so love I thee', Hippolito tells Isabella, quite sincerely, yet committing himself to an incestuous affair which will cause both of their deaths (I ii 217). The original version is equally ill-judged, but leads to the comic alternative of marriage: 'I love thee . . . as one loves a woman for a wife', Follywit of *A Mad World* tells Frank Gullman, innocently contracting himself to a prostitute who is out to trap him (IV v 98–9). Leantio's speech extolling wedlock on his return home is closer to its source in tone and effect. Leantio celebrates the 'comforts . . . in woman's love', and declares, 'What a delicious breath marriage sends forth – / The violet-bed's not sweeter' (III ii 4–8). Compare the newly-married Hoard in *A Trick*: 'Who would not wed? the most delicious life! / No joys are like the comforts of a wife' (v ii 41–2). Each is about to discover that he is married to a courtesan. Parallels of this kind bear out Robert Ornstein's claim that 'even though *Women Beware Women* is set in Italy, its characters are London citizens, blood brothers of the *personae* of Middleton's city comedies . . . . While his contemporaries pondered man's tragic relation to the universe, Middleton studied the comic relation between human appetites and the social environment which conditions them'.[19]

Despite the similarities of style and theme discussed above, *Women Beware Women* and *The Changeling* are also strikingly different. The world of the former is more obviously mercenary and debased, and more overtly committed to a male-centred relegation of its women to the status of commodities. The Ward subjecting Isabella to degrading physical inspection merely embodies in a coarser form the Duke's view of her as 'a jewel of unvalued worth' (III iii 162), or Leantio's assumption that Bianca is his 'best treasure' which must be locked up, 'a gem no stranger's eye must see' (III ii 94, 166). Puns on *business*, examined below by Christopher Ricks, stress the merging of sex and money, and in a less rib-nudging way than Wycherley achieved later in *The Country Wife*: 'Who for his business from his wife will run, / Takes the best care to have her business done' (II i 575–6). A similar patriarchal oppressiveness operates in *The Changeling*, and here too a woman is threatened with an arranged marriage; but the sense of economic reductivism is less acute. Hints remain, however, as when Alsemero terms Beatrice 'My absolute treasure' (v i 83).

The Changeling, on the other hand, invests its action and characters with a mythic suggestiveness that *Women Beware Women* only intermittently attempts. One myth, noted below by David Frost, is that of the Creation and the Fall; this is glanced at in *Women Beware Women* when the Duke tells Bianca that she 'lights on a tree that bears all women's wishes', and invites her to 'pluck fruit there' (II ii 371–2). Another is that of Beauty and the Beast. As Robert Jordan remarks, in *The Changeling* 'the fairy-tale ending is subject to a bitter reversal. Instead of the beast being revealed as a prince, the process of this story is to reveal that the princess is in fact a beast'.[20] There is also a repeated suggestion of diabolic possession. Of Bianca we learn that 'the devil's in her' (*Women Beware Women*, III i 72), but in *The Changeling* the idea informs the whole of Beatrice's relationship with De Flores, as J. L. Simmons shows.[21]

Critics have disagreed sharply over the relevance of Rowley's subplot in *The Changeling*, and that of the masque in *Women Beware Women*. These questions are dealt with below.[22] One further issue requires discussion. Many critics of *Women Beware Women*, unwilling to accept Bianca's abrupt acquisition of a new identity after her encounter with the Duke, have claimed to detect it in her earlier appearances. We are told that Bianca 'behaves with subtle immodesty' in I i and is 'cunningly compliant' with the Duke's advances; that her attitude to Leantio is 'lustful'; that her 'seduction' is 'an event in which she plays an active part'; and that the Duke's 'appeal to her vanity and mercenary instincts is enough, apparently, to, overcome her scruples . . . . The pair go off together, perhaps arm in arm'.[23]

All of these comments are seriously mistaken, as a glance at the text will show. There is nothing to suggest that Bianca regards herself as anything other than Leantio's loyal and loving wife, up to and including her arrival in Livia's art gallery. Trapped by the Duke, she rejects all of his arguments, and her last words imply that he will have to use force: 'Why should you seek, sir, / To take away that you can never give?' (II ii 367–8). The point is that the rape is a rape, not a seduction. When she reappears she decides to abandon herself to immorality because she now regards herself as contaminated, and made immoral, by the rape that has been inflicted on her: 'mine honour's leprous', she believes, and 'sin and I'm acquainted'; she has been 'abused, and made for use' (II ii 424, 436, 440).

The twisted thinking involved here is shared by other Middleton rape victims. In *The Ghost of Lucrece* Lucrece sees herself as defiled and made into a whore. Delivering her complaint from hell, she attributes her damnation to what has happened to her. In *The Revenger's Tragedy* Antonio's wife is spoken of as 'fall'n' and her rapist as a 'defacer'; she has taken poison rather than 'live with shame' (I iv 2, 47, 68). Castiza in *Hengist* also thinks she will be damned: 'take not from me', she begs, 'That which must guide me to another world, / And leave me dark forever' (III ii 87–9). After the rape she argues that only 'consents in sin' receive 'punishments' (IV ii 187), but the play hedges on this because Castiza was blindfolded at the time and the rapist was actually her husband.

Bianca likewise assumes that she is now morally and spiritually polluted, but her response is different. Rather than taking actual poison, she cries, 'Come poison all at once' (II ii 426), resolving to accept the fact of her corruption by bringing her personality into alignment with it. We seem to have a choice of interpretations here. If we stress the play's Calvinism, we may incline to G. R. Hibbard's view that through her response to the rape 'a latent potentiality for evil in Bianca has now become actual'.[24] But we can also see Bianca's reaction as a connivance in the very patriarchal values of which the rape itself, in the way that it treats her as an object open to proprietorial seizure, is an expression. Such values dictate that women are fragile vessels whose commercial and moral 'worth' depends on their undamaged condition, and Bianca accepts that her worth is now lost.

NOTES

1. 'The Authorship of *The Revenger's Tragedy*', *Studies in Philology*, XXIII (1926), pp. 157–68.

2. David J. Lake, *The Canon of Thomas Middleton's Plays* (1975); MacDonald P. Jackson, *Studies in Attribution: Middleton and Shakespeare* (Salzburg, 1979). Students of the play who are bemused or intimidated by the vast and complex literature which has grown up around the question of its authorship could make no better beginning than Jackson's clear and undogmatic closing chapter (pp. 159–78).

3. *The Moral Vision of Jacobean Tragedy* (Madison, 1960), p. 110.

4. *The Jacobean Drama*, rev. edn (1958), p. 153.

5. *Themes and Conventions of Elizabethan Tragedy* (Cambridge, 1935), p. 165.

6. '*The Revenger's Tragedy*: A Study in Irony', *Philological Quarterly*, XXXVIII (1959), p. 245.

7. *Preaching in Medieval England* (Cambridge, 1926), p. 344.

8. See M. D. Anderson, *Drama and Imagery in English Medieval Churches* (Cambridge, 1963), p. 55.

9. For discussion of the influences outlined in this paragraph, see the essays of Bowers and Salingar below, and the following: R. T. Brucher, 'Fantasies of Violence: *Hamlet* and *The Revenger's Tragedy*', *Studies in English Literature 1500–1900*, xxi (1981), pp. 257–70; P. Hyland, 'The Disguised Revenger and *The Revenger's Tragedy*', *Southern Review*, xv (1982), pp. 254–62; A. Kernan, *The Cankered Muse* (New Haven, 1959), pp. 221ff.; S. McMillin, 'Acting and Violence: *The Revenger's Tragedy* and Its Departures from *Hamlet*', *Studies in English Literature 1500–1900*, xxiv (1984), pp. 275–91; J. Peter, *Complaint and Satire in Early English Literature* (Oxford, 1956), pp. 255ff.; S. Schoenbaum, '*The Revenger's Tragedy*: Jacobean Dance of Death', *Modern Language Quarterly*, xv (1954), pp. 201–7; and P. S. Spinrad, *The Summons of Death on the Medieval and Renaissance English Stage* (Columbus, 1987), pp. 229–49.

10. Jonas A. Barish, 'The True and False Families of *The Revenger's Tragedy*', in *English Renaissance Drama*, ed. S. Henning *et al.* (Carbondale, 1976), p. 143.

11. 'The Tongue and Its Office in *The Revenger's Tragedy*', *PMLA*, xcii (1977), p. 61.

12. L. G. Salingar, 'Tourneur and the Tragedy of Revenge', *The Pelican Guide to English Literature: The Age of Shakespeare* (Harmondsworth, 1955), p. 343.

13. John Peter, *Complaint and Satire in Early English Literature*, p. 266.

14. e.g. R. Huebert, '*The Revenger's Tragedy* and the Fallacy of the Excluded Middle', *University of Toronto Quarterly*, xlviii (1978–9), p. 21.

15. '*The Revenger's Tragedy*', *Essays in Criticism*, vi (1956), p. 484.

16. M. P. Tilley, *A Dictionary of the Proverbs in England in the Sixteenth and Seventeenth Centuries* (Ann Arbor, 1950), G200.

17. Calvin, *On Secret Providence*, quoted by B. Armstrong, *Calvinism and the Amyraut Heresy* (Madison, 1969), p. 33, n. 90. Compare 1 Corinthians, i:19: 'I will destroy the wisdom of the wise, and will bring to nothing the understanding of the prudent'.

18. Una Ellis-Fermor, *The Jacobean Drama*, pp. 153–4.

19. *The Moral Vision of Jacobean Tragedy*, pp. 171, 192.

20. 'Myth and Psychology in *The Changeling*', *Renaissance Drama*, iii (1970), p. 165.

21. 'Diabolical Realism in *The Changeling*', *Renaissance Drama*, xi (1980), pp. 135–70.

22. On the subplot of *The Changeling*, see N. W. Bawcutt below, and R. Levin, *The Multiple Plot in English Renaissance Drama* (1971), pp. 34–48. Hints for the thematic integration of the subplot appear earlier in Middleton, in *The Second Maiden's Tragedy*, i ii 313, where Leonella says of her mistress and herself, both of whom have taken lovers, that 'we shall make but a mad house betwixt us', and in *1 The Honest Whore*, where a feigned madwoman refers to barley-break, and an asylum of lunatics and a character named Lollio appear. On the relation of this last play with *The Changeling*, see C. Hoy, *Introductions . . . to Texts in the Dramatic Works of Thomas Dekker*, 4 vols. (1980), ii, pp. 9–10, 64. On the masque in *Women Beware Women*, see R. V. Holdsworth below; also M. R. Golding, 'Variations in the Use of the

Masque in English Revenge Tragedy', *Yearbook of English Studies*, III (1973), pp. 44–54, and S. P. Sutherland, *Masques in Jacobean Tragedy* (New York, 1983), pp. 87–100.

23. G. B. Shand, 'The Stagecraft of *Women Beware Women*', *Research Opportunities in Renaissance Drama*, XXVIII (1985), pp. 29–31; M. S. Lancaster, 'Middleton's Use of the Upper Stage in *Women Beware Women*', *Tulane Studies in English*, XXII (1977), p. 75; N. Taylor and B. Loughrey, 'Middleton's Chess Strategies in *Women Beware Women*', *Studies in English Literature 1500–1900*, XXIV (1984), p. 353; S. Schoenbaum, *Middleton's Tragedies* (1955), p. 120.

24. 'The Tragedies of Thomas Middleton and the Decadence of the Drama' *Renaissance and Modern Studies*, I (1957), p. 51.

PART ONE

The Revenger's Tragedy

1. CRITICAL COMMENT, 1878–1930

John Churton Collins (1878)

Like Juvenal and Marston, [Tourneur] loves to satirise that he may secure for himself the luxury of prurient description. He did not hate men because he hated vice, but he hated vice because he hated men. . . . I am certainly inclined to suspect that he had some acquaintance with the Greek tragedians. That his purely sensual conception of the passion of love, however, in which he stands in unenviable solitude among his fellow dramatists, does not arise from any Hellenic bias, but springs purely from his own diseased and perverted consciousness, cannot, of course, be seriously doubted. It has, it is easy to see, narrowed and damaged his work. . . .

[The defects of *The Revenger's Tragedy*] lie principally in the delineation of the subordinate characters, who want colour and complexity. Hippolito, for instance, is a mere shadow; Ambitioso and Supervacuo are simply what their names imply, they are not men so much as abstractions; they enact a set part, and reveal no capabilities for anything else. Castiza never appears except to assert or defend her chastity, a treasure much too cheap, and necessarily, to justify her wearisome eulogies. There is something unsatisfactory and unpleasantly rapid about the change in the character and position of the mother, though her repentance at the dagger's edge probably left her as base as it found her – but Tourneur should have marked it. The action of the play sometimes flags when it should hurry on, and sometimes hurries on when it might with advantage slacken its pace. But through this chaos of bleared, rapid and uneven work spring into fierce and vivid light a series of scenes and positions unique in conception, brilliant and powerful in execution. . . . The character of Vindice in its appalling and unrelieved intensity, in its savage and devilish energy, bitter cynicism, and angry grandeur is unrivalled among the creations of an age which abounds in similar portraits. . . .

Tourneur's great defect as a dramatic poet is undoubtedly the

narrowness of his range of vision – of his insight and sympathies. . . .
None of his dramatis personæ are at all complex; they are either the
personifications of certain attributes – tragic studies of tragic
humours, as Ben Jonson's masterpieces are comic studies of comic
humours – or they are abstractions, phantoms, failures. . . .

In closing our review of these works it is difficult to leave them
without pausing for a moment over the memory of their author,
who, with obvious but perhaps unconscious egotism, has evidently
left in their strange and melancholy pages no inconsiderable frag-
ments of his own strange and melancholy autobiography. . . .
Nothing, it is true, is so idle, so easy, and so presumptuous as to
speculate and theorise on subjects like these; but here it is no
officious recreation, but an imperative duty, with such lyric intensity
and passionate abandonment has a poet stamped on his writings
the terrible traces of so much bitter experience, of so much suffering,
cynicism, and despair. Never, indeed, with the single exception of
Byron, has a dramatist, while preserving successfully a certain
superficial and technical consistency in the delineation of subordinate
characters altogether out of the range of his care, comprehension
and sympathy, so obviously and so defiantly interwoven and
interpenetrated objective embodiment with an intense all-absorbing
subjectivity. . . . It is the egotism of a powerful and distorted mind,
which narrowed as it hardened and gained in intellectual vigour as
it lost in sensuality and enthusiasm. It would seem that he united
the not uncommon anomaly of a fiery and restless soul with a cold
and logical intellect. Where such a perilous union, no longer mutually
corrective, fails to secure in consistent purpose the principle of
healthy and harmonious actions, or to find at all events a narcotic
in the possession of humour, it must either work its own speedy
destruction, or, tortured into morbid and irritable action, become
the fruitful parent of 'all monstrous, all abhorred things'.

Nature, who had in many respects endowed him so richly, had
altogether denied him this sense of humour, and consequently the
balance and insight which humour is usually able to bestow. Hence,
no doubt, the diseased, warped and chaotic character of much of
his work. . . . Like Marlowe, he hungers and thirsts after the
sensuous, the defiant and the forbidden, but he has none of Marlowe's
glory, grandeur and idealism. Like Webster, he loves to live among
horrors till he has become 'native and indued unto that element'
[Hamlet, IV vii 179]; but he moves not with the same firm tread

through tangled labyrinths of gloom and wreck with 'Look you, the stars shine still' [*The Duchess of Malfi*, IV i 100] as creed at once and comment. Sin and misery, lust and cynicism, fixed their fangs deep in his splendid genius, marring and defacing his art, poisoning and paralysing the artist.

SOURCE: extracts from Introduction to *The Plays and Poems of Cyril Tourneur*, 2 vols. (1878), vol. I, pp. xliii, xlvi–xlvii, lii–lvi.

John Addington Symonds   (1888)

The Revenger's Tragedy is an entangled web of lust, incest, fratricide, rape, adultery, mutual suspicion, hate, and bloodshed, through which runs, like a thread of glittering copper, the vengeance of a cynical plague-fretted spirit. Vindice emerges from the tainted crew of Duke and Duchess, Lussurioso, Spurio and Junior, Ambitioso and Supervacuo, with a kind of blasted splendour. They are curling and engendering, a brood of flat-headed asps, in the slime of their filthy appetites and gross ambitions. He treads and tramples on them all. But he bears on his own forehead the brands of Lucifer, the rebel, and of Cain, the assassin. The social corruption which transformed them into reptiles, has made him a fiend incarnate. Penetrated to the core with evil, conscious of sin far more than they are, he towers above them by his satanic force of purpose. Though ruined, as they are ruined, and by like causes, he maintains the dignity of mind and of volition. The right is on his side; the right of a tyrannicide, who has seen his own mistress, his own father, the wife of his friend, done to death by the brutalities of wanton princelings. But Tourneur did not choose to gift Vindice with elevation of nature. In the strongest scene of the play he showed this scorpion of revenge, stooping to feign a pander's part, tempting his mother and his sister as none but a moral leper could have done. In the minor scene of the duke's murder, he made him malicious beyond the scope of human cruelty and outrage. It was inherent apparently in this poet's conception of life that evil should be proclaimed predominant. His cynicism stands self-revealed in the sentence he puts into Antonio's mouth, condemning Vindice to death: 'You that would murder him would murder me'.

Even justice, in his view, rests on egotism. And yet Tourneur has endowed Vindice with redeeming qualities. The hero of this crooked play is true to his ideal of duty, true to his sense of honour. He dies contented because he has perfected his revenge, preserved his sister's chastity, and converted his mother at the poniard's point. Where all are so bad and base, Vindice appears by comparison sublime. If we are to admire tone and keeping in a work of art, we certainly find it here; for the moral gradations are relentlessly scaled within the key of sin and pollution. The only character who stirs a pulse of sympathy is vicious. Castiza is a mere lay figure, and her mother one of the most repulsive personages of the Jacobean drama.

Source: extract from Introduction to *The Best Plays of Webster and Tourneur* (1888), pp. xiv–xv.

William Archer (1923)

Tourneur, as we know, ranks very high in the esteem of orthodox criticism. Swinburne places him 'higher than Ford', and declares that he 'recalls the passion and perfection, the fervour and the splendour and the harmony which we . . . recognise in the dialogue or the declamation of Aeschylus himself'.[1] . . . I will not harp on the amazing parallel between Tourneur and Aeschylus. I will only ask whether such monstrous melodrama as *The Revenger's Tragedy*, with its hideous sexuality and its raging lust for blood, can be said to belong to civilised literature at all? I say it is a product either of sheer barbarism, or of some pitiable psychopathic perversion. I say it is ludicrous to find critics solemnly aestheticising in this slaughterhouse. . . . *The Revenger's Tragedy* is a mere farrago of sanguinary absurdities, which might have been amusing had it been presented as a burlesque of the prevailing style of tragedy. One cannot, indeed, quite repress a suspicion that Tourneur wrote it with his tongue in his cheek, and would have been amazed and amused to think of Vindice being taken seriously by a whole school of critics after three centuries.

SOURCE: extracts from *The Old Drama and the New* (1923), pp. 70, 74, 76.

NOTE

1. A. C. Swinburne, *Contemporaries of Shakespeare* (1919), pp. 169, 177.

T. S. Eliot   (1930)

Webster, in his greatest tragedies, has a kind of pity for *all* of his characters, an attitude towards good and bad alike which helps to unify the Webster pattern. Tourneur has no such feeling for any of his characters; and in this respect is nearer, as Professor Stoll has pointed out and Professor Nicoll has reminded us, to the author of *Antonio and Mellida*.[1] Of all his other contemporaries, Middleton is the nearest. But Mr Nicoll, we think quite rightly, rejects Mr E. H. C. Oliphant's theory that Middleton is the author of *The Revenger's Tragedy*, and with Mr Dugdale Sykes restores the play to Tourneur.[2] And, in spite of Mr Oliphant's weight of probabilities, there is one quality of Middleton which we do not find in the two plays attributed to Tourneur. The finest of the tragic characters of Middleton live in a way which differs from Tourneur's, not in degree but kind; and they have flashes of a kind of satiric wit unknown to Tourneur, in whom wit is supplied by a fierce grotesquerie. In reading one play of Middleton, either *The Changeling* or *Women Beware Women*, for instance, we can recognise an author capable of considerable variety in his dramatic work; in reading either of Tourneur's plays we recognise a narrow mind, capable at most of the limited range of Marston.

Indeed, none of the characters of Tourneur, even the notable Vindice, the protagonist of *The Revenger's Tragedy*, is by himself invested with much humanity either for good or evil. But dramatic characters may live in more than one way; and a dramatist like Tourneur can compensate his defects by the intensity of his virtues. Characters should be real in relation to our own life, certainly, as even a very minor character of Shakespeare may be real; but they must also be real in relation to each other; and the closeness of emotional pattern in the latter way is an important part of dramatic merit; The personages of Tourneur have, like those of Marston, and perhaps in a higher degree, this togetherness. They may be distortions, grotesques, almost childish caricatures of humanity, but they are all distorted to scale. Hence the whole action, from their appearance to their ending, 'no common action' indeed,[3] has its own self-subsistent reality. For closeness of texture, in fact, there are no plays beyond Shakespeare's, and the best of Marlowe and Jonson, that can surpass *The Revenger's Tragedy*. Tourneur excels in three virtues of the dramatist: he knew how, in his own way, to construct a plot, he was cunning in his manipulation of stage effects, and he was a master of versification and choice of language. *The Revenger's Tragedy* starts off at top speed, as every critic has observed; and never slackens to the end. We are told everything we need to know before the first scene is half over; Tourneur employs his torrent of words with the greatest economy. The opening scene, and the famous Scene v of Act III, are remarkable feats of melodrama; and the suddenness of the end of the final scene of Act v matches the sudden explosiveness of the beginning. . . .

Accepting the canonical order of Tourneur's two plays, *The Atheist's Tragedy* adds nothing at all to what the other play has given us; there is no development, no fresh inspiration; only the skilful but uninspired use of a greater metrical variety. Cases are not altogether wanting, among poets, of a precocious maturity exceeding the limits of the poet's experience – in contrast to the very slow and very long development of Shakespeare – a maturity to which the poet is never again able to catch up. Tourneur's genius, in any case, is in *The Revenger's Tragedy*; his talent only in *The Atheist's Tragedy*.

Indeed, *The Revenger's Tragedy* might well be a specimen of such isolated masterpieces. It does express – and this, chiefly, is what gives it its amazing unity – an intense and unique and horrible vision of life; but is such a vision as might come, as the result of few or slender experiences, to a highly sensitive adolescent with a gift for words. We are apt to expect of youth only a fragmentary view of life; we incline to see youth as exaggerating the importance of its narrow experience and imagining the world as did Chicken Licken.[4] But occasionally the intensity of the vision of its own ecstasies or horrors, combined with a mastery of word and rhythm, may give to a juvenile work a universality which is beyond the author's knowledge of life to give, and to which mature men and women can respond. Churton Collins's introduction to the works[5] is by far the most penetrating interpretation of Tourneur that has been written; and this introduction, though Collins believed *The Revenger's Tragedy* to be the later play, and although he thinks of Tourneur as a man of mature experience, does not invalidate this theory. 'Tourneur's great defect as a dramatic poet', says Collins, 'is undoubtedly the narrowness of his range of vision:' and this narrowness of range might be that of a young man. The cynicism, the loathing and disgust of humanity, expressed consummately in *The Revenger's Tragedy*, are immature in the respect that they exceed the object. Their objective equivalents are characters practising the grossest vices; characters which seem merely to be spectres projected from the poet's inner world of nightmare, some horror beyond words. So the play is a document on humanity chiefly because it is a document on one human being, Tourneur; its motive is truly the death motive, for it is the loathing and horror of life itself. To have realised this motive so well is a triumph; for the hatred of life is an important phase – even, if you like, a mystical experience – in life itself.

The Revenger's Tragedy, then, is in this respect quite different from any play by any minor Elizabethan; it can, in this respect, be compared only to *Hamlet*. Perhaps, however, its quality would be better marked by contrasting it with a later work of cynicism and loathing, *Gulliver's Travels*. No two compositions could be more dissimilar. Tourneur's 'suffering, cynicism and despair', to use Collins's words, are static; they might be prior to experience, or be the fruit of but little; Swift's is the progressive cynicism of the mature and disappointed man of the world. As an objective comment on the world, Swift's is by far the more terrible. For Swift had himself enough pettiness, as well as enough sin of pride, and lust of dominion, to be able to expose and condemn mankind by its universal pettiness and pride and vanity and ambition; and his poetry, as well as his prose, attests that he hated the very smell of the human animal. We may think as we read Swift, 'how loathsome human beings are'; in reading Tourneur we can only think, 'how terrible to loathe human beings so much as that'. For you cannot make humanity horrible merely by presenting human beings as consistent and monotonous maniacs of gluttony and lust. . . . What gives Tourneur his place as a great poet is this one play, in which a horror of life, singular in his own or any age, finds exactly the right words and the right rhythms.[6]

SOURCE: extracts from 'Cyril Tourneur', *Times Literary Supplement* (13 November 1930), pp. 925–6; reprinted in *Selected Essays* (1934), pp. 182–92.

NOTES

1. [Ed.] John Marston; see E. E. Stoll, *John Webster* (1905), pp. 105–6; and Allardyce Nicoll (ed.), *The Works of Cyril Tourneur* (1930), pp. 6, 39.

2. [Ed.] Nicoll, op. cit., pp. 18–20; E. H. C. Oliphant, 'The Authorship of *The Revenger's Tragedy*', in *Studies in Philology*, XXIII (1926), pp. 157–68; and H. Dugdale Sykes, 'Cyril Tourneur: *The Revenger's Tragedy*: *The Second Maiden's Tragedy*', in *Notes and Queries*, CXXXVII (1919), pp. 225–9.

3. [Ed.] Eliot is quoting *The Revenger's Tragedy*, III v 71.

4. [Ed.] In the nursery tale, an acorn drops on Chicken Licken's head and she thinks the sky has fallen.

5. [Ed.] See the extracts, above, in this section of Part One.

6. [Ed.] Eliot's essay, a review of Allardyce Nicoll's *The Works of Tourneur*, provoked a correspondence in *The Times Literary Supplement* among Eliot, Oliphant and others, mainly over the authorship issue; see 18 December 1930, p. 1087, and, in 1931, 1 January, p. 12; 5 February, p. 99; 16 April, p. 307; 23 April, p. 327; 18 June, p. 487. See also Oliphant's 'Tourneur and Mr T. S. Eliot', *Studies in Philology*, XXXII (1935), pp. 546–52.

2. MODERN STUDIES

L. G. Salingar   *The Revenger's Tragedy* and the
Morality Tradition   (1938)

Tourneur's plays have too often been described as if they were texts
for illustration by an Aubrey Beardsley. They have suffered as a
result. Symonds read *The Revenger's Tragedy* as a melodrama with
agreeable thrills and some needless moralising; and, on this reading,
it was not difficult for William Archer, applying the standards of
naturalism, to make the play appear ludicrous.[1] Though Mr Eliot
has supplied a corrective by pointing out that the characters are not
to be taken as studies in individual iniquity, but as figures in a
pattern with a poetic life of its own, his essay on Tourneur again
misrepresents him. He is made 'a highly sensitive adolescent with a
gift for words'. [Quotes the passage in Eliot's essay, excerpted above,
beginning 'The cynicism, the loathing and disgust of humanity' to
the end of the paragraph – Ed.] This is the reading of the 'nineties
again. Tourneur's poetry, however, unlike the Romantic poetry of
decadence, has a firm grasp on the outer world. Cynicism, loathing
and disgust there are in *The Revenger's Tragedy*; but if Tourneur were
merely giving expression to a neurotic state of mind, he could hardly
have written successful drama at all. The 'object' of his disgust is
not the behaviour of his characters, singly or together, so much as
the process they represent, the disintegration of a whole social order.
It is this theme, particularised and brought to life by the verse, that
shapes the pattern of the play; and it is developed with the coherence,
the precise articulation, of a dramatist assured that his symbols are
significant for his audience as much as for himself. Tourneur is
writing in the contemporary Revenge convention; but behind the
Revenge plays is another dramatic influence, working in harmony
with Tourneur's narrowly traditionalist outlook, that of the Moralities. *The Revenger's Tragedy* is a logical development from the mediaeval
drama.

The Moralities had been the staple of popular drama when

Marlowe began writing, and their methods were absorbed into the blank verse narrative play. That they were absorbed, not abandoned, is clear from *Faustus*; and L. C. Knights has pointed out that their influence on Jonson and his contemporaries was considerable and varied.[2] They offered the Elizabethans a group of stock situations, types and themes which had been utilised for the representation of social and religious problems throughout the changes of a century; and the later drama could rely on their familiarity in presenting fairly complex situations simply and effectively on the stage. The Morality influence makes itself felt, under the Senecanism and the literary satire, through the conventions of the Revenge plays themselves, and in *The Revenger's Tragedy* most strongly of all. The characters in the Moralities are personified abstractions and moral or social types, representing the main forces making for or against the salvation of the individual and social stability; they have no dramatic functions outside the doctrinal scheme. The actions on the stage are symbolic, not realistic, and the incidents are related to each other logically, as parts of an allegory or as illustrations of the argument. *The Revenger's Tragedy* is constructed on closely similar lines. Miss Bradbrook has analysed the narrative into 'a series of peripeteia', representing 'the contrasts between earthly and heavenly vengeance, and earthly and heavenly justice'[3] – linked as the parts of an allegory rather than as a natural sequence of events. The characters are exclusively the instruments of this movement, and it is from this point of view that they explain themselves to the audience; their speeches reveal their world rather than individual minds. The Duke and his court are simply monstrous embodiments of Lust, Pride and Greed; Vindice and the other revengers, despite the intensely personal tone of their speeches, are portrayed in the same way. The characters' motives are generalised and conventional – Lussurioso, for example, is an extreme case of Pride and Lust – and many of the speeches are general satiric tirades, spoken in half-turn towards the audience. This is a narrower dramatic pattern than Marston's, and more like those of the Moralities; but Tourneur gains in dramatic coherence from the earlier examples. With Jonson, he was the last writer to apply them successfully.

'I see now', says Ambitioso in the underplot – the traditional comic underplot in which the Vices are confounded – 'there is nothing sure in mortality, but mortality.' The contrast between the skeleton and the specious overlay provided by wealth and sensuality is fundamental to Tourneur and the Morality-writers alike. When Pride, in Medwall's *Nature*, leads Man to debauchery, he prepares for him 'a doublet of the new make':

> Under that a shirt as soft as silk,
> And as white as any milk
> To keep the carcass warm.

These lines might have provided Tourneur with his text. Medwall, however, writes with an equanimity, a sense of security in the values of Nature, that Tourneur has lost. His sense of decay, of the skull, is overpowering:

> Advance thee, O thou terror to fat folks,
> To have their costly three-pil'd flesh worn off
> As bare as this; for banquets, ease, and laughter,
> Can make great men as greatness goes by clay;
> But wise men little are more great than they.

The Stoical conclusion is feeble beside the savage intensity of the first lines. Death has triumphed, and the only course left open to Vindice is to convert a horrified recoil into a grim acceptance, turning the forces of death against themselves. Nevertheless, the fascination of physical decay has not corrupted Tourneur's satiric purpose; there is nothing mechanical in Vindice's wielding of the lash. The changes of tone in this first soliloquy with the skull imply an attitude active and controlled:

> When two heaven-pointed diamonds were set
> In those unsightly rings – then 'twas a face
> So far beyond the artificial shine
> Of any woman's bought complexion,
> That the uprightest man (if such there be
> That sin but seven times a day) broke custom,
> And made up eight with looking after her.
> O, she was able to ha' made a usurer's son
> Melt all his patrimony in a kiss,
> And what his father fifty years told,
> To have consum'd, and yet his suit been cold.
> But O, accursed palace!
> Thee when thou wert apparell'd in thy flesh
> The old duke poison'd . . .
> O 'ware an old man hot and vicious:
> *Age, as in gold, in lust is covetous.*

The contrasts between life and death, between natural virtue and the effects of lust and greed, are not merely presented – they are shown as a unified process in Vindice's mind, a process which extends through the whole world of the play. The imagery associated with the skull is concrete, exact and dramatically useful; Tourneur builds up a system of relationships between images and situations which gains in cumulative effect – these lines, for example, have a bearing on the ironic undertones of the scene where the Duchess tempts Spurio, who is wearing her jewel in his ear ('had he cut thee a right diamond . . .'), and, again, on the second appearance of the skull, poisoned with cosmetics. The pun in the first line is flat but not extraneous; it emphasises the way in which the symbols are to be taken – the physical world is treated, in a peculiarly direct and consistent manner, as emblematic of the moral order, man in relation to the divine will. This moral order is rigidly identified with the traditional social hierarchy of ranks and obligations; but the narrowness of Tourneur's outlook makes for concentration, and his poetic material is ranged and ordered by reference to the experience of society as a whole. In this passage, the physical contrast between the 'diamonds' and their sockets, visible on the stage, prepares for, and supports, the crude cynicism of the parenthesis, which marks the change of tone. The complete degeneration of virtue is represented by placing the 'usurer's son' on the same footing of sensuality as 'the uprightest man', the mock inflation overturning any protest from respectability. Here, however, the tone changes again: the 'patrimony', by implication the ill-gained result of greed, is itself 'melted' away, and, though virtue cannot be reinstated, divine justice is vindicated in the rhyme. Vindice's tone mounts again as he reverts to the palace; but the Duke, with the 'infernal fires' burning in his 'spendthrift veins', has already been paralleled with the usurer's son – the two types of social disintegration are juxtaposed throughout the play – so that Vindice's exultant determination on revenge appears as part of an inevitable cycle of feelings and events.

The trite 'sentences' at the end of Tourneur's most passionate speeches are meant to enforce this sense of inevitability by lowering the tension and appealing to the commonplace. Tourneur himself calls them 'conceits', and continually draws attention, in Marston's manner, to his virtuosity in using them. The resemblance to Marston, however, is only superficial; they are more closely akin to the popular moralists and the Morality writers. Vindice's emblem is an example:

'A usuring father to be boiling in hell, and his son and heir with a whore dancing over him' [IV ii 88–9]. Again:

> O, you must note
> Who 'tis should die:
> The duchess' son; she'll look to be a saver;
> *Judgement in this age is near kin to favour.*   [I iv 52–5]

> Could you not stick? see what confession doth!
> Who would not lie, when men are hang'd for truth?   [v i 131–2]

These popular aphorisms and tags of Seneca Englished gave Marston and Tourneur a large part of the raw material from which their more ambitious speeches are developed. But while Marston works up his material as a self-conscious litterateur, Tourneur adheres to the Morality mode. The language of the latter is plain and colloquial, but adequate, as a rule, to the simple didactic purpose; a speech to the audience from Lupton's *All for Money* is typical:

> Is not my grandfather Money think ye of great power
> That could save from hanging such abominable whore,
> That against all nature her own child did kill?
> And yonder poor knave that did steal for his need
> A few sort of rags, and not all worth a crown,
> Because he lacks money shall be hanged for that deed,
> You may see my Grandsire is a man of renown:
> It were meet when I named him that you all kneeled down.
> Nay, make it not so strange, for the best of you all,
> Do love him so well, you will come at his call.

The audience is included in the framework of the play, the function of the speeches being to expound the theme to them from their own point of view. Marston's sophisticated railing has quite a different effect; it draws attention to itself [as between Pietro and Mendoza in *The Malcontent*]:

> PIET. Tell me – indeed, I heard thee rail –
> MEND. At women, true; why, what cold phlegm could choose,
> Knowing a Lord so honest, virtuous,
> So boundless-loving, bounteous, fair-shaped, sweet,
> To be contemned, abused, defamed, made cuckold?
> Heart! I hate all women for't: sweet sheets, wax lights, antic bedposts, cambric smocks, villainous curtains, arras pictures, oiled hinges, and all the tongue-tied lascivious witnesses of great creatures' wantonness.[4]

The lively phrasing here is at odds with the ostensible moral purpose – it is true that Mendoza is gulling Pietro, having cuckolded him himself, but his speech is in the same style as the Malcontent's own speeches; the literary exhibitionism accompanies a confusion of dramatic motives. Tourneur's railing in *The Revenger's Tragedy* is more surely realised; it is presented in the older and simpler dramatic mode:

> Now 'tis full sea abed over the world;
> There's juggling of all sides. Some that were maids
> E'en at sunset are now perhaps i'th' toll-book.
> This woman in immodest thin apparel
> Lets in her friend by water; here a dame,
> Cunning, nails leather hinges to a door,
> To avoid proclamation; now cuckolds are
> A-coining, apace, apace, apace, apace;
> And careful sisters spin that thread i'th' night
> That does maintain them and their bawds i'th' day.

HIPP. You flow well, brother.

VIND.   Puh, I'm shallow yet,
> Too sparing and too modest – shall I tell thee?
> If every trick were told that's dealt by night,
> There are few here that would not blush outright.

[II ii 136–49]

The direct appeal to the audience, as Miss Bradbrook remarks, is bathetic (*Themes and Conventions*, p. 173); but it is significant of the condition of success for the first speech, Tourneur's single-minded attitude towards subject and audience together. The shaping influence is that of the Moralities, transmitted directly through Jonson. . . .

The disguises and deceptions which compose the plot are symbolic, not naturalistic – an occasion is even created for making Castiza herself appear in a false character. Vindice is disguised three times – when, as Piato, he enters 'the world' and becomes 'a man o' the time', a court pander; a second time, when he appears as a fantastic 'character' of himself, a melancholy, litigious scholar; and finally, as a masquer. The disguises are distinguished from the disguiser; what Vindice does in his assumed roles affects his character as Vindice, but the relationship is circumscribed and conventional; no provision is made to render it plausible, realistically, that Vindice would or could have sustained his roles.[5] When he tempts his sister, he is not Vindice in disguise, he is Vindice-become-Piato; Piato and Vindice are sharply distinguished. Nevertheless, Vindice suffers for what Piato has to do; and the separate roles, moreover, are complementary to each other. At first, Vindice is the honest malcontent, the nobleman wronged and depressed by poverty; then he becomes a member of the society that has wronged him. He is sardonically aware of himself in his role, as if necessity, not policy, had changed him, just as it threatens to change his mother – (this is the way in which Flamineo [in *The White Devil*] and Bosola [in *The Duchess of Malfi*] fuse the roles of villain and critic). He is morally involved in his actions as Piato; and when he appears in the conventional fatal masque, he is justly the victim as well as the instrument of heavenly vengeance. The second disguise is a carica-ture of his original position. Thus the different roles are not linked together by reference to circumstantial probability, but by reference to the dramatic and social functions of the original character, as with Edgar in *Lear*. The disguisings are related symbols of a transformation within the moral and social order.

Symbolic disguising with a similar dramatic purpose was a stock convention of the Moralities; sometimes there is a change of dress, sometimes only of name. This was not merely a convention of the stage; it embodied popular beliefs about the methods of the Deceiver – 'the devil hath power / To assume a pleasing shape' [*Hamlet*, II ii 599]. Thus, in Medwall's *Nature*, Pride and Covetise beguile Man under the names of Worship and Worldly Policy, the other Deadly Sins being disguised in the same way. Moreover, the disguisers, besides their attributes as moral types, are usually given, more specifically than any other figures in the play, the attributes of a particular social class. Man, in *Nature*, is a noble, but he is made representative of humanity in general; it is emphasised, on the other hand, that Pride is a knight, and the Deadly Sins only appear as officers of the household. In the later Moralities, social themes, as distinct from theological, become more prominent; and the moral role of the disguisers is often completely merged into their role as the agents of social change. In the Marian play, *Respublica*, for example, the Reformation is engineered by the profiteer Avarice disguised as Policy; and the characters with aliases in *The Tide Tarrieth No Man* are the broker, Hurtful Help, who operates under the deceptive title of Help, and his accomplices.

The disguisers are contrasted with the other characters in that the latter represent the permanent and unequivocal moral standards which maintain social stability. Even in the middle-class Moralities of the sixteenth century, the disguisers – and the vices in general –

frequently stand for 'usury' in its various forms; the other characters, for its opponents and victims. Traditional ethics under the Tudors subsume social and economic questions directly under moral categories; the system rests on the belief that the social order has been established by Nature in accordance with the divine will. This is expounded by Nature herself at the beginning of Medwall's play:

> Th' almighty God that made each creature,
> As well in heaven as other place earthly,
> By His wise ordinance hath purveyed me, Nature,
> To be as minister, under Him immediately,
> For th' enchesoun [*the reason*] that I should, perpetually,
> His creatures in such degree maintain
> As it hath pleased His grace for them to ordain.

This is the ethic of a society predominantly agricultural, in which 'everything . . . seemed to be the gift of nature, the obvious way of life, and thus the result of the Divine ordering, whether as a good gift or as a penalty.'[6] In order to enjoy the divine bounty, to maintain each individual in the sufficiency appropriate to the station in which he was born, it was necessary to observe the conditions on which it was given; and the satisfaction of the profit-motive, of 'greed', or, equally, the wasteful gratification of selfish pleasure, whether on the part of knight, burgher or peasant, interfered with this primary necessity. They were 'against nature', contrary to the obvious expression of the divine will. Opportunities for personal aggrandisement, by means of capital investment, organising ability or technical innovation, were, relatively, too few and unimportant, before the sixteenth century, seriously to disturb this traditional order; and it seemed evident that they could only be taken at someone else's expense. By the end of the century, as commercial enterprise, money power and new industrial techniques began to dominate economic life, they seemed to involve a change in the whole relationship between man and nature, between the individual and his vocation.[7] To conservative minds, it meant the substitution of appearances for realities.

Hence, while the Elizabethans applied the Morality conventions of disguise to a variety of new purposes, the earlier associations were not lost. The tradition of dramatic allegory, with disguising as an essential part, was also maintained by the court masque; and Jonson's *Cynthia's Revels*, in particular, with its satire on the social climbers and rootless adventurers infesting the court, is avowedly a combination of masque and Morality. 'The night is come', says one of the Children in the Induction, explaining the plot, 'and Cynthia intends to come forth . . . All the courtiers must provide for revels; they conclude upon a masque, the device of which is . . . that each of these Vices, being to appear before Cynthia, would seem to be other than indeed they are; and therefore assume the most neighbouring Virtues as a masquing habit.' Here Jonson turns the popular ethic against the courtly, the Morality against the masque; for it was the convention of the masques that the courtiers who came to dance as virtues or deities were in fact the incarnations of the qualities they assumed; the masque itself was a social institution, representing the court as the magnificent embodiment of the virtues by right of which it claimed to govern. *The Malcontent, Women Beware Women* and *The Revenger's Tragedy* make ironic use of this function of disguisings in the masque. In Tourneur's case, especially, the masque, as a symbol of courtly riot, is treated from the point of view of the Morality. The courtiers in the masque described by Antonio are Morality Vices –

> Putting on better faces than their own,
> Being full of fraud and flattery;

and, throughout the play, descriptions of revels form the nucleus of the satire, leading up to the fatal masque at the end. They are associated with the references to bastardy and prostitution and to 'patrimonies washed a-pieces', and with the images of cosmetics and of justice 'gilt o'er' with favour. Against the 'forgetful feasts' is set the image of the skeleton. The corruption of the court by wealth and luxury, and its violation of the moral order which justifies high rank, is set beside the effects of usury, both alike overthrowing the standards of Nature. Virtue and honour, on the other hand, are identified, as in Castiza's first soliloquy, with the norms of the traditional manorial order, which Tourneur makes to stand for social norms in general. Several of his metaphors are taken from the payment of rents – vengeance, for example, is a 'quit-rent'.

G. Wilson Knight's description of the structure of a Shakespearean play, then, is peculiarly appropriate to *The Revenger's Tragedy* also: it is 'an expanded metaphor, by means of which the original vision has been projected into forms roughly correspondent with actuality, conforming thereto . . . according to the demands of its nature.'[8] The central metaphors and the technique of presentation are the products of mediaeval ways of thought, as they had taken shape on the stage in the conventions of the Moralities. With his narrow and hypersensitive mentality, his imperviousness to the psychological make-up of individuals and his intense preoccupation with ethics, Tourneur could not have written successful drama except by means of their example.

The total impression created by the development of his plot, by the figures of the lecherous old Duke and his court, by the imagery and rhythms of the verse, is that of a hectic excitement, a perverse and over-ripe vitality on the verge of decay; the themes of the danse macabre, suggested in *Hamlet* and *The Malcontent*, dominate *The Revenger's Tragedy*. But the satire is not hysterical; Tourneur maintains an alert sardonic irony which makes its objects grotesque as well as disgusting. The sense of proportion expressed in the style is not that of the Revenge plays; it comes from the Moralities, and from Jonson. Jonson's influence is most apparent in the scene [II i] where Vindice tempts his mother and sister; the subject is from *The Malcontent*, the style from *Volpone*[9]:

> Would I be poor, dejected, scorn'd of greatness,
> Swept from the palace, and see other daughters
> Spring with the dew o' th' court, having mine own
> So much desir'd and lov'd – by the duke's son?
> No, I would raise my state upon her breast,
> And call her eyes my tenants; I would count
> My yearly maintenance upon her cheeks,
> Take coach upon her lip, and all her parts
> Should keep men after men, and I would ride
> In pleasure upon pleasure . . .
> How blest are you, you have happiness alone;
> Others must fall to thousands, you to one,
> Sufficient in himself to make your forehead
> Dazzle the world with jewels, and petitionary people
> Start at your presence.

These passages are not mere echoes of Jonsonian phrasing; they have the energetic hyperbole and the finely measured scorn of Jonson's best manner. The scene continues with a passage of brilliant extravaganza:

> O, think upon the pleasure of the palace;
> Secured ease and state; the stirring meats,
> Ready to move out of the dishes, that
> E'en now quicken when they're eaten;

> Banquets abroad by torch-light, music, sports,
> Bare-headed vassals, that had ne'er the fortune
> To keep on their own hats, but let horns wear 'em;
> Nine coaches waiting, – hurry, hurry, hurry.
>
> CAST. Ay, to the devil.
> VIND. [*Aside*] Ay, to the devil – [*To her*] To th' duke, by my faith.
> GRAT. Ay, to the duke. Daughter, you'd scorn to think o'th' devil
> and you were there once.

The excitement of these passages is hardly the product of a nightmare vision. On the contrary, it is controlled and directed by a sense of the crude realities underlying the court's fantastic behaviour. The source and character of Tourneur's grotesquerie is indicated, again, by Spurio's soliloquy in Act II, scene ii:

> Faith, if the truth were known, I was begot
> After some gluttonous dinner, some stirring dish
> Was my first father, when deep healths went round,
> And ladies' cheeks were painted red with wine,
> Their tongues as short and nimble as their heels,
> Uttering words sweet and thick; and when they rose,
> Were merrily dispos'd to fall again.

The nervous and sinister tones of the mockery are balanced by the 'primitive' realism.

Nevertheless, Tourneur does not escape from his cycle of decay; there is nothing in the play, in its scheme of moral and social values, to compensate for Vindice's fall. In the process of commercial development, which had brought new hopes and possibilities to the middle classes, Tourneur saw only that the court had been uprooted from the people and the soil, while the old-fashioned gentry were left to their honour, their poverty and their discontent. As, throughout the sixteenth century, landlord and ploughman alike had been submitted to a growing dependence on money, and their customary incomes had proved inadequate to meet rising costs and a rising standard of living, the stability of the old hierarchy had broken down. Many of the nobility and gentry were forced to give up their 'hospitality' or to sell their estates; and their successors and survivors, knowing, with Burghley, that 'gentility is nothing else but ancient riches', had acted accordingly. The nobility themselves had become enclosers, joint-stock-holders, company-promoters, monopolists; the court, at the turn of the century, was the happy-hunting-ground for adventurers and profiteers. Until the end of Elizabeth's reign, this commercialisation of the nobility was in harmony with the main economic and political needs of the middle classes: but when the latter had outgrown their royal tutelage, the powers of the court became obstructive; and when titles were sold and honours conferred on irresponsible favourites, it became clear that the system of court privileges opened the way to the machiavellian and the sycophant. The fount of honour was poisoned at the source. While 'the disproportion between honour and means' became more glaring, large numbers of the lesser gentry, deprived of the security of the old order, found themselves landless men, dependent on an uncertain or an insufficient patronage, men without 'vocations'.[10] Tourneur's Vindice is one of the dramatic spokesmen of these malcontents. His independence belongs to the past; the present is contaminated by the values of 'gold'. On the basis of this contrast, which is extended to society as a whole, Tourneur's poetry formulates an exceptionally coherent response to the life of his time. But the business of buying and selling, the accumulation of wealth without social responsibility, which has hoisted sensuality to its evil eminence in his court, is accepted as normative and final; it becomes a process by which the values of Nature and the impulses which go to maintaining a civilised life are inevitably decomposed into their opposites. This conception forms the organising principle in Vindice's second speech to the skull [III v 43ff.], where the complex themes and symbols of the whole play are concentrated into a single magnificent passage.

The irony of this speech is reinforced by the dramatic situation: 'all the betrayed women are in a sense represented by the poisoned skull of Vindice's mistress – not only she herself, but Antonio's wife, Castiza, who would have been betrayed, and the imaginary "country lady" whom the Duke thought he was about to seduce.'[11] Similarly, 'yon fellow' is the imaginary profligate turned highwayman, the approaching Duke, and the Duchess's youngest son, who has already appeared under judgement for rape, and is ironically despatched in the next scene. Thus the skull becomes the fitting symbol, as it is the final result, of the process represented by the action and the imagery, by which solid realities are exchanged for treacherous appearances. The metaphor of 'exchange' is important; Vindice's irony turns, in this speech, on the ambiguities of the word 'for', referring both to equivalence in exchange and to purpose or result. In the first lines, a complex group of relationships are associated in the image contrasting the 'labours' of the worm – physically present in 'expend' and 'undo' – with the silken bedizenment of the lady for whom they are undertaken, a contrast which appears, at the same time, as one between the silk and the skeleton it covers; it is for the skull that the labours are ultimately intended. The 'silk-worm' is also the worm of the grave; it suggests, too, the poor weaver, 'undone' for the sake of the wealthy – the contrast between rich and poor is made explicit in the next speech; – and the colours of the silk and of the gold which is paid for it are made flat and wan by the suggested comparison with her 'yellow' face. The speech is developed round a further series of exchanges:

> Does the silk-worm expend her yellow labours
> For thee? for thee does she undo herself?
> Are lordships sold to maintain ladyships
> For the poor benefit of a bewitching minute?
> Why does yon fellow falsify high-ways,
> And put his life between the judge's lips,
> To refine such a thing? keeps horse and men
> To beat their valours for her?
> Surely we are all mad people, and they
> Whom we think are, are not; we mistake those:
> 'Tis we are mad in sense, they but in clothes.

In the third and fourth lines, the process of commercial exchange is again ironically invoked; the social stability implied by 'lordships' and 'maintained' is undermined in the colloquial sarcasm of 'lady-ships', and the 'bewitching minute' of lust is a 'poor benefit' to exchange for an inherited estate – 'poor', too, in the sense that procreation is made futile. 'Bewitching' recalls the earlier scene in which it was suggested that Gratiana's attempt to prostitute her daughter was due to diabolic possession; it detaches Vindice from the dissolution he contemplates and yet implies that it is inescapable. 'Yon fellow' implicates the Duke and his stepson as well as the broken gallant, so that 'falsify' attaches to the royal justice itself together with the royal high-way. There is also a suppressed pun on counterfeit coinage, which, with the corrosive impression of 'falsify', is carried on in the next lines: by his emphasis on the root senses of the verbs ('maintain', 'falsify', 'refine'), Tourneur sets up a characteristic tension between the imagined activities and the ideal relationships to which they ought to conform. In the old dispensation – as in Medwall's play – Nature had appointed Reason to govern Sensuality; here, Reason has been overturned. It takes its revenge, against the irrationality of the 'bewitching minute', in the contrast between the life and the moment of sentence. The judgement is also the Last Judgement. As before, the mounting rhythm then returns, after a pause, to the slow, heavy syllables referring to the skull, the final cause, it is suggested, as it is the final stage, of the whole movement – 'to refine such a thing'. The phrase, coming at this point, implies both that the overlay of 'refinement' on her 'ladyship' is as futile, and as deathly, as the poisoned cosmetic on the skull, and that this comparison actually clarifies a state of affairs present wherever bones are clothed with flesh. The next phrase again catches in its puns the self-destruction of a powerful stimulus; 'keeps' relates it to 'maintains', four lines above; 'beat their valours' refers primarily to the fierce courage of the highwaymen, but 'beats' also means 'abates', and 'valours' are 'values' – once again the purchase of death for life. Thus the perversion of the impulses making for life finds its culminating expression in the image of violent action, and the activity is simultaneously nullified by means of the puns. The last three lines generalise what has already been revealed to the senses. Just as the great lady of the first lines has dissolved into her 'ladyship', so all seeming realities have been reduced to the skull; so that to murder the Duke with the poisoned skull is a fully appropriate revenge.

Tourneur's symbols, then, are organised by applying to the contemporary world the standards of the mediaeval social tradition, as it had survived through the sixteenth century. But *The Revenger's Tragedy*, with its alternation between finely wrought passages of high mental and nervous tension and passages of clumsy sententious generalisation, represents an emotional equilibrium which Tourneur evidently could not maintain. He had profited by the example of Jonson, who had remodelled the Morality drama, with its barely delineated types and its sparse, loosely connected incidents, into something solid and closely-knit; but Jonson's mind was the more elastic, more confident of the permanent validity of his standards, more independent and detached. His dramatic structures allow of a varied interplay of motives and experiences; Tourneur's do not. In *The Revenger's Tragedy* he succeeded in directing the response to his situation by presenting Morality figures who express, or arouse, acute and powerful but narrowly restricted emotions. When, instead of dealing with types, he tried to examine individual motives, and to argue out the reasons for his judgements, he failed. . . .

With Jonson and *The Revenger's Tragedy*, the influence of the mediaeval tradition virtually came to an end. None of the Stuart dramatists whose main work came later – with the partial exception of Massinger, in his comedies – attempted to revive it; the trend of dramatic writing was towards semi- or pseudo-naturalism. Webster fumbled with the Revenge conventions in the effort to develop something relatively new to the stage – to excite varied or conflicting sympathies for individuals at odds with their surroundings. His picture of society resembles Tourneur's; but the Morality elements, which had represented for the latter the dramatic equivalents for a central core of judgements and feelings, have disappeared; and Webster, unable to come to rest on any attitude, from which to value his people, more stable or more penetrating than a pose of stoical bravado, could not write coherent drama at all. Where they are not simply melodrama, his plays depend on exploiting immediate sensations, disjointed from their dramatic contexts; and this applies not only to his stagecraft, but to his verse, which works by analogous means, and which gains, as Tourneur's loses, from quotation in short passages. His plays, with their unrealised 'sense of tragic issues' in the individual, point towards a dramatic reorientation, a development from Shakespeare, which they do not themselves achieve. After Shakespeare, the only dramatist to achieve such a reorientation was Middleton.

SOURCE: essay, '*The Revenger's Tragedy* and the Morality Tradition', in *Scrutiny*, VI (1937–38), pp. 402–22.

NOTES

[Abbreviated and renumbered from the original – Ed.]

1. [Ed.] See Symonds' and Archer's comments, above, in this selection.
2. See L. C. Knights, *Drama and Society in the Age of Jonson* (1937), p. 188; and compare M. C. Bradbrook, *Themes and Conventions of Elizabethan Tragedy* (Cambridge, 1935), p. 70.
3. Bradbrook, op. cit., ch. VII, 'Cyril Tourneur'.
4. Marston, *The Malcontent*, ed. G. K. Hunter (Manchester, 1975): I vii 40–8.
5. Cf. Bradbrook, op. cit., pp. 66–72, 166–7. The speech in which he describes his motives (at the end of I iv) makes it clear that they belong to the situation, not his character. Similarly, his behaviour in his second disguise would be ridiculous if it were really addressed to Lussurioso; but it is addressed primarily to the audience, on the assumption that every stage disguise is successful.
6. E. Troeltsch, *The Social Teaching of the Christian Churches* (Tübingen, 1912; trans. 1931), I, 249.

7. See Troeltsch, loc. cit. The capitalist economic system, he points out, is 'based on money': it 'depersonalises values, makes property abstract and individualistic . . . raises men above natural conditions of life . . . replaces the idea of providence and the spirit of mutual help . . . by products which are all times ready for use . . . It is the cause of the development of a formal abstract law, of an abstract, impersonal way of thinking, of rationalism and relativism. *As a result, it leads to a restless and changing social differentiation which is based not upon the unchanging land, but upon accidental accumulations of money which can change anything into anything else*' (my italics).

8. G. Wilson Knight, *The Wheel of Fire* (1930), p. 16.

9. Cf. the wooing of Celia in *Volpone*, and L. C. Knights, *Drama and Society*, pp. 185–8.

10. See Bacon's essay 'Of Nobility': 'A numerous nobility causeth poverty and inconvenience in a state, for it is a surcharge of expense; and besides, it being of necessity that many of the nobility fall in time to be weak in fortune, it maketh a kind of disproportion between honour and means'. L. C. Knights has shown how widespread was unemployment or misemployment among the lesser gentry about the turn of the century, and how closely this was connected with the literary fashion of melancholy (*Drama and Society*, Appendix B).

11. I have again made use of Miss Bradbrook's analysis (*Themes and Conventions*, pp. 169–72).

Fredson Bowers   'The Revenger's Tragedy as a Revenge Tragedy'   (1940)

With *The Revenger's Tragedy*, usually attributed to Cyril Tourneur and doubtfully dated 1606–7, we come to one of the last of the great tragedies composed under the specific influence of the Kydian formula. Almost twenty years, however, had passed since the first performance of *The Spanish Tragedy*, and in that time other playwrights had been subtly varying the pure tradition. Two of these authors, Chettle and Marston, exercised, indeed, a more important guidance over Tourneur than did Kyd.

Chettle in *The Tragedy of Hoffman* (1602), in his endeavor to please the developing taste for a highly colored villain, had instituted an important change in the form by endowing his villainous protagonist with the revenge motives of a Kydian hero. The audience, however, had never been in doubt about Hoffman's real character. But with Vindice in *The Revenger's Tragedy* there is that doubt, directly caused by the curious moral atrophy of the play. In spite of the assertion sometimes made that his revenge is no longer a solemn duty justified as a code and approved by the audience, but springs from a malicious desire for retaliation,[1] Vindice's wrongs as first portrayed to the audience are as real as any hero revenger's. His betrothed has been poisoned after she had repulsed the duke's lustful advances. Owing to the seriousness of the Elizabethan betrothal, Vindice is seeking revenge for the murder of a woman who was, in effect, his wife. To supplement this central motive Tourneur adds the traditional revenge for a father, although in a very feeble manner, for Vindice's father is supposed merely to have died from discontent at his disgrace by the duke.[2]

Last, and quite important for the audience's sympathy, Vindice is seen in the light of a moral purger of a corrupt court. The rape of Antonio's wife did not touch him except as Antonio was his brother's friend. Yet this revenge for Antonio, long quiescent after the first solemn oath, plays an extremely important part in the catastrophe, for the device of the masque in which Vindice slays Lussurioso is aided by two lords who are, presumably, the friends of Antonio. Vindice is not content with the death of the duke, his logical victim, but must scourge from the court all his vicious progeny and set up a new and righteous succession. He has no ambitions to usurp the ducal seat, and he believes himself to be a good man and a virtuous revenger. Deciding on the trial of his mother and sister, he says,

> though I durst almost for good
> Venture my lands in heaven upon their good.   [I iii 184–5][3]

Here, then, is presented to the audience a revenger with entirely adequate motives of blood-revenge, one who is a purifier of the state and, unlike the traditional villain, firmly believes in his own salvation.

That Tourneur has actually formed Vindice as a villain and so at the last exposes him, is a triumph in objective character-portrayal – a very rare occurrence on the Elizabethan stage. Every previous thoroughgoing villain had known he was a villain, and was excessively anxious to make that fact clear to the audience: thus he was a completely self-conscious individual who had no illusions about himself and was anxious that the audience should have none. Chettle's *Hoffman* marked the first change towards objectivity, but the transformation was incomplete because Lorrique, in the capacity of chorus, exposed Hoffman's true character. With Tourneur the objectivity is complete. The spectators were forced to decide for themselves as to Vindice's true character and to trace, step by step if they were analytical, his self-deluded downfall.

Indeed, the action of the play and the characters are so feverish and abnormal that the audience may well have been carried along unthinkingly until the common sense horror of Antonio at the revengers' deeds came like a shock of cold water both to the listeners and to Vindice. Not until the startling anti-climax does the cold reason of a normal person with whom the audience can identify itself enter the play. The moment Antonio speaks, the spectators are oriented and the true horror of the smirking admissions of Vindice and his brother is realised. This lack of a normal character to act as a touchstone accounts in a great measure for the at least partial acceptance of the lurid deeds of the revenger, particularly when the playwright's own views are so completely hidden. In fact, one might be tempted to believe that Vindice would have remained a hero if Tourneur had not felt the lure of an unexpected climax.[4] But as it is, the unique situation where the revengers of blood are hustled off to prison and execution like common criminals, removes all possible glamour clinging to a revenger.

Tourneur, then, took over the villain revenger from Chettle but changed him into a far more artistic being by a strict objective characterisation. There are other reminiscences, also, which show his influence. Vindice preserves the skull of his beloved as Hoffman the skeleton of his father, and thunder rolls as a portent. The last lesson involves a total change in the revenger's code. Hieronimo in *The Spanish Tragedy* and Titus in *Titus Andronicus* had been openly boastful and exultant once their revenge was consummated. The reason was simple: their revenge had been aimed at only a few persons and had been concentrated in one single action. Hoffman and Vindice, however, are in a society where every man's hand would be against them if they were known. Furthermore, they have not one but several revenges to perform; therefore they must strike secretly and then preserve themselves for their further revenges.

Although the character of the protagonist is indebted to *Hoffman*, perhaps the strongest influence on *The Revenger's Tragedy* came from Marston's *Malcontent*, itself not uninfluenced by Chettle. All three plays contain the central situation of a revenger living disguised in the midst of his enemies and endeavoring to secure his revenge by setting them one against another or by fobbing off his own deeds on one of his enemies for punishment. As in *The Malcontent*, the disguised revenger is hired as an accomplice by his enemy, and so secures his chance for revenge. Part of the duty of each is to attempt for his master the seduction of a woman of his own family. Both revengers create the initial discord in the ranks of their enemies by reports of adulteries in their households. Lastly, both protagonists are malcontents, and an important part of the revenge is completed by the use of a masque.

Marston's *Antonio's Revenge* has also left its mark. The brutal and long drawn out revenge on the duke parallels the torture of Piero. Most important, however, is the communal character of the revenge where the revenger is aided by his friends and by supporters of vengeance for another man – Pandulfo in *Antonio's Revenge* and Antonio in *The Revenger's Tragedy*. Owing to this alliance of revengers, the protagonist does not die in the final slaughter. Ironically, in *The Revenger's Tragedy* the alliance itself afterwards ruined the revenger. Tourneur has not hesitated to take striking incidents from other plays. The meditative speech on a skull comes from *Hamlet* and perhaps the solemn swearing to revenge over crossed swords; the stabbing of a body thought to be alive is from *The Jew of Malta*; and, lastly, murder by poisoned lips is found in *Soliman and Perseda*.

Both Chettle and Marston had worked with the complete plot as the unit, but with Tourneur, as later with Fletcher, the scene was the unit and the plot is composed of a series of strong, brilliant situations, each occupying a single scene, somewhat loosely strung together. Complicated intrigue on the parts of all the characters against one another is elaborated from *The Malcontent* and completely displaces the simple dual conflict of the Kydian plot already revolutionised by Chettle. But what Tourneur gains in brilliance of scene he relinquishes in coherence. There are so many intrigues that the revenger loses control and is lost in the maze. The opposing forces are stronger than he, and he is frequently of no purpose in the plot. By turning his revenger protagonist into a villain, Chettle had centered in him the audience's increasing interest in villainy which had already in other plays caused the enlargement of the villain's part at the expense of the revenging hero's. But Tourneur created so many villains, each struggling against the others but none against Vindice, that Vindice is too often submerged, and the play lacks on occasion a controlling protagonist.

The fact, also, that Vindice has no one clear-cut opponent against whom he can direct every scheme, adds to the confusion. Presumably the duke is his chief victim, but most of Vindice's revengeful plans center on Lussurioso, who has injured him so slightly in comparison that Vindice seems to wander from his true revenge. At no time does he hold the reins tightly. He has waited nine unexplained years[5] without opportunity for vengeance and has at last come to court hoping that circumstances will somehow prove favorable. His enemies are so powerful that the most he can do is to try to set them to destroying each other. But the solidarity of the court has disintegrated before his arrival, and the villains do not need his help to be at each other's throats: most of their internecine warfare occurs without Vindice's instigation or even his knowledge. His direct plot against Lussurioso is laid aside as early as II ii when he refuses a golden opportunity as did Hamlet and Antonio in *Antonio's Revenge*. Thereupon he transfers his attentions to the duke and thus does succeed in his revenge on the original injurer.

After this murder of the duke [III v], the action is continued by the strife among the duke's ambitious sons. The brothers determine to work revenge for the death of their younger brother on Lussurioso, but this action proves abortive when the revengers are before them in the masque and the brothers are themselves destroyed. Vindice evolves an elaborate plan to murder Lussurioso over the body of his father, but the unexpected presence of witnesses causes it to be abandoned. After Spurio has determined to kill Lussurioso, and Ambitioso to kill Spurio once the deed is done, the fatal masque is presented. The revengers achieve their purpose in slaying Lussurioso but there is no indication that the destruction of Spurio and the other brothers is anything more than an unexpected accident in the general tussle.

Hoffman, at least, conceived a far-reaching plan, and carried it through to the result he wished. It is he who pulls the strings and motivates each action. But *The Revenger's Tragedy* is full of uncompleted situations for which the ground has been laid. In *Hoffman* clarity was achieved and the interest of the audience held by watching the cause and effect, the inception and the result, of Hoffman's schemes, even though the basic law of drama – conflict – was missing from a major part of the action because of Hoffman's disguise. Tourneur has so constructed his play that the conflict chiefly occurs among the foes of the revenger without the revenger's instigation. Vindice, therefore, is not so firmly placed in the plot as

Hoffman or Malevole in *The Malcontent*; in addition, the continual promises of actions which never come off, the maze of intrigue and counter-intrigue, serve in the light of cold analysis virtually to disintegrate the plot. Where Tourneur saves himself is in his emphasis on scene and strong situation. The testing of Gratiana, the murder of the duke, the ghastly even though theatrically arranged irony, the unfathomed lust and brutality of the characters – these make the play.

The Revenger's Tragedy stands practically at the crossroads of Elizabethen tragedy. Henceforth with few exceptions the taste of the next period into which the tragic drama was entering led to the portrayal of extreme villainy, already foreshadowed, where the villains are the protagonists and the depiction of horror and tortuous intrigue is of such prime importance that revenge, while still the leading motive of the plot, does not carry the main interest of the audience except as a means to an end. *The Revenger's Tragedy*, while obviously linked to the past, is the distinct forerunner of the new school of true horror tragedies which were to break temporarily with the narrower tradition of the Kydian revenge play.

Source: extract from *Elizabethan Revenge Tragedy 1587–1642* (Princeton, N.J., 1940 paperback edn, 1966), pp. 132–8.

NOTES

[Reorganised and renumbered from the original – Ed.]

1. C. V. Boyer, *The Villain as Hero in Elizabethan Tragedy* (New York, 1914), p. 145.
2. Vindice is serious about the worth of this motive, for when the duke lies dying Hippolito cries: 'And let this comfort thee: our lord and father / Fell sick upon the infection of thy frowns, / And died in sadness; be that thy hope of life' [III v 169–71].
3. [Ed.] Several modern editions, including that of R. A. Foakes in the Revels series (1966), emend the second 'good' to 'blood' but a play on 'good' meaning 'virtue' is surely intended.
4. In his liking for the unexpected and the strained situation, Tourneur fairly anticipates the methods of Fletcher. The whole situation of the testing of the mother, with the daughter's pretended acquiescence, while undoubtedly derived from *The Malcontent*, is handled in just the manner Fletcher employed to titillate a jaded audience with strong situations.
5. This long wait for vengeance before the opening of the play gradually became a semi-convention, as in Massinger's *Duke of Milan*. Presumably the audience was to be impressed with the revenger's tenacity of purpose

and fierceness of resolve. Seldom is this period of inactivity well motivated, for the revenger's ultimate course of action could as well have been adopted at the beginning as at the end. Since only rather villainous revengers are presented as waiting such a period, the suspicion is well founded that the information is given to illustrate their over-bloodthirsty characters. No normal, sympathetic person by Elizabethan standards would harbor his wrath for such a time and withstand the promptings of religion for forgiveness.

Inga-Stina Ekeblad (Ewbank)   'The Structure of *The Revenger's Tragedy*'   (1960)

Without an understanding of the form and structure of *The Revenger's Tragedy*, it is not possible to give an objective explanation of the features of the play which make it, in some respects, different from *The Atheist's Tragedy*, and, in some, reminiscent of Middleton's plays. The need to make clear what the author was really meaning to do becomes obvious when we meet with definitions of *The Revenger's Tragedy* as varied as:

. . . a true tragedy in the revenge-horror style.[1]
. . . an outlet for the expression of his better judgement on man and his essentially gloomy view of human life.[2]
. . . a logical development from the medieval drama . . . The actions on the stage are symbolic, not realistic, and the incidents are related to each other logically, as parts of an allegory, or as illustrations of an argument.[3]

Yet, contradictory as the judgements above may seem, they all contain *part* of the truth about *The Revenger's Tragedy*. Taken together they at least point to a fact that it is essential to recognise: namely that in this play there operate various traditions, and that the play is a fusion of various traditional dramatic forms, each with its own characteristic mode of expression. For in *The Revenger's Tragedy* can be detected the following main components:

1. The Revenge play in the Senecan-Kydian tradition.
2. The dramatic Satire, risen to popularity around the turn of the century.
3. The Morality play, and the medieval homiletic tradition from which it emerged.

Of those components it is the tradition of the Revenge play that governs the plot. From Vindice's opening soliloquy, closely parallel to the opening of Chettle's *Hoffman*, to the final masque, which, via *The Malcontent* and *Antonio's Revenge* can be traced back to *The Spanish Tragedy* itself, the dramatic structure, with its whole web of revenges, shows that elements have been absorbed from all the chief plays in the tradition popularised by Kyd some fifteen years earlier. The most spectacular dramatic effects draw upon the common stock of thoughts, phrases, and incidents belonging to the Revenge tradition: the central situation of Vindice, the Revenger, moving around in the midst of his enemies, the brooding over the skull, the portentous thunder, and the fiendish physical and mental torture of the old Duke, are just a few examples.[4]

The element of Satire is also partly inherent in the plot itself. The intrigue which is formed by Vindice's various disguises is a vehicle for the exposure and scourging of villainy; of vices such as they are personified by characters whose mere names place them in the satiric, 'humorous', tradition. The satiric intent of the play is made especially clear in speeches where the author seems to interrupt the Revenge action in order to give us a piece of poetry which – considering for the moment only its content – might have been part of a non-dramatic Satire of the period. Such a piece are the Bastard's words:

> Faith, if the truth were known, I was begot
> After some gluttonous dinner, some stirring dish
> Was my first father, when deep healths went round,
> And ladies' cheeks were painted red with wine,
> Their tongues as short and nimble as their heels,
> Uttering words sweet and thick; and when they rose,
> Were merrily dispos'd to fall again, –
> In such a whisp'ring and withdrawing hour,
> When base male-bawds kept sentinel at stair-head,
> Was I stol'n softly . . .   [I ii 180–9]

Thanks to the subject matter of imagery, often in seemingly non-satiric contexts – as when Vindice broods over his mistress's skull:

> O, she was able to ha' made a usurer's son
> Melt all his patrimony in a kiss,
> And what his father fifty years told,
> To have consum'd . . .   [I i]

– we are, despite the trappings of Italianate Revenge, kept in constant touch with early seventeenth-century England and its

changing economic and social world: with the breaking up of the
traditional manorial order, 'farmers' sons' washing their hands and
becoming City gentlemen, exchanging simple country manners for
'the pleasure of the palace'; and with the growing acquisitive spirit,
the amassing of wealth. From one point of view, then, the play is to
be seen as a Satire on all the features of the early Jacobean period
of material progress and spiritual and moral decay which are
compressed in the two figures recurring in action and imagery: the
whore and the usurer.[5] The immediacy of the satiric attacks is shown
by the frequent repetition of phrases like 'in this luxurious day', or
'in these days'.

What, however, distinguishes the satire of the play from that of,
for instance, Marston's plays, is its backbone of orthodox *moral*
purpose. Social, economic, or sexual, satire of seemingly topical
import is constantly made ethical. It is, indeed, impossible to draw
a borderline between what was denoted as the second and the third
traditional component in *The Revenger's Tragedy*. Satire and Morality
here form a unity – that unity of realistic satire and dogmatic
moralising which is characteristic of the medieval homily. No less
than in a traditional Morality does the pattern of the seven deadly
sins underlie and shape the play. When, for example, Vindice is
speaking over the skull:

> Does every proud and self-affecting dame
> Camphor her face for this? and grieve her maker
> In sinful baths of milk, when many an infant starves
> For her superfluous outside – all for this?   [III v 84–7]

we are very far from the conventional harping on ladies and their
cosmetics. The key to these lines lies in 'proud' and 'sinful': as in
the medieval Morality the imagery of finery is pursued down to its
moral significance, to its connection with pride, the deadliest of the
sins, and with the homiletic theme of waste and extravagance versus
the suffering inflicted upon innocents. As has often been observed,
the skull is here used as a true *memento mori*. It provides the occasion
for a parade of sins:

> Here's an eye
> Able to tempt a great man – to serve God;
> A pretty hanging lip, that has forgot how to dissemble:
> Methinks this mouth should make a swearer tremble,
> A drunkard clasp his teeth, and not undo 'em
> To suffer wet damnation to run through 'em.

Here's a cheek keeps her colour, let the wind
Go whistle; . . .
⠀⠀⠀⠀⠀⠀⠀⠀It were fine, methinks,
To have thee seen at revels, forgetful feasts,
And unclean brothels; sure, 'twould fright the sinner,
And make him a good coward, put a reveller
Out of his antic amble,
And cloy an epicure with empty dishes.
Here might a scornful and ambitious woman
Look through and through herself . . .

This scene strongly recalls the medieval homily, and not only in subject but also in the handling of the dramatic situation: the explicit case-by-case moralising which does not shrink from breaking the dramatic illusion in order to drive home its points. To understand this passage as its author conceived of it, we should pay attention to how parts of Vindice's speech, while organically related to the rest of what he is saying, simultaneously serve as a kind of stage-directions. We must picture Vindice, with the skull 'dressed up in tires', coming downstage to make a direct appeal to the male members of the audience: 'Who now bids twenty pound a night, prepares / Music, perfumes and sweetmeats?' But no one 'bids'. So he continues: 'All are hush'd.' Similarly, at the end of his speech, he again comes downstage, now to address the female audience: 'see, ladies, with false forms / You deceive men, but cannot deceive worms.' It is worth noticing how the return to theatrical illusion is accomplished through Vindice's ambiguous words: 'Now to my tragic business'. Vindice is now retiring upstage, to the action-area where Hippolito is lingering, in order to go on with what in two senses is his 'tragic business'.

Even in situations which at first sight have no element of moralising in them, the dramatic treatment, and the language, are controlled by traditional religious morals. The scape-goats of the early seventeenth-century Satires are treated as deadly sins: in action by the structure of the plot which conveys to death every misdoer – first, of course, the lechers and gluttons, but eventually even Vindice since he has overstepped the bounds of human revenge and neglected the words *Vindicta mihi*; in language by the recurrence of words like 'sin' and 'damnation'. *Luxuria* is a main theme of action and language alike. The descriptions of the feasting at court, the 'gluttonous dinner', and the 'stirring meats, / Ready to move out of the dishes', parallel condemnatory descriptions of immoderate feasts in medieval poetry, just as the concern with 'lordships sold to maintain ladyships', or with 'Fair meadows cut into green foreparts', shows the medieval attitude to 'getting and spending': an attitude governed, primarily, not by economic theory but by religious morality.[6] Love in the play is seen only as lust, and lust as a way to damnation. Vindice's speech: 'Now 'tis full sea abed over the world . . .', fascinated as it is with the vice it is supposed to scourge, could at first sight be taken from any of the contemporary Satires. But, again, in its disconcerting accusation of the very audience watching this play – 'If every trick were told that's dealt by night, / There are few here that would not blush outright' – it also shows its relationship to the Morality.

The speech just referred to shows how important it is to recognise that *The Revenger's Tragedy*, unlike many of the Satires of the period, never leaves us at a loss as to how to take, in the sense of how to place within a moral scheme, a speech or an incident. In Vindice's tempting of Castiza the excited, accelerated, movement of images and rhythm almost seems to outstrip the listener's or reader's imagination, so as to drive him from a proper moral viewpoint:

> O, think upon the pleasure of the palace;
> Secured ease and state; the stirring meats,
> Ready to move out of the dishes, that
> E'en now quicken when they're eaten;
> Banquets abroad by torch-light, music, sports . . .
>
> [II i 199–203]

But then, in its dramatic context of the *Comus*-like situation, Vindice's speech is the beguiling of the archfiend, and thus ethically impressive through its very quality of allurement. Besides, characteristically, the sequel of the speech makes its true value abundantly clear:

> Nine coaches waiting, – hurry, hurry, hurry.
> CAST.   Ay, to the devil.
> VIND.   [*Aside*] Ay, to the devil – [*To her*] To th' duke, by my faith.

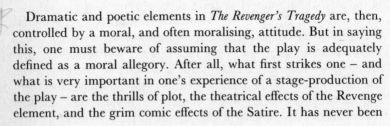

Dramatic and poetic elements in *The Revenger's Tragedy* are, then, controlled by a moral, and often moralising, attitude. But in saying this, one must beware of assuming that the play is adequately defined as a moral allegory. After all, what first strikes one – and what is very important in one's experience of a stage-production of the play – are the thrills of plot, the theatrical effects of the Revenge element, and the grim comic effects of the Satire. It has never been sufficiently stressed, I think, that in a sense *The Revenger's Tragedy* is a *farce*, just as *Volpone* and *The Jew of Malta* are farces.[7] The play is permeated by a kind of grotesque humour which stretches from details of imagery to whole scenes like the stabbing of the already dead body,[8] or Vindice's 'dialogue' with the 'bony lady':

> Madam, his grace will not be absent long.
> Secret? Ne'er doubt us, madam; 'twill be worth
> Three velvet gowns to your ladyship. Known?
> Few ladies respect that! Disgrace? a poor thin shell . . .
>   [III v 43–6]

This, if played right – with skilful ventriloquism – should be extraordinarily funny on the stage. Again, this gargoylish grin, the blending of farcical joking with tremendous moral seriousness, reaches, through Jonson and *The Jew of Malta*, back to medieval dramatic and homiletic traditions. We need only think of Chaucer's *Pardoner's Tale*.

What I am trying to say, however, is that we must be aware that any disentanglement of the various components of *The Revenger's Tragedy*, such as has been done above, is artificial. The various traditional elements do not exist separately, but are fused together; and exactly in this fusion lies the key to the peculiar qualities of *The Revenger's Tragedy*.

Using the traditional components that we have just traced, the author, by an astonishing power of assimilation and creation, achieves a unity of effect. We may first see in single features of the play how this is accomplished. The skull is a melodramatic device of Revenge plays, but it is also a device for conveying moral meaning. The masque, spectacular climax of many Revenge plots, is also part of the satire on courtly revelling; it yet also possesses an allegorical value. The thunder, used purely for theatrical effect in a Revenge play like *Hoffman*, here also betokens God's active intervention. It is *God's* warning and vengeance, and so is the spectacular blazing star. Vindice is the arch-Revenger, but he is also the detached commentator of the satiric drama, and the traditional Malcontent, as well as being a moralising preacher and an active moral agent, now of good, now of evil, depending on his disguise. The tempting of Castiza is clearly a Morality situation, with the disguised tempter assailing the 'crystal tower' of virginal virtue; but it would be unfair to overlook the purely dramatic value of the way the situation is handled. Vindice disguised and using all his powers of allurement

to wreck his sister, while hoping with all his heart that she will resist
temptation – that is a situation dramatically even more effective
than the Celia-scene in *Volpone*, which may or may not have
influenced it, and infinitely more so than the pure good-evil
opposition in *Comus*. In short, whether we consider the plot of the
play, its characters, or its language, we find the elements of the
three traditions co-existing and co-operating.

The unity of the play as a whole is a product of the balance of
the various components of the play with each other. The tone of
realism demanded by the 'decorum' of satiric verse serves in the
total effect of the play to control the melodramatic effect of the
Revenge plot. To illustrate this, we need only put side by side
Vindice's introductory speech over his mistress's skull, with its
startling directness of imagery, and the rhetoric in the – outwardly –
similar situation in *Hoffman*. Satiric verse, on the other hand, is
constantly deepened in significance by the ever-present moral framework, and often – again the skull-speech is the best example – by
an allegorical situation where it occurs. Moral allegory, finally,
never appears pure, with the theatrical gauntness of the Morality
play. It is made dramatically effective, and even theatrical, by the
handling of intrigue and incidents. As for the language of the play,
its characteristic quality lies, again, in its fusing of various modes.
A single example will have to suffice, Vindice's words which are
part of the central skull-speech:

> Why does yon fellow falsify high-ways,
> And put his life between the judge's lips?   [III v 76–7]

Through the image of the 'judge's lips' this harks back to the trial
of the Younger Son in Act I, and the Duchess's words: 'Death too
soon steals out of a lawyer's lip'. It thus has a kind of plot relevance;
but also, in the two lines together, satirical references to actual high-
way robbery and its legal consequences fuse with suggestions of the
symbolical high-way to Heaven and the impending Judgement. And
all this is simultaneous with the audience's picture of the skull,
which makes the words into a *memento mori*. Here, as in all the
climactic points of the play, a three-fold tradition is activated.
Building on, and drawing strength from, the traditions of Revenge
tragedy, satiric drama, and Morality, *The Revenger's Tragedy*, when
approached from the point of view of its artistic form, shows the

tightness and coherence of a play composed with a firmly realised purpose.

SOURCE: extract from 'On the Authorship of *The Revenger's Tragedy*', in *English Studies*, XLI (1960), pp. 227–33.

NOTES

[Reorganised and renumbered from the original – Ed.]

1. Allardyce Nicoll, *British Drama* (1925), p. 185.
2. C. E. Vaughan, 'Tourneur and Webster', *The Cambridge History of English Literature*, 15 vols. (Cambridge, 1907–27), VI, p. 168.
3. L. G. Salingar [see his essay, above, in this selection].
4. Cf. for the disguise-intrigue *The Malcontent* and *The Tragedy of Hoffman*; for the skull and the thunder *Hamlet* and *Hoffman* respectively; and for the torture, e.g. the treatment of Piero in *Antonio's Revenge*.
5. Cf. Vindice's 'conceit': 'A usuring father to be boiling in hell, and his son and heir with a whore dancing over him' [IV ii 88–9].
6. See John Speirs, '*Wynnere and Wastour* and *The Parliament of the Three Ages*', *Scrutiny*, XVII (1950), pp. 132–53, especially pp. 134, 136. Note also the sermon story of the English knight who fleeced the poor to secure the money to provide his wife with new elaborate headgear – G. R. Owst, *Literature and Pulpit in Medieval England* (Cambridge, 1933), p. 321, n. 5 – and cf. II i 225–6: 'Fair trees, those comely foretops of the field, / Are cut to maintain head-tires.'
7. Cf. T. S. Eliot's comment on *The Jew of Malta* in 'Christopher Marlowe', *Selected Essays*, rev. edn. (1934), p. 123.
8. This, one might note, is a direct 'parallel' with *The Jew of Malta*: Jacomo's 'killing' of Bernadine's corpse in IV i.

Peter B. Murray   'The Revenger's Tragedy and Transformation'   (1964)

The action *The Revenger's Tragedy* imitates through the forms of plot, characters and diction is the effort to make moral and physical transformations. The play depicts a world of inverted values, a dark world in which torchlight makes an 'artificial noon' for scenes of evil [I iv 27], and there is always a sense that the day is 'out o'th' socket / That it is noon at midnight' [II iii 44–5]. People disguise themselves and dissemble their true intentions, and their expectations are transformed by ironic reversals in action and word. Transforming puns, metaphors and personifications are everywhere.

We must not be tempted to associate this theme of transformation exclusively with Tourneur's *Transformed Metamorphosis* and thus to use it as an argument for his authorship of the play. The corrupt world, especially the world spawned by the hectic imaginings of Englishmen fascinated by Italy, was commonly represented as 'transformed' in Jacobean literature. Besides the transformed world of Tourneur's poem, there is the world of Jonson's comedies:

> Call devils angels; and sin piety;
> Let all things be preposterously transchang'd.[1]

There are also the 'Mad World' of Middleton's *A Mad World, My Masters*, and the Spain of his *Changeling*. Perhaps closest to what we find in *The Revenger's Tragedy* is the Italianate hell of John Marston:

> Lorenzo Celso the loose Venice duke
> Is going to bed: 'tis now a forward morn
> 'Fore he take rest. O strange transformed sight,
> When princes make night day, the day their night![2]

In the transformed world of *The Revenger's Tragedy* nothing is as it should be: 'Time hath several falls; / Griefs lift up joys, feasts put down funerals' [v i 164–5]. Revels for funerals! and the revels, in which courtiers should masque as virtues, are instead the vehicles for murder and rape.

'Judgement in this age is near kin to favour' and speaks 'all in gold' [I iv 55, 61]. Ethical principles of justice are lost to sight, and replacing them is a demonic, ironic justice, oblivious of good and evil, but working to destroy evil-doers. Honesty is but 'heaven's beggar', chastity a 'foolish country-girl' [II i 183, 82]. 'Faiths are bought and sold, / Oaths in these days are but the skin of gold' [III i 6–7]. The people in the ducal family are so depraved that they are ready to 'call foul incest but a venial sin' [I ii 171]. They find true delight only in stealth [I iii 105]; 'there's no pleasure sweet but it is sinful' [III v 208]. 'Forty angels can make fourscore devils' [II i 89], and the court is so given up to evil that those who would purge it must disguise themselves as Vices, reversing the normal process of the morality play, in which Vices disguise themselves as Virtues. The members of the ducal family are overcome only by treachery and force, and at the last the opening wish of the bastard, Spurio, comes true, and all the court is 'turn'd into a corse' [I ii 36].

The society controlled by this devilish ducal court is described by Vindice as corrupted by gold and sensuality. The taking of Lussurioso's gold in a demonically inverted ritual of sacrament is a symbol of Vindice's moral poisoning, and Vindice regards the commercial society as capable of similar evil transformations of everything it touches. 'A right good woman in these days' is easily 'chang'd / Into white money' [II ii 27–8], lordships are sold to maintain whoredoms, ironically called 'ladyships' [III v 74], and fruitfields are 'turned into bastards' [I iii 51]. 'It was the greatest blessing ever happen'd to women, / When farmers' sons agreed, and met again, / To wash their hands and come up gentlemen; / The commonwealth has flourish'd ever since' [II i 219–22]. A mother who lives off her daughter's whoredom may call her eyes her 'tenants', count her 'yearly maintenance upon her cheeks', and take 'coach upon her lip' [II i 96–8].

Family relations are out of joint. Lussurioso is twice duped into attacking his father, and Hippolito and Vindice brandish daggers against their mother; thus sons are 'turn'd monsters' [IV iv 4]. The Duke and Duchess have no children in common, and the paternity even of Lussurioso, the Duke's heir, is held doubtful [I ii 197–9]. Spurio suggests that 'some stirring dish / Was my first father' [I ii 181–2]. Brothers murder brothers and undertake to act as panders to their sisters. The name of bawd 'Is so in league with age that nowadays / It does eclipse three quarters of a mother' [I iii 156–7], and Gratiana is 'bewitch'd' or 'transported' by a 'fury' into being a bawd to Castiza [IV iv 33, 93], who implores God 'Henceforth to make the mother a disease' [II i 243]. Castiza sums up much of this in the commonplace:

> The world's so chang'd, one shape into another,
> It is a wise child now that knows her mother!   [II i 166–7]

For the action of the play the central symbol of the evil transformations this hellish world has wrought is the transformation of the head of the poisoned Gloriana to a skull, 'death's vizard' [I i 50]. By means of this skull, a mask or 'shell' of death [I i 15], the disguisings, paintings and dissimulations of the play are immediately related to the traditional theme of *memento mori* and its moralising on the vanity of sin in a world where even Ambitioso is taught that 'there is nothing sure in mortality, but mortality' [III vi 88–90]. Vindice contrasts the bare truth of the skull to the falseness of the heavily painted or gorgeously masked faces of the courtiers and ladies who dance and feast by the deceptive light of torches [I i 14–48; III v 53–98]. Human flesh is but another mask, struck off by death, and penetrable, like other masks, by the eye of God [I iii 63–6].

Repeated allusions to human brows, faces and heads keep the image of Gloriana's skull ever before our minds, as it is constantly before the mind of Vindice. The head of the Duchess's youngest son, Junior, actually appears on stage, and faces are disguised, painted or figuratively burned with hot irons [II i 238]. The standard Elizabethan idea that on the brow of a person is charactered his honor or dishonor is used everywhere in *The Revenger's Tragedy*. The most common of these brow-ornaments are of course the cuckold's horns, but also the Duke is concerned for the 'forehead of our state' [I ii 4], Ambitioso speaks of the 'iron forehead' of the law [I ii 33], Vindice tells Castiza her forehead will 'dazzle the world with jewels' if she submits to Lussurioso [II i 191–2], and had Gratiana succeeded as a bawd 'that office would have cling'd unto' her forehead [IV iv 63]. All these allusions to brow heraldry unite with the symbol of the skull in the revenge of Vindice on the Duke. The incestuous kisses of Spurio and the Duchess, one of which the lecherous Duke is forced to watch as he dies, eat into his forehead 'like strong poison' [II ii 162–3], even as the corrosive poison from the skull of Gloriana hideously transforms his face.

The 'grave' transformation of Gloriana, besides acting as a symbol of all the evil transformations in the world, is related in several ways to the tragic transformation of Vindice that the play dramatises. 'Still sighing o'er death's vizard', Vindice is immediately shown to be obsessed [I i 50]. Gloriana's death is the motivating force driving him to seek revenge, and we can trace the degeneration of his character through subtle changes in his attitude toward Gloriana and her skull: transformation begets transformation.

Gloriana's skull undergoes a fearful transformation into a painted and masked semblance of a living woman when Vindice obtains his revenge. The power of paint and a mask to disguise death with the semblance of life indicates that masks and disguises are agents transforming more than the mere superficial appearances of things. Vindice disguises himself as Piato, thinking he can return to his 'true' character at will, but as Piato he experiences a disillusionment that must permanently alter his outlook and his actions.

Vindice's lines referring to his entrance into the identity of Piato always suggest that the process is a transformation: 'I'll quickly turn into another' [I i 134]; 'What brother? am I far enough from myself?' [I iii 1]. He even invokes 'Impudence', the 'goddess of the palace', to alter his countenance and character:

> Strike thou my forehead into dauntless marble,
> Mine eyes to steady sapphires; turn my visage,
> And if I must needs glow, let me blush inward . . .   [I iii 5–10]

And when his disguise leads him to pretend to be Lussurioso's pander to Castiza, Vindice, having allowed himself to be 'entered' by the 'Indian devil' of gold, cries 'Now let me burst; I've eaten noble poison. / We are made strange fellows, brother, innocent villains' [I iii 169–70]. A little later Hippolito rages against Lussurioso, 'O villain, / To make such an unnatural slave of me' [II ii 10–11].

Masks and dissimulations abound as evil characters try to transform evil into a semblance of good, to rub 'hell o'er with honey' [II ii 23], and as the virtuous try to test the evil by pretending to be evil themselves. Thus Castiza as well as Vindice tempts Gratiana, pretending in IV iv to be ready to serve the pleasure of Lussurioso.

'A masque is treason's licence, that build upon; / 'Tis murder's best face when a vizard's on' [v i 181–2]. Vindice builds upon this by appearing as Piato in the murder of the Duke, as a railing malcontent under his own name at the 'murder' of Piato, and in the masque that is to end with the murder of Lussurioso. Junior and his cohorts had worn 'better faces than their own, / Being full of fraud and flattery' when they raped Antonio's wife during a masque [I iv 29–30]. Ambitioso and Supervacuo dissemble their true feelings under false tears and false rhetoric when they receive the report of what they presume to be the death of Lussurioso [III vi 39–52]. The ludicrous irony of their failure to secure Lussurioso's death through dissembling at this juncture does not deter them from wearing masks as 'murder's best face' in the revels of Act v in order to make another attempt on his life. Their earlier wiles have cost them the life of Junior, their younger brother; this time they are the agents of their own well-merited destruction.

The crucial transformations in the play are effected by poisoning, figurative or literal. One of those the Duke refers to when he says 'Many a beauty have I turn'd to poison' is Gloriana [II iii 129], and in repayment her skull poisons him. Vindice eats the 'noble poison' of Lussurioso's gold, and, as we have noted, the society as a whole is poisoned by gold. The transforming power of poisonous gold is related to the other symbols of transformation through the name 'Piato' which Vindice chooses when he masks himself. This word meant several things in Italian, including 'flat, squat, cowered down, hidden'. More subtly related to the meaning of the play is 'plated'. As 'Oaths in these days are but the skin of gold' [iii i 7], the disguise of Vindice, after he is sacramentally poisoned by gold, is metaphorically a 'plating' of gold over his features.[3] . . .

The play's structure can be best perceived if we define its unifying action of *transformation* as going out in one form and returning in another. This formulation is broad enough to describe the arrangement of events in the plot structure, to define the dramatic and verbal ironies and poetic justices, and to shed some light on the tragedy of Vindice-Piato.

The action develops scene by scene to the climax at the virtual center of the play in the murder of the old Duke [iii v]; in the second half a series of scenes parallel in reverse the scenes of the first half and so afford ironic contrasts with them. Thus in i iii, Vindice hires himself to Lussurioso as Piato in order to penetrate the court and get his revenge. This action leads him to subvert and then to curse his mother. Paralleling this, in iv i–ii, Vindice hires himself to Lussurioso, ostensibly so that Lussurioso can get *his* revenge on Piato, and Lussurioso is led to attack and unwittingly to curse his dead father.

In ii i Vindice overcomes Gratiana, and she attempts to subvert Castiza. Reversing this, in iv iv Gratiana is reconverted to good and Castiza pretends to try to subvert *her*.

In i ii the Duke, conducting the trial of Junior for a crime of which he, too, is guilty, lets him *escape* for the time and seems concerned only for his own 'honor', not for justice. At the end of the play the wheel comes full circle, and Antonio, the new duke, *condemns* Vindice and Hippolito for a crime of which he, too, may be morally guilty, and appears to be concerned primarily for his own welfare. Human justice is lacking at the end of the play as at the beginning.

The incidents of the play also imitate the action of 'going forth in one form and returning in another' in dramatic irony and poetic justice. Reversals of action occur at every point in the development of the plot. The multiple reversals of the denouement, bloodily transforming the expectations of Lussurioso and his stepbrothers, culminate in the irony of Vindice's fate. Even though he knows that only 'an ass' would reveal himself as a murderer, and that he has been secure in the ducal palace only because he has masked his identity and dissembled his true intentions, his pride in his wit is so great that he cannot resist bragging about the clever way the old Duke was murdered. Antonio is the one man in the court whom Vindice trusts to be of a mind with himself, since the wrongs they have suffered at the hands of the ducal family are so alike; yet it is Antonio who destroys him.

The irony in all these incidents is 'that in the imminent shadow of death man should strive to damn himself'.[4] Vindice see this, and in the closing lines of his opening soliloquy and in his long speeches in the climactic III v he preaches sermons on the vanity of sin, opposing the reality of the skull to the sensuality of the court. Nevertheless – and this is the tragic irony of Vindice's character – his obsessions drive him likewise to embrace damnation.

At the end of the seventeenth century, evidently through the error of Gerard Langbaine, *The Revenger's Tragedy* acquired an alternate title, *The Loyal Brother*.[5] This title was no doubt preserved by subsequent editors because it focuses so many ironies of the play and reveals important elements in the structure of the plot. First consider Vindice and Hippolito as loyal brothers. Loyal they are to each other, yet they lead one another into a course of action that can end only in death. And in what does their loyalty to Castiza consist? They would preserve her honor at any cost, but behave as though they hoped to corrupt her! Ambitioso, Supervacuo and Junior are stepbrothers of Lussurioso, who is a half-brother of Spurio. There is little loyalty between Lussurioso and Spurio or between either of them and any of their stepbrothers. The relation of Ambitioso and Supervacuo to their youngest brother is, however, remarkably similar to that of Vindice and Hippolito to Castiza. The 'loyalties' and the events they motivate are arranged so that there are many ironic contrasts-in-parallel between the quest of Vindice and Hippolito for revenge and of Supervacuo and Ambitioso for power.

Thus the desire of Vindice and Hippolito to guard their sister is paralleled in the desire of Ambitioso and Supervacuo to save Junior. In each case the brothers enter into false pleading that ironically endangers their intentions. Ambitioso's hypocritical 'We are sorry / That we are so unnaturally employ'd / In such an unkind office, fitter far / For enemies than brothers', spoken when he and Supervacuo hope to have Lussurioso executed, would be sincere if he knew the result would be the death of Junior, and could as well be spoken by Vindice in reference to his attempt to procure Castiza [III iii 4–7].

Later this parallel is carried further in juxtaposed scenes of Act IV [iii–iv]. First we see Ambitioso and Supervacuo considering when to use their rapiers to end the dishonor caused by their mother's incestuous lust for Spurio. Then '*Enter* VINDICE *and* HIPPOLITO, *bringing out their mother one by one shoulder, and the other by the other, with daggers in their hands*', preparing to purge her of the dishonorable office of bawd to her own daughter. At the end of the play the 'parallel' gives way to virtual fusion, and the author makes us see that the drive of Vindice and Hippolito to transform an evil court into a good one by violence ends in the same way as the drive of Supervacuo and Ambitioso to overthrow the state and obtain power for themselves. Supervacuo and Ambitioso mask themselves in the revels to murder Lussurioso, and Vindice and his party do the same. In fact, Vindice and Hippolito will be physically indistinguishable from Supervacuo and Ambitioso:

> The masquing suits are fashioning; now comes in
> That which must glad us all – we to take pattern
> Of all those suits, the colour, trimming, fashion,
> E'en to an undistinguish'd hair almost.   [v ii 14–17]

Nearly every character in the play makes an attempt to transform something or someone. Those who are not busy trying to subvert justice, overturn the state or seduce others are trying to reform sinners or purge the evil court and make it good through blood revenge. Vindice is, of course, chief among those pursuing this last course of action. *Vindice* signifies 'a revenger of wrongs, a redresser of things and abuses, a defender, one that restoreth and setteth at liberty or out of danger, a punisher of things done amiss'.[6] But it would be a mistake to assume that the title of *The Revengers Tragædie* refers only to the revenge of Vindice. Nearly all the evil figures of the ducal court are motivated at some time in the play by a desire for revenge: the Duchess against the Duke for not sparing Junior, Spurio against the Duke for his bastardy, Supervacuo and Ambitioso against Lussurioso for the death of Junior, Lussurioso against Piato for leading him to attack his father's bed, and Ambitioso and Supervacuo against Spurio for his incest with their mother. These peripheral revenge actions parody the aims of Vindice, keeping ever in view the possibility that 'Revenge' may serve no good purpose. . . .

Although Vindice believes his revenge to be necessary and just, the play makes clear his ultimate realisation that in his betrayal of chastity he has been 'nimble in damnation' [IV iv 34]. His moral perception is blinded at the moment when disillusion cuts through to his sexual obsession, and he is driven to seek *sadistic* revenges. Then the Duchess's accusation of the judges who condemn Junior applies as well to Vindice: 'Your too much right, does us too much wrong' [I ii 80]. . . .

The virtue of chastity comes to stand for the spiritual values that must be preserved or restored. This is made clearest in the important speech of Lussurioso commissioning Vindice to seduce Castiza:

> Go thou, and with a smooth enchanting tongue,
> Bewitch her ears, and cozen her of all grace;
> Enter upon the portion of her soul,
> Her honour, which she calls her chastity,
> And bring it into expense.   [I iii 111–15]

There is no avoiding the sexual implications of 'enter' here, for almost immediately Vindice and Lussurioso make obscene jokes about what will 'put a man in' [130]. The use of 'enter' to suggest a corrupting intercourse immediately relates this passage to lines nearer the beginning of the scene, when Lussurioso pays Vindice to become his servant:

> LUSS.   So; thou'rt confirm'd in me,
>   And thus I enter thee.
> VIND.   This Indian devil
>   Will quickly enter any man.   [84–6]

In both these passages corruption is represented as 'entrance' by the devil or one of his agents. So later, when he is about to overcome Gratiana, Vindice-Piato says aside 'I fear me she's unmother'd, yet I'll venture. / That woman is all male whom none can enter' [II i 111–12]. Gratiana immediately 'forgets heaven' for Lussurioso's gold, and her transformed state is regarded as possession by the devil. Castiza says that there is a 'poisonous woman' who is 'too inward' with her mother [II i 239–41]. The theme of 'entering' is linked to the use of daggers and especially of poison as agents of the devil. The corrupting effect of evil pleading on the pleader is best described in Gratiana's remark after her conversion: 'O see, / I spoke those words, and now they poison me' [IV iv 135–6].

The entrance of Lussurioso's gold into Vindice symbolises the beginning of his evil transformation, and it also is the moment when Vindice, like Richard II's antic death, 'Comes at the last and with a little pin / Bores through' the ducal 'castle wall'.[7] The theme of 'entering' is thus related to the structure of the play, for this penetration of his enemy's stronghold is only through the outermost wall, and Vindice must yet penetrate further, beyond Lussurioso to the Duke himself – a penetration consummated at the inmost part of the play, its very center in the murder scene at III v.

In his temptation of Gratiana and Castiza, Vindice insists that their choice is absolute: they can enjoy riches only if they become corrupt. Thus what L. G. Salingar calls the play's 'social dilemma' is presented in essentially moral terms of 'pollution on entry into "the world" '.[8] If Gratiana can 'forget heaven' she can be rich [II i 121]. Wordly salvation is contrasted with heavenly salvation,[9] and 'angels', like Vindice, are active agents of both good and evil, the contrasting significances of the word as heavenly beings and as coins ironically emphasising the abyss between the moral poles of the play:

GRAT.   O fie, fie; the riches of the world cannot hire a mother to such a most unnatural task!
VIND.   No, but a thousand angels can;
Men have no power, angels must work you to't.
The world descends into such base-born evils
That forty angels can make fourscore devils.   [II i 84–9]

But at the end of the scene, when 'celestial soldiers' have successfully defended the heart of Castiza, Vindice calls on 'angels' to 'give this virgin crystal plaudities' [II i 140, 245–6]. The world is so evilly transformed that even the agents which should serve good ends – Vindice and the angels – are alike corrupted, 'plated' with gold masks.

'Time hath several falls' in the structure of *The Revenger's Tragedy*. The action is rapid; the old virtues are contrasted with the decadence of this transformed age; moral transformations occur in a 'minute' despite the sinners' despairing belief that repentance requires a long time, and the vanity of transitory worldly pleasure is exposed through contrast with the eternity that lies beyond life. In the transformed world of the play Vindice becomes Piato, of whom Hippolito says 'This our age swims within him, and if time / Had so much hair, I should take him for time, / He is so near kin to this present minute' [I iii 24–6]. By torchlight night becomes day and age becomes unnaturally youthful in its lusts. Vindice rails against this unnatural lust in his opening speech, and the Duke himself admits later that 'Age hot is like a monster to be seen; / My hairs are white, and yet my sins are green' [II iii 131–2]. Similarly, when Lussurioso asks Vindice 'Is't possible that in this / The mother should be damn'd before the daughter?' the witty reply is 'O, that's good manners, my lord; the mother for her age must go foremost, you know' [II ii 47–50].

People *rush* to death and damnation: the 'Indian devil' of Lussurioso's gold 'quickly' enters Vindice, and Vindice sets 'golden spurs' to Gratiana, which 'put her to a false gallop in a trice' [II ii 45–6]. 'Cuckolds are / A-coining, apace, apace, apace, apace', and Vindice-Piato urges Castiza to go to the court: 'Nine coaches waiting – hurry, hurry, hurry', to which Castiza replies, 'Ay, to the devil' [II ii 142–3; II i 206–7]. The first gentleman is sent 'straight' to execution, and at the end, when Vindice is made to bring himself forward as a murderer by 'time' (Piato?), he is borne to 'speedy execution' [v i 127; v iii 116, 102].

The emphasis on speedy damnation and death is greatest in the bizarre execution of the Duchess's youngest son. Ambitioso and Supervacuo pretend to plead for Lussurioso's life, but actually want the Duke to execute him. The Duke, to test them, says 'he shall die / E'er many days. Make haste' – to which Ambitioso replies 'All speed that may be', and off Ambitioso and Supervacuo rush with the Duke's signet to have Lussurioso executed [II iii 100–2]. The Duke releases Lussurioso, and the order for execution is applied to the Youngest Son, while Ambitioso congratulates himself that he shall be 'duke in a minute' [III i 13]. The officers tell the treacherous brothers 'we'll not delay / The third part of a minute' in executing their victim [III iii 17–18]. The whole of III iv is an ironic 'knavish exposition' upon the letter the Youngest Son has received from his brothers:

Brother, be of good cheer ... thou shalt not be long a prisoner ... We have thought upon a device to get thee out by a trick ... And so rest comforted; be merry, and expect it suddenly.   [III iv 10–15]

The joke plays back and forth over not *long* a prisoner and *suddenly*:

Junior 'must straight suffer'; he is to be granted 'no delaying time' [III iv 28, 45].

> JUNIOR BRO. . . . Look, you officious whoresons, words of comfort:
> 'Not long a prisoner'.
> 1.OFFIC. It says true in that, sir, for you must suffer presently.
> [III iv 61–3]

Damnation can come in a single minute, often associated with midnight at noon or noon at midnight. Midnight is 'the Judas of the hours, wherein / Honest salvation is betray'd to sin', the 'hour of incest' [I iii 69–70, 61]. In revels, 'When torchlight made an artificial noon', occurred the 'vicious minute' of the rape of Antonio's wife and the damning conception of Spurio, 'By one false minute disinherited' [I iv 27, 39; I ii 168]. At the beginning of the play Vindice calls upon vengeance to keep its 'day, hour, minute', and in the 'unsunned lodge, / Wherein 'tis night at noon' he damns himself as he crowds 'Nine years' vengeance . . . into a minute' [I i 41; III v 18–19, 123]. Recapitulating these fatal minutes and the mad, whirling pace of the play and all its revels, disguises and murders, is the microcosmic Dance of Death in the masque that closes the action. Pleasure-seeking permits enemies to penetrate the court in disguise, and 'Within a strain or two' of music Vindice and his accomplices turn the hopes of Lussurioso that he 'shall ne'er die' into blood [v ii 19; v iii 34].

Although the evil characters believe death and damnation can be crowded into a minute, they think the processes of salvation are slow. Supervacuo and Ambitioso fear the Duchess and Spurio will 'sin faster than we'll repent' [IV iii 18], and the Duke speaks of his need for days and months to clear his soul of sin. The author, of course, believes in the efficacy of instantaneous grace, as it is dramatised in the re-conversion of Gratiana.

The most thoroughly evil of the characters never sincerely think of repentance, and though they believe in damnation, they usually do not think sin has long-lasting evil effects while one is living. Thus the Duke has no real desire to repent – he only wants Lussurioso to spare his life – and Ambitioso and Supervacuo speak of repentance in a merely figurative manner. Ambitioso thinks that now Antonio's wife is dead, 'people's thoughts will soon be buried'; but we know such crimes are not soon forgotten, that Vindice has spent nine years brooding over his dead lady [III i 19; I i 50]. Vindice, Hippolito and Gratiana after her re-conversion are the characters most aware of the enduring consequences of sin. Hippolito speaks of being 'eternally wretched' as a consequence of riches, and Gratiana finally sees that 'when women are young courtiers, they are sure to be old beggars: / To know the miseries most harlots taste' [IV iv 74, 142–4]. Vindice, who sees these evil consequences from a somewhat different angle, is perhaps alluding to the relationship between the Duke and Spurio when he says: 'You shall have one woman knit more in an hour than any man can ravel again in seven and twenty year' [II ii 67–9].

The climactic and morally the most significant expression of the vanity of sin is Vindice's *memento mori* sermon in III v. Here the 'bewitching minute' of sin is directly opposed to the skull and its moral:

> . . . it were fine, methinks,
> To have thee seen at revels, forgetful feasts,
> And unclean brothels; sure, 'twould fright the sinner,
> And make him a good coward . . .   [III v 90–3]

These dramatic and symbolic structures develop and support the central moral dialectic of the play – the struggle between the powers and the ways of life working toward salvation and those working toward damnation. The drama is now external – as in the transformations brought about through seduction and revenge – and now internal – within the character of Vindice or between opposed meanings of a single word.

The author's approach to man in *The Revenger's Tragedy* is primarily moral, but in one instance at least it is also psychological. Most of his characters are intellectually conceived as allegorically 'good' or 'evil' abstractions. Vindice, however, develops as a living person who changes in response to experience. He may have begun in his creator's mind as one more allegorical character, ambivalent only in being 'polluted', one thing 'entered' by another, but he has also been provided with complex emotions and allowed the freedom to act as these dictate. The result is one of the most believable portraits of neurotic perversion in all the Jacobean drama.

The Revenger's Tragedy dramatises the traditional Christian doctrine of fallen man and the traditional pattern of sin and redemption. The world of the play is the *fallen* world, a world transformed by the loss of its innocence into an Italianate hell which caricatures the depravity caused by the Fall, and at the same time depicts the terrible consequences of man's refusal of God's grace: 'Is there a hell besides this, villains?' Dramatically contrasting with the exaggerated corruption of 'the world' is the comparative innocence of the home of 'Chastity' and her mother, 'Grace'. But the devil enters even the havens of innocence, and man is corrupted and falls. Gratiana's later redemption suggests the restoration that is possible through divine aid.

All of the play's impure characters conform to the traditional conception of the fallen state of man. They are corrupted in will, and although they can still dimly distinguish right from wrong, their reason has been so weakened and subverted by their appetites that it is unable to move the will toward good. In critical moments these characters are blinded by passion and lack insight into the truth of their situation. Caught up in the traditional Christian warfare with the World, the Flesh and the Devil, they are overcome; the ducal family by the temptations of the Flesh, Gratiana by the World, and Vindice by the Devil of malice. In this unequal conflict, Elizabethans believed, man has only one great hope; he may be saved by the direct intervention of the grace of God, the greatest of all agents of transformation:

... grace, no matter how it came, was by all churches thought of as irradiating the entire character. It calmed and assuaged the passions, rectified the will, opened the eye of reason to spiritual truths, and by cleansing the motives enabled men to practice true Christian charity in their daily lives. So incredible was the change that a person having a justifying grace might be said to be reborn, 'a new creature ... endued with a new nature or disposition'.[10]

Source: extracts from *A Study of Cyril Tourneur* (Philadelphia, 1964), pp. 190–7, 200–5, 223, 240–8.

NOTES

[Reorganised and renumbered from the original – Ed.]

1. Jonson, *Every Man in His Humour* (Quarto version), v iii 288–9; ed. J. W. Lever (1971).
2. Marston, *What You Will*, I i 364–7; ed. M. R. Woodhead (Nottingham, 1980).
3. [Ed.] Middleton took the name *Piato*, along with most of the other names in the play, from John Florio's English-Italian dictionary *A World of Words* (1598); for a full list see R. A. Foakes' Revels edition of *The Revenger's*

Tragedy, p. 2. In a part of his study not reprinted here, Murray notes that Florio cites two other relevant senses of *Piato* (or *Piatto*), in addition to 'hidden' and 'plated': (1) 'a platter, a dish, a charger, a plate, a mess or dish of meat ... a course served in at any feast'. Murray finds this appropriate because 'the common idea that lust is an appetite is projected everywhere in the play. Sexuality thrives amid banquets and revels, and the characters speak of lust in terms of eating' (p. 213); (2) 'a plea, a suit in law, a controversy, a pleading'. Murray comments: 'Vindice as pander is to be Lussurioso's "sin's attorney" [ii i 35], to go "and with a smooth enchanting tongue, / Bewitch her ears, and cozen" Castiza "of all grace" [i iii 111–12]' (p. 237). On *Piato* meaning 'secret' as well as 'hidden', see John Stachniewski's essay on Middleton below.

    4. Peter Lisca, '*The Revenger's Tragedy*: A Study in Irony', *Philological Quarterly*, xxxviii (1959), p. 246.

    5. In *The Lives and Characters of the English Dramatic Poets*, 'First begun by Mr Langbaine', ed. Charles Gildon (1699?), p. 142, appears the entry '*The Loyal Brother; or The Revenger's Tragedy, 4to*'.

    6. Florio, *A World of Words* (1598), p. 449.

    7. Shakespeare, *Richard II*, iii ii 169–70.

    8. L. G. Salingar, 'Tourneur and the Tragedy of Revenge', in *The Age of Shakespeare (Pelican Guide to English Literature)*, vol. ii (Harmondsworth, 1955), p. 348.

    9. Compare iv iv 105 ('the hope you look to be sav'd in') and iv iv 155 ('Faith, and thy birth hath sav'd me') with ii i 103 ('You brought her forth, she well may bring you home'); and note the use of 'salvation' in the usual religious sense elsewhere in the play, e.g. ii ii 22, 'Hast thou beguil'd her of salvation?'

    10. Paul H. Kocher, *Science and Religion in Elizabethan England* (San Marino, 1953), p. 311. [Kocher is quoting Henry Bullinger's *Decades*, an influential Protestant theological work of the period – Ed.]

R. V. Holdsworth   *The Revenger's Tragedy* as a Middleton Play (1989)

This is not another attempt to prove that Middleton wrote *The Revenger's Tragedy*. Proof was provided by E. H. C. Oliphant sixty years ago,[1] and many new, objective and mutually independent tests have been applied since, all of which return the same result. No doubt there always will be people who, because of a refusal to inspect the evidence or a failure to understand it, will go on asserting Tourneur's claim; there is still a Flat Earth Society four centuries after Galileo. But that should not delay the step which the labours of Oliphant and his successors impel us towards, and which in this essay I shall attempt to take: the critical assimilation of the play into the Middleton canon. The task is not difficult, for one of the chief fascinations in the study of Middleton is his self-repetitiveness. Each of his plays, pageants, poems and prose pieces is, in terms of both style and ideas, an intricate web, in which modes of thought and expression are retrieved from his own earlier work, questioned, modified, recombined and handed on to works which come later. From every point of view *The Revenger's Tragedy* fits into this constantly unfolding pattern of continuities.

At the same time, it would be disingenuous to pretend that discussing the play in this way is not in itself a contribution to the authorship debate. If the play really is by Middleton, treating it as his should, given his self-cannibalising tendencies, yield more illuminating insights, or at least a stronger sense of rightness, than would flow from treating it as by somebody else. One should, too, be able to trump what the Tourneurians have always regarded as their strongest card: that is the claim that – however uniquely Middletonian *The Revenger's Tragedy* might be in its spellings, its linguistic contractions, its oaths and exclamations, its vocabulary, its phraseology, its versification, and its character names – the play cannot be by Middleton because it is not written in his style. Quite what is meant by style when these elements have been removed is not fully clear, but there is no need to quibble. The play's broadest literary qualities are compatible with Middleton's authorship, just as the linguistic details of the text make his authorship certain.

The Revenger's Tragedy is often praised as a remarkable fusion of discrete components. Largely through the speeches and actions of Vindice, the author has been able to marry a revenge-tragedy structure with homiletic denunciations of sin and vanity, satiric tirades against court vices and abuses, and a more particularised social vision of an ancient agrarian economy crumbling away into a tawdry urban one based on money and prodigal display, meadows and acres being transformed into satins and silks. Each of these constituents is separately anticipated in Middleton's earliest non-dramatic writings, and one could say that he merely put them together to make the play. *The Wisdom of Solomon Paraphrased* (1597), written when Middleton was seventeen, is a numbingly verbose and monotonous poem; it is also one long homily on worldly vanity recklessly pursued in the shadow of death and judgement, and offers immediate evidence of the passionate moral urgency which defenders of Tourneur like to claim Middleton shows no sign of possessing. Middleton next turned to verse-satire with *Microcynicon* in 1599; subtitled *Six Snarling Satires*, it covers some of Vindice's favourite topics, such as panderism, avarice, gaudy clothes and face-painting. *The Ghost of Lucrece* followed in 1600. This postscript to Shakespeare's *Rape of Lucrece* demonstrates Middleton's early interest in the theme of blood-revenge, for it is a kind of revenge poem spoken by Lucrece's ghost who decries the 'moth' of lust, demands the death of Tarquin who has raped her and driven her to suicide, and receives Revenge's promise 'to avenge / Her chaste untimely blood'. The Lucrece motif reappears in *The Revenger's Tragedy* in the shape of Antonio's wife, raped by Junior Brother ('that moth to honour') and dead by her own hand before the play begins. Finally, there are the five pamphlets Middleton wrote alone or with Dekker in 1603–4: *Plato's Cap, News from Gravesend, The Meeting of Gallants at an Ordinary, The Black Book* and *Father Hubburd's Tales* – all of which are satirical depictions of urban vice and rural decay.

To take a few cases of specific indebtedness. In a passage in *The Wisdom of Solomon Paraphrased* not in Middleton's biblical source, he imagines the stark polarity of sin and virtue as an opposition between midnight and noonday. God's stern presence makes 'midnoon midnight . . . Midnight with sin, midnoon where virtue lay; / That place was night, all other places day' [xvii xix 4–5].[2] Middleton recycles the image to express the morally debased worlds of his plays, where the distinction is levelled or confused. Witgood in *A Trick to Catch the Old One* (1604–6) boasts of his 'brothel at noonday, and muscadine and eggs at midnight' [iii i 93–4]. In *The Revenger's Tragedy* (1606), Antonio's wife was raped 'When torchlight made an artificial noon'; the Duke's lustful encounters occur 'in this unsunned lodge, / Wherein 'tis night at noon'; and, in the hubbub that follows Lussurioso's attempt to kill the Duchess, Spurio demands, 'is the day out o'th' socket, / That it is noon at midnight?' [*R.T.,* i iv 27, iii v 18–19, ii iii 44–5]. Middleton is still using the idea as late as *Women Beware Women* (c. 1621), where the incestuous affair between Hippolito and Isabella is preceded by their being 'heard / In argument at midnight, moonshine nights / Are noondays with them', and Leantio fatally 'tells the midday sun what's done in darkness' [*W.B.W.,* i ii 63–5, iv i 152].

A less appealing feature of *The Wisdom of Solomon* is its shrill anti-feminism, which exceeds anything in its source. Another of Middleton's additions is the notion that 'The far-fet chastity of female sex / Is nothing but allurement into lust' [VI xiv 1–2]. Whether or not the teenaged Middleton really believed this, the characters in his plays who come out with such sexist abuse, as Vindice constantly does, are ones we are meant to disapprove of, and who often receive ironic endorsement of their prejudice where they least welcome it. This happens to Captain Ager in *A Fair Quarrel* (1615–16). Reluctant to stake his honour on his mother's chastity in the knowledge that 'she's but woman', he probes her reputation only to learn that the ritual insult he has been offered, 'son of a whore', is apparently true. It also happens to Vindice, who gratuitously resolves, 'for the salvation of my oath', to test the chastity of his mother Gratiana, and promptly discovers that she is willing to act as bawd to his sister. Since her name means 'grace', his earlier cynical quip, 'Save Grace the bawd, I seldom hear grace nam'd!' [*R.T.*, I iii 16], has rebounded against him. Vindice's anti-feminism outdoes Captain Ager's, however, by its scatological tendencies. 'Why are men made close', he asks, meaning physically sealed as well as tight-lipped, 'But to keep thoughts in best?. . . . Tell but some woman a secret overnight, / Your doctor may find it in the urinal i'th' morning' [*R.T.*, I iii 80–3]. Only Middleton's more incorrigibly depraved characters, such as Francisca in *The Witch* (1614–16) jeering at the integrity of Isabella, achieve this level of crude innuendo: 'She can keep it secret? / That's very likely, and a woman too! . . . 'Twould ne'er stay with me two days – I have cast it' [III ii 121–5]. Leonella in *The Second Maiden's Tragedy* (1611) has a terser version: ''Has frayed a secret from me . . . from a woman a thing's quickly slipped' [II ii 175–6].[3] By contrast, the virtuous Fitzgrave in *Your Five Gallants* (1606–7), checking the loyalty of the Courtesans, is allowed to say merely, 'you're women, and are hardly secret' [V i 55].[4]

Microcynicon and *The Ghost of Lucrece* launch Middleton's ever-deepening interest in sexual corruption, a theme passed on to *The Revenger's Tragedy* along with much of the verbal equipment for dealing with it. In *Microcynicon* the existence of 'Lust-breathing lechers' prompts the ironic cry 'O 'tis a gallant age!' [p. 122]. In the plays the atmosphere of lust is often all-enveloping. Tailby, the 'whore-gallant' of *Your Five Gallants*, marvels 'What an age do we breathe in!' [IV viii 78], Lussurioso finds Vindice 'well experienc'd / In this luxurious day wherein we breathe' [*R.T.*,

I iii 109–10], and the Black Bishop's Pawn of *A Game at Chess* (1624) knows that only bottling up one's sinful thoughts prevents 'The very air we breathe' from being 'unblest' [I i 107]. In *The Ghost of Lucrece* the figure of Iniquity is arraigned principally for 'luxury': 'Thou hast burnt out the humour of thy bones, / And made them powders of impiety . . . all thy sinews, O Iniquity, / Are so dried up' [323– 7]. The 'plague pamphlet' *News from Gravesend* contains a similarly grotesque portrait of an 'adulterous and luxurious' sinner, 'through whose blood / Runs part of the infernal flood . . . The heat of all his damn'd desires / Cool'd with the thought of gnashing fires . . . His marrow wasted'.[5] Middleton conflated these two sketches to furnish Vindice with his opening cameo of the Duke: 'grey-haired adultery . . . impious steep'd . . . O, that marrowless age / Would stuff the hollow bones with damn'd desires, / And 'stead of heat, kindle infernal fires / Within the spendthrift veins of a dry duke, / A parch'd and juiceless luxur'. 'Luxur' (lecher) has been added from *The Black Book* (1604) and *Father Hubburd's Tales* (1604), a Middleton coinage that has not been found anywhere else, while the assimilation of the Duke to a concept, adultery, crops up again in *The Changeling*, where De Flores, Alsemero tells Beatrice, is 'Your adultery' [v iii 54].

The Black Book, besides supplying many more details of language, is the first Middleton work to use the plot-device shared in some form by nearly all his early plays: that of the disguised observer anatomising the time's deformities. Middleton states in his preface that he aims to 'dive into the deep of this cunning age', seek out the 'monsters of nature' and 'strip their villanies naked' – phrases which recall the motives and comments of earlier disguised railers, such as Jonson's Asper in *Every Man out of His Humour* (1599) and Marston's Altofronto in *The Malcontent* (1603). Asper and Altofronto, though, remain uncontaminated by the folly and wrong-doing they witness and are virtuously aloof from their roles (as, respectively, the envious Macilente and the ill-willing Malevole), whereas the role-playing agent Middleton employs in *The Black Book* is Lucifer, who is inseparable from the evil he studies. Lucifer declares: 'I haunt invisible corners as a spy, / And in adulterous circles there rise I . . . I must turn actor and join companies, / To share my comic sleek-ey'd villanies' [pp. 7–8].[6] Although Middleton elsewhere tried his hand at virtuous disguisers, Vindice's primary kinship is with Lucifer, and not merely in that he follows his forebear by embodying the maxim of pride coming before a fall. Vindice is another student of evil with an underlying corrupt identity who turns actor and spies into the corners of the court, including the 'luxurious circle' where the Duke meets his harlots, and who becomes morally indistinguishable from the victims he pursues ('we are ourselves our foes', he finally perceives). Like Lucifer, too, Vindice discovers that he is hardly needed. England turns out to be a hotter place than hell, and the monsters Vindice encounters would soon be at each other's throats without his help. The implication of this redundancy is made explicit in a later Middleton tragedy, *Hengist, King of Kent* (1616/20): 'sin needs/No other destruction than it breeds/In its own bosom' [v ii 76–8].

Among the instances of moral decay which Lucifer sees is 'an honest field of wheat . . . changed into white money' [p. 16]. It is typical of Middleton's subsequent concern to connect economic with sexual corruption, rather than treating them separately, that in the plays this metaphor is redirected. The Captain of *The Phoenix* (1603/4), aiming to prostitute his wife Castiza, determines 'to turn her into white money' [I iv 246], and Vindice, having failed to corrupt his sister, who is also called Castiza, complains, 'A right good woman in these days is chang'd/Into white money with less labour far' [*R.T.*, II ii 27–8]. The idiotic Tim of *A Chaste Maid in Cheapside* (1613) requires the same image to describe the illness of his sister, brought on by her resolution to remain chaste: 'Gold into white money was never so chang'd,/As is my sister's colour into paleness' [v ii 16–17]. As 'white money' is silver coin, Middleton's ultimate source is no doubt the thirty pieces of silver for which Judas exchanged his loyalty to Christ.

The one area of moral excoriation not fully anticipated in these early non-dramatic works is eating. This triggers some typically bold metaphoric combinations in *The Revenger's Tragedy*, where it is predictably fused with lust. The bastard Spurio believes 'I was begot/After some gluttonous dinner, some stirring dish/Was my first father', and Vindice imagines 'the stirring meats,/Ready to move out of the dishes, that/E'en now quicken when they're eaten' [*R.T.*, I ii 180–2, II i 200–2]. Here one is dealing with a starting-point rather than with an act of retrieval. The idea of the impregnatory power of food reappears in *The Inner-Temple Masque*, written in 1619 for one of those revels which the play treats as symptomatic of social and moral collapse, where the character Fasting-Day declares, 'maids have had fuller bellies,/Those meals that once were sav'd have stirr'd, and leapt, / And begot bastards' [137–9]. Curiously, the masque's title-page states that it was 'presented as an entertainment for many worthy ladies'. Just how the worthy ladies greeted Fasting-Day's announcement as they tucked into their food is not easy to guess. Middleton's final version of the idea is more congruous: the Black Knight of *A Game at Chess* rhapsodises about gluttons who have 'Lust swimming in their dishes, which no sooner / Was tasted but was ready to be vented' [v iii 26–7].

Defenders of Tourneur often assert that 'Middleton's plays known to have been written before, or soon after, the composition of *The Revenger's Tragedy* are all comedies'.[7] This is of course wrong: Middleton had written or had helped to write five other tragedies by 1608. But the objection would be empty anyway, for the proximity of *The Revenger's Tragedy* to satiric comedy, particularly the sardonic comedy of self-inflicted come-uppance at which Middleton excels, is conspicuously clear. Commenting on the Duke's teeth, destroyed by poison, Vindice observes, 'those that did eat are eaten' [*R.T.*, III v 163] – a literal formulation of the law of biter-bit which governs the play in which the two of them are appearing, and which both of their careers will eventually illustrate. Other notable casualties in the play include Spurio, whose prayer 'Would all the court were turn'd into a corse' [I ii 36] is answered, but naturally includes him since he too is a courtier; Ambitioso, who gets his wish to be 'duke in a minute' [III i 13], for his reign is entirely contained in that span; and Lussurioso, who warns Junior Brother 'do not jest thy doom' [I ii 49], but then follows the same cheerful course to self-invited ruin. 'How strangely does himself work to undo him', muses Hippolito [IV i 60].

This law of ironic repayment operates throughout Middleton's plays, whatever their ostensible genres. 'Through the world' – as Follywit puts it in *A Mad World, My Masters* (1604–6) – 'either in jest or earnest . . . craft recoils in the end' [III iii 10–11]. An arch exponent of craft, he ends, of course, by having the same lesson read over him: 'Who lives by cunning, mark it, his fate's cast; / When he has gull'd all, then is himself the last' [v ii 298–9]. *Women Beware Women*, a tragedy, sticks to the formula. 'Jest on', the Mother tells Livia over their chess-game, "ere now, lady, / I have seen the fall of subtlety' [*W.B.W.*, II ii 307–8]. Livia proceeds to exemplify the comment, finally acknowledging 'My subtlety is sped', just as Guardiano is 'caught by some springe of his own setting', and

Bianca's fall demonstrates 'What shift sh'has made to be her own destruction' [*W.B.W.*, v ii 132, 161, 217].

It is true that Vindice thinks he is performing 'tragic business' [*R.T.*, III v 99], whereas Follywit and the trickster-heroes of Middleton's other comedies know they are engaged in 'comic pranks' (*A Mad World*, II i 130). But the deaths Vindice inflicts on his victims are merely an extreme form of the discomfiture the comic schemers inflict on theirs; they are engineered with the same glee and with the same aesthetic concern to achieve a witty matching of punishment with sin. Self-tricked in the finale, Vindice realises what kind of play he is in, appreciatively remarking, 'Is't come about? . . . 'Tis time to die, when we are ourselves our foes' [*R.T.*, v iii 106–10]. Follywit in *A Mad World* jauntily concurs, with due allowance for his non-lethal self-assassination: 'Is't come about? tricks are repaid, I see' [v ii 288]. In *The Revenger's Tragedy* it is left to Antonio, the only character on stage who has been exempt from the pattern of biter-bit reversals, to put the case for the play's nominal genre: the closing massacre is in his view 'a piteous tragedy', stocked with 'tragic bodies' [*R.T.*, v ii 60, 127]. The Cardinal of *Women Beware Women*, another outsider, makes the same attempt as he stands among the corpses of his court: 'Sin, what thou art, these ruins show too piteously' [*W.B.W.*, v ii 222]. In fact, these last-minute demands for the requisite tragic emotion only point up our inability to supply it. The cold tit-for-tat symmetries of both plays' retributive logic, coupled with the displays of insouciant moral blindness which have abetted them, have already manoeuvred us into that detached attitude which for satiric comedy is the norm. *A Yorkshire Tragedy* (1605–8), host to another blindly self-destructive sinner, is more forthright: 'Where justice claims all, there must pity fail' [vii 26].[8]

Vindice is close relative to all Middleton's early comic protagonists. Closest is Follywit, who is at once a shape-changing revenger plotting against an old lecher, a moralist who inveighs against others but complacently excludes himself, and ultimately a victim of his own pride in chicanery. Constant verbal transferals signal Middleton's awareness of their kinship. Here is Follywit hatching his plot to masquerade as my Lord Owemuch: 'Peace, 'tis mine own, i'faith; I ha't! . . . Thanks, thanks to any spirit / That mingled it 'mongst my inventions . . . nay, 'tis in grain; I warrant it hold colour' [*A Mad World*, III iii 68–82]. And this is Vindice coming up with his scheme to dress the Duke's corpse in his diguise: 'But I have found it; / 'Twill hold, 'tis sure; thanks, thanks to any spirit / That mingled it 'mongst my inventions ... Nay, doubt not, 'tis in grain; / I warrant it hold colour' [*R.T.*, IV ii 200–24].

In one way the ironies that attend Follywit's career are more fully exploited. Vindice, entranced by the 'betwitching minute' of sex as he contemplates the face of Gloriana's skull [*R.T.*, III v 75], yet preserves enough detachment and self-command to inflict his 'punitive union with a whore' device (versions of which occur throughout Middleton's plays) on his intended victim, and he continues to be one jump ahead until the last few lines, so that his self-imposed downfall has no narrative logic. Despite the psycho-logic which precipitates it – amoral craft having become for him the pre-eminent value to which he assumes everyone must subscribe – in terms of the plot it has the air of being an afterthought. Follywit, on the other hand, who is also captivated by the 'bewitching minute' he spends contemplating the face of the Courtesan [IV v 18], resolves to marry her himself in the belief that she is a bashful virgin. Since, as we know, she is the whore of his intended victim, he thus springs Vindice's trap on himself. This sets a time-bomb ticking for the rest of the play, heard by us but not by him, and puts an ironic distance between our perception of the schemer's supposedly superior skill and his own perception of it which the plot of *The Revenger's Tragedy* can only allow to be retrospective.

Another comic kinsman is Quomodo of *Michaelmas Term* (1605 / 6). After a Volpone-like staging of his own death so that he may 'in disguise, note the condition of all' [IV i 111], Quomodo finds that his wife is unfaithful and his children disloyal, ruins himself financially, and learns 'deceit is her own foe' [v iii 74]. This matches Vindice's disguising himself and discovering that his mother is willing to be a bawd, as well as his mortal self-beggarment and his concluding insight 'we are ourselves our foes'. In *Michaelmas Term*, Vindice's other role as disguised railer against the time's enormities is split off into the Father of the sub-plot who comes to London in pursuit of his daughter, the Country Wench, now working as a trainee prostitute. He disguises himself as her servant, thus witnessing corruption at first hand, as Vindice does when in disguise he becomes the servant of Lussurioso. The Father's service does not, however, extend to active assistance in his daughter's corruption – on the contrary, he feels that 'he that can / Be bawd to woman never leapt from man' [III i 265–6]; whereas Vindice, while uttering similar denunciations, contrives to play the bawd in earnest. The countryside which the Wench has left stands for the world of innocence and decency which city-livers have lost. 'Lay by my conscience . . . that weed is for the country' are the play's opening words, spoken by the spirit of Michaelmas Term as he exchanges his white cloak for a black one. Vindice agrees: 'Let blushes dwell i' th' country', he declares, as he dons his pander's disguise [*R.T.*, i iii 5].

Three other early Middleton comedies have protagonists who escape the biter-bit law while imposing it on others. *A Trick to Catch the Old One* (1604–6), besides offering a title one might adopt for the central business of *The Revenger's Tragedy*, is a revenger's comedy in which an ambiguous hero, Witgood, contrives the union of his ageing victim with a whore as his revenge. Witgood, though, retains the rewards of his cunning: an ending which gives this play a cynicism which in the tragedy is dispelled by Vindice's fall. (Unless one takes it that Antonio's motives are tainted: see Introduction, above.) But of course, as cannot happen in that play, the victim, Walkadine Hoard, is still alive at the close to deliver a spot of healthy didacticism: 'Curs'd be all malice! black are the fruits of spite, / And poison first their owners' [v ii 155–6]. The note is oddly bitter and solemn for what is most of the time a breezy city comedy, and shows how unstable the divide was for Middleton between comic and tragic idioms; the one is always likely to flow into the other, just as between generically separate plays there is a constant exchange of narrative material. Hoard's insight would, indeed, be an apt epitaph for Vindice to deliver on his own career, if he had the self-perception to achieve it. Vindice has revelled in the 'quaintness' of his 'malice' [*R.T.*, iii v 109], and we are invited to see him as poisoned by spite from the very start. Addressing the skull in his opening speech, he calls it 'Thou sallow picture of my poison'd love'. By *love* he means 'true-love', but we can understand the sense 'my poisoned love for Gloriana', which is what the stage-picture of him standing alone cradling her skull represents: a love poisoned by the hatred and vengefulness which her murder has provoked in him. The 'black condition' [*R.T.*, iv i 69] Lussurioso detects in Vindice is not acquired only in the course of the play.

The other two comedies have protagonists who, like Vindice, are fulminators against society, but they are virtuous disguisers, and Middleton disperses Vindice's negative aspects through the rest of the cast. *The Phoenix*, which probably predates *The Revenger's Tragedy*,

anticipates its quasi-Italian setting in a ducal court, its nest of
treacherous courtiers (one of whom is called Lussurioso), its chaste
female in distress (also named Castiza), and its plot-device of a
villain who inadvertently recruits the disguised protagonist to attack
his own parent. But other components differ, in order to express a
view of vice as more of a temporary infection than an incurable
disease. The Duke is virtuous and the protagonist is his son, who
disguises himself solely to protect his parent and preserve the state.
Establishing his function as a moral doctor in the opening scene,
Phoenix announces his aim 'to look into the heart and bowels of
this dukedom, and, in disguise, mark all abuses ready for reformation
or punishment' [I i 100–2]. Middleton takes care to prohibit the
idea that Phoenix's false role might imply a taste for deceit or might
alter his nature for the worse, even having him retain his true name
while disguised, which unaccountably fails to arouse the suspicions
of the courtier who hires him. Vindice's worldly cynicism is possessed
only by Phoenix's victims. The Captain, for example, husband of
Castiza, welcomes the attentions of her would-be seducer in the
court as 'a sign we shall live in the world' [I ii 43], while in *The
Revenger's Tragedy* it is Vindice who resolves to be 'a right man then,
a man o'th' time; / For to be honest is not to be i'th' world' [*R.T.*,
I i 94–5].[9] Phoenix does threaten to develop some Vindice-like
symptoms of malaise in response to the evils he uncovers – 'I'm sick
of all professions; my thoughts burn', he confesses at one point
[IV ii 101] – but elsewhere he steadies himself by asking, 'why so
rashly for one villain's fault / Do I arraign whole man?' [I iv 203]:
a question which never occurs to Vindice. Thus, when Phoenix
masquerades as a malcontent who can admit 'treason into his
bosom, / And keep it safe nine years' [II ii 251–2], there is no
question of hidden morbidity; but with Vindice, who really has
brooded on political (if not moral) treason for 'nine years'
[*R.T.*, III v 123], there certainly is. At the end of the play Phoenix's
medical credentials are recalled and endorsed: 'thou hadst piercing
art: / We only saw the knee, but thou the heart' [v i 178–9]. In the
darker world of *The Revenger's Tragedy* diagnostic penetration of this
order is possessed only by God, 'that eternal eye, / That sees through
flesh and all' [*R.T.*, I iii 65–6].

The other virtuous disguiser is Fitzgrave of *Your Five Gallants*
(1606–7), who duplicates Vindice's tactics by adopting a deviously
apt alias ('Bowser', payer-out) and posing as a melancholy loner,

'infected / With fashion, time, and humour', in order to 'wind myself / Into the bosoms' of his enemies and 'find these secret mischiefs out' [I ii 91–4; II ii 7]. Like Vindice, he defeats his opponents by means of a masque (pairing them with whores afterwards), and he rages against the same vices, including 'Thou Impudence, the minion of our days' [IV v 82], where Vindice, with more localised focus, decries 'Impudence, / Thou goddess of the palace' [*R.T.*, I iii 5–6]. But Fitzgrave, harking back to Phoenix and Marston's Altofronto, remains uninfected by the diseased personality he assumes, and Middleton is careful to sanitise him by off-loading the more detailed and lacerating tirades (which might suggest an unhealthy fascination with the immorality he opposes) onto the villains. It is Tailby, a real pander, who inveighs against women 'Whose clothes / E'en stand upright in silver, when their bodies / Are ready to drop through 'em; such there be, / They may deceive the world, they ne'er shall me' [II i 332–5]. This is the authentic voice of Vindice, who uses the skull to point out that 'here might a scornful and ambitious woman / Look through and through herself; see, ladies, with false forms / You deceive men, but cannot deceive worms' [*R.T.*, III v 96–8]. Similarly, it is Goldstone, the cheater-gallant, who reasons, 'since the world rolls on dissimulation, / I'll be the first dissembler' [II i 139–40]: an argument advanced by Vindice when he renounces honesty because it is not 'i' th' world' [*R.T.*, I i 95].

Nevertheless, *Your Five Gallants*'s condemnation of false appearance leaves it in a muddle which does not afflict *The Revenger's Tragedy*. When Fitzgrave, in disguise, exclaims, 'O thou world, / How art thou muffled in deceitful forms!' [III ii 146–7], we are arbitrarily not expected to think that his words pass negative judgement on him; while Vindice's repudiation of 'false forms' has an ironic relevance to the speaker which *The Revenger's Tragedy* never ceases to exploit. Middleton runs into this problem again in *A Game at Chess* (1624), where the White Knight, about to pretend blackness in order to trap the Black Knight, is first made laboriously to muse, 'What a pain it is / For truth to feign a little!' [IV iv 16–17].

There is one other early comedy to mention. It has been largely ignored by Middleton critics, perhaps partly because it is a collaboration with Dekker, but no doubt mainly because A. H. Bullen left it out of his *Works of Middleton*. This is *The Honest Whore Part One* (1604). Its neglect is unfortunate, for it furnishes all the remaining elements of *The Revenger's Tragedy* which the unassisted comedies lack. Here we have Hippolito and Matheo, close equivalents of Vindice and Hippolito in the revenge play, except that more is made of the subordinate partner's chirpy scepticism as a means of off-setting the protagonist's death-obsession. The setting of *The Honest Whore* is Italy, and this Hippolito's true-love, Infelice, has apparently been killed by the cruelty of her father the Duke (Hippolito calls him a murderer in the first scene). As a result Hippolito declares 'I shall forget myself' and collapses into a state of neurotic morbidity, which issues as a tendency to inflamed fantasising under the guise of moral denunciation. Among his favourite topics are 'full suppers, midnight revels, / Dancing, wine, riotous meetings' and 'that devil, lust' [ii i 403–9].[10] Above all, he gives way to a violent, undiscriminating anti-feminism, on the grounds that 'One woman serves for a man's damnation': an argument which so impresses the whore Bellafronte that she sees 'The foul black spots that stick upon my soul', curses the 'minute' of her corruption ('So soon a maid is changed into a whore'), and joins Hippolito in condemning the 'shallow son and heir' eager to 'waste all his inheritance to purchase / A filthy, loathed disease' [ii i 427–8; iii iii 12, 60–2; iv i 139].

All this anticipates, often in close verbal detail, Vindice's decision to 'forget my nature', his social and sexual moralisings, and his reforming of Gratiana (who ejects 'this infectious spot out of my soul'), as well as the 'vicious minute' and the 'false minute' of sexual knowledge which distress Antonio and Spurio [*R.T.*, i ii 168; i iii 182; i iv 39; iv iv 51]. What is more, the *Honest Whore*'s Hippolito equips himself with a skull. It is not that of Infelice, who it turns out was drugged not dead, but its 'bare bone' [iv i 63] supports the same mortuary ruminations that the 'bare bone' of Gloriana's skull inspires in Vindice [*R.T.*, iii v 53]. 'Here's a fellow', Hippolito grimly notes, whose 'colours' will last 'Till doomsday' [iv i 79–82], anticipating Vindice's 'Here's a cheek keeps her colour' [*R.T.*, iii v 60]; and Hippolito buttonholes the audience by demanding 'And must all come to this?' [iv i 76], as does Vindice with 'all for this?' [*R.T.*, iii v 87].

These shared features do not, however, stop *The Honest Whore Part One* from being the vastly inferior play; indeed they cause it. The prevailing tone of cheery farce collides jarringly with Hippolito's fevered broodings, which seem contextually marooned and too obviously overheated. And because he is destined to snap out of it at the end and fall into the arms of the resurrected heroine, Middleton and Dekker have to pretend that his turbulent obsessions are romantically ennobling. Bellafronte's, comment, for example, 'I warrant he's an honest fellow, if he take on thus for a wench' [II i 212], seems an amazingly obtuse way of viewing the pathological behaviour to which Hippolito actually succumbs. More problems arise in the skull scene [IV i], where Hippolito ponders Infelice's death. Since, as we know, she is not really dead (a knowledge that in itself robs the scene of much of its power), Hippolito has to brandish not only a skull – whose it is we worryingly never learn – but Infelice's picture, addressing that as 'Thou figure of my friend', and forcing it to yield mortuary instruction ('here the worms will feed', he somewhat debatably claims). In *The Revenger's Tragedy*, on the other hand, the skull itself can be for Vindice both 'Thou sallow picture of my poison'd love' and the means by which he reveals the worm's eye-view of humanity. His brother can ask him 'Is this the form that living shone so bright?', and he can reply with dark and mordant emphasis (since he makes no distinction between the living and the dead), 'The very same' [*R.T.*, III v 67–8].

As a student of Middleton, I am quite prepared to put these failures down to the baleful impact of Dekker. The main cause of them, however, is that Middleton wants to make the Hippolito scenes, for which he was responsible, an occasion to explore the psychological consequences of an obsessive linking of sex and death, but the exigencies of the plot constantly strain against this desire. Hippolito *talks* about 'lust and murder' 'hitting' [II i 350], and a comic servant suggests that if he turns his back Hippolito and the skull 'will be naught' (unchaste) 'together' [IV i ii]. But these ideas remain a matter of words only, whereas the plot of *The Revenger's Tragedy* provides the means by which they can be embodied in action, and become central images of what the play is about.

None of Middleton's other tragedies matches the satiric exuberance he achieved in *The Revenger's Tragedy*, though shared motifs continually appear. The Wife of *A Yorkshire Tragedy* (1605/8) is a Castiza-figure who has ended up married to an English Lussurioso, appropriately more demented about money than sex, but equally unabashed by his reprobate's addiction to the promptings of the 'blood'. 'It is our blood to err, though hell gap'd loud', Lussurioso explains [*R.T.*, I iii 72], and so does the *Yorkshire Tragedy*'s Husband:

''tis our blood to love what we are forbidden' [iv 61].[11] It is a measure of Middleton's Calvinist commitment to the idea of man's wilful depravity that he puts *blood* to this syntactical use, as though it were a force capable of independent volition; I have not found another writer who couples the word with an infinitive construction. The Husband also partly replicates Vindice's career in being 'mad to be revenged' and thus becoming a case of 'Bad turned to worse', which provokes the comment, 'Alas, that hate should bring us to our grave' [ii 36 167, 181].

There are much more intricate links with *The Second Maiden's Tragedy* (1611). Govianus, whose mistress kills herself to avoid being raped by the Tyrant, copies Vindice's stratagem of disguising himself as the criminal's hireling and annointing the corpse's lips with poison for him to kiss; but here the revenger is to survive with his nobility reaffirmed, so extensive readjustments are required. The death occurs within the play, which makes the retaliation seem more justified, and Govianus, who disguises himself only while springing his trap, is primarily motivated by a desire not for revenge but to reinter the Lady's body – for it is the Tyrant who is the necrophiliac who excavates the woman's corpse and gloats over it, and who finally discovers 'I talk so long to death, I'm sick myself' [v ii 121]. Vindice's 'bony lady' thus passes to the victim, while Govianus has the holier stimulus of the Lady's spirit. Castiza, as well as Gloriana, is assimilated into the Lady of *The Second Maiden's Tragedy*, and the job of corrupting her is given wholly to her parent, who is put up to it by the Tyrant himself; and while Vindice has to 'set spurs' to Gratiana [*R.T.*, II ii 45], the Lady's father 'needs no spur' to set about the task [I i 239]. Like Castiza, the Lady conveys her revulsion by pretending not to recognise her parent when the approach is made.

These realignments leave the protagonist morally uncompromised, apart from the question of the revenge itself, and Govianus is made to enact it in a very grave and pious spirit, with none of Vindice's sadistic glee. 'Give me a sober fury', he prays, 'A rage that may not overcharge my blood / And do myself most hurt' [v ii 51–3]. Nevertheless, the transplantation of Vindice's ghoulish method of revenge, while permitting a similar, and similarly appropriate, coupling of lust and death, brings with it doubts about the revenger's purity of motive, and indeed sanity, which in the earlier play were deliberately aimed at, but which the new context cannot absorb. In

The Revenger's Tragedy there was nothing which compelled Vindice
to make Gloriana one of the 'villains all three' who killed the Duke
[*R.T.*, III v 154], and his dressing her up as a court whore was of a
piece with his cynical anti-feminism, signalled by his constant sneers
at female constancy, his corrupting of his mother, his attempt to
prostitute his sister, and his belief that Gloriana's skull, since it
represents the ultimate exposure of universal female duplicity, should
persuade him to 'chide myself / For doting on her beauty' [*R.T.*,
III v 69–70]. In *The Second Maiden's Tragedy*, though the method of
killing is equally gratuitous (the Tyrant, like the Duke, is unguarded),
we are not supposed to feel that Govianus is being fiendish, or
dishonouring the Lady's corpse, or that he is self-deluded in claiming
'this act . . . honours me / Unto my mistress' spirit' [v ii 148–9].
Middleton works hard to head off such suspicions. As Govianus
paints on the poison, he experiences 'a religious trembling' which
'bids me put by such unhallowed business', but then he vaguely
adds, 'revenge calls for't, and it must go forward'. As soon as it has
gone forward the Lady's ghost comes on to congratulate him and
tell him he will go to heaven, and he gives the assurance that he
'cannot reverence chastity too much' [v ii 91–2, 163–4, 209]. The
result is to blur the savage neatness of Vindice's revenge by wrapping
it in a haze of pious sentiment, and without the compensation of
convincing us that the moral questions which this revenge raised no
longer apply.

What of Middleton's last two tragedies, *Women Beware Women*
(c. 1621) and *The Changeling* (1622)? The links have diminished by
this time – due partly to the number of years, and plays, which
intervene; and partly because Middleton's later characters, from the
tragicomedies onwards, are more internally complex and free-
standing, and not, or not so obviously, interdependent units in a
larger moral design. The need for an expositor figure disappears as
the characters become more spontaneously able to explore or declare
themselves. The earlier tragedy continues, nevertheless, to exert an
influence.

Like Vindice, Leantio in *Women Beware Women* is driven by the
sexual depredations of a duke into becoming an embittered railer
against the court, and he too exhibits a perverse tendency to value
the woman he professes to love in proportion to her destructive
potential. Vindice admires Gloriana because 'she was able to ha'

made a usurer's son / Melt all his patrimony in a kiss' [*R.T.*, i i 26–7]; and Leantio admires Bianca because she is 'Able to shoot destruction through the bloods' of the youth of Florence [*W.B.W.*, i i 164] – an ability which he himself will later confirm. While he lacks Vindice's manic gleefulness, in other respects Leantio is virtually a Vindice whose Gloriana yields to the Duke; certainly they are alike in regarding themselves as living dead men once deprived of their partners. 'My life's unnatural to me', says Vindice, 'As if I liv'd now when I should be dead' [*R.T.*, i i 120–1], and Leantio shares this feeling: 'Methinks by right, I should not now be living, / And then 'twere all well' [*W.B.W.*, iii iii 320–3]. Neither has long to wait.

Other motifs reappear. As the Duchess inveigles Spurio into incest by suggesting that the Duke may not be his father, so Livia lies to Isabella about her parentage in order to propel her into an affair with her uncle. The finales of the two plays are also related, and not just in that both employ masques as mechanisms for revenge. Lussurioso cries 'We're ready now for sports, let 'em set on' [*R.T.*, v iii 38], invoking suggestions of the Danse Macabre since he is unwittingly calling for death to come and claim him in the midst of worldly pleasures; and Bianca too cries 'Let sports come on apace' [*W.B.W.*, v ii 71], and with the same result. Corpse-kissing then makes a double come-back. The dying Hippolito kisses the dead Isabella, whom he has seduced: 'I kiss thy cold lips, and applaud / This thy revenge in death'; and Bianca kills herself by kissing poison from the lips of the Duke whose death she has caused: 'Thus, thus, reward thy murderer', she tells the corpse, 'and turn death / Into a parting kiss' [*W.B.W.*, v ii 134–5, 195–6]. The Duke's death in *The Revenger's Tragedy* stands behind these deaths, but the ironies are more complex: Middleton has not closed down the possibility that some form of genuine love has been present in both of the pairings.

The main link with *The Changeling* is in the ironic self-exposure of both Vindice and Beatrice-Joanna through moral blindness and overconfidence. Both own up to their criminality expecting to be congratulated, and are promptly rebuffed, with death as the result. Vindice asks Antonio, 'was't not for your good, my lord?' [*R.T.*, v iii 103], just as Beatrice urges Alsemero, 'Forget not, sir, / It for your sake was done' [*Ch.*, v iii 77–8]. She also tells him 'I have kiss'd poison for't', thus fleetingly recalling the Duke's demise as well. Both protagonists end by acknowledging the force of the moral law they have flouted: ''Tis time to die, when we are ourselves our foes', observes Vindice, which Beatrice closely echoes while disclosing a deeper sense of guilt: ''Tis time to die, when 'tis a shame to live'. Editors are silent, but these exit lines surely derive some of their resonance from the famous passage in Ecclesiastes: 'To everything there is a season, and a time to every purpose under the heaven: a time to be born, and a time to die' [iii:1–2].

It remains to consider why Middleton redeployed the same verbal and narrative material so frequently, and felt able to switch it back and forth between his comedies and tragedies largely unadjusted. The clue lies in his thorough-going Calvinism (brilliantly explored by John Stachniewski in the essay in section 2 of Part Two, below). Calvin allowed no distinction between venial and mortal sins: to him folly and selfishness were just as symptomatic of a reprobate identity as were blasphemy and murder. He preached instead the total depravity of human nature redeemable only by the inscrutable miracle of God's grace, which was predestined, at conception, to be extended only to a certain few. Otherwise the vast mass of mankind was irremediably damned. In his *Confessio Fidei Gallicana* of 1559 Calvin proclaimed the damnation 'even of little children in the mother's womb',[12] and English theologians accepted this. Donne, for example, contended that 'There in the womb we are fitted for works of darkness, all the while deprived of light; and there in the womb we are taught cruelty by being fed with blood, and may be damned though we be never born'.[13] The spiritual identity conferred on us in the womb held the key to our destiny to election or reprobation, and could never be certainly known. Intimations might be possible through a relentless scrutiny of one's innermost propensities, but all the time the unregenerate impulses of the 'blood' would hinder access to this secret, inner self.

The impact of these cheering doctrines on Middleton's thinking and on his dramatic strategies is very far-reaching. They help to explain, for a start, the presence of bitter invectives in his comedies and of emotionless ironic patterning in his tragedies, for a determination to view all forms of wrong-doing as equally revelatory of the fallen state of humanity would naturally promote a levelling of generic distinctions. The delayed come-uppances that Middleton's comic and tragic wrong-doers share can also be traced to Calvin, who thus describes God's typical method of dealing out punishment:

> He doth oftentimes so bear with the wicked, that as one asleep He doth
> not only suffer them to take many wicked things in hand, but also He
> maketh them rejoice at the success of their wicked enterprises, that at the
> last He may make their fall the greater . . . [In Genesis] God showed
> himself a revenger by little and little, and as it were fair and softly.[14]

This sums up Middleton's presentation of the careers of both Vindice
and Follywit, and suggests as well the source of his famous
detachment. Middleton as vengeful moralist keeps his distance,
showing his hand only in his finales in the form of abrupt peripeteia.

A Calvinist stress on the depravity of mankind and the inevitability
of sin flows through and directs all Middleton's work, comedies
included. 'All', Phoenix is convinced, are 'by nature vicious' [*The
Phoenix*, III ii 250]; and Penitent Brothel in *A Mad World*
acknowledges – as do Lussurioso in *The Revenger's Tragedy* and the
Husband of *A Yorkshire Tragedy* – 'an appetite I know damns
me, / Yet willingly embrace it' [I i 104–5]. Even 'the uprightest
man', according to Vindice, sins 'seven times a day' [*R.T.*, I i 23–
4], and Alsemero believes 'There's scarce a man amongst a thousand
sound, / But hath his imperfection' [*Ch.*, I i 117–18]. If he means
by this that one in a thousand can expect salvation, he is being
wildly optimistic, for Calvin had calculated that no more than thirty
thousand souls, in the whole history of the world, would be numbered
among the elect. Given this arithmetic, many of Calvin's followers
might have agreed with Samuel Beckett that the best thing of all is
not to have been born.

Middleton's characters, having been born, show an intense interest
in the circumstances of their conception, together with a tendency
to see themselves as wholly determined by it, and always for the
worse. 'If the truth were known', reasons the impecunious Skirmish
in *The Puritan* (1606), 'I was begot when my father had never a
penny in his purse' [I ii 86–8], a gambit repeated by the sensually
inclined Spurio: 'if the truth were known, I was begot / After some
gluttonous dinner' [*R.T.*, I ii 180–1]. Spurio is told that he is 'The
curse o'the womb . . . Half-damn'd in the conception' [*R.T.*,
I ii 161–3], and the same suspicion overwhelms Beatrice-Joanna
when she is trapped by De Flores: 'Was my creation in the womb
so curs'd?' [*Ch.*, III iv 165]. Middleton shared similar anxieties, to
judge from a passage in *The Wisdom of Solomon*: 'I was conceiv'd with
seed, deceiv'd with sin . . . The seed of man did bring me into

blood, / And now I bring myself, in what? no good' [vii ii 7–12].

The conviction of being damned at (and by) conception triggers other preoccupations. It helps to explain why Middleton's characters constantly liken the present world to hell, the residence of the damned,[15] and it suggests a deeper reason why Vindice and Leantio think of themselves as already dead. The masked skull is Vindice's way of projecting this perception onto all humanity, a tactic anticipated in *The Wisdom of Solomon* where the living are said to 'die in sin, and mask in death's disguise' [ii i 9]. Calvin, too, tended to assimilate life into death: God, he declared, 'has barred the door of life to those whom he has given over to damnation' [*Institutes*, 3.21.7].

Above all, the idea of damnation in the womb fuelled Middleton's ceaseless interest in the connection of sex and death, for given the statistical probabilities virtually every act of impregnation becomes not a giving of life but an act of murder. Captain Ager puts this succinctly in *A Fair Quarrel*, when he accuses women of having 'let in death to all mankind' [ii i 29] – *let in* being a phrase Middleton employs elsewhere to denote sexual penetration.[16] It is thus not surprising that innocent sexuality is all but absent from Middleton's work. Instead, the 'bewitching minute' of copulation is presented as a spiritually ruinous event, and all sex becomes lust, 'an eternal act of death' [*Hengist*, iii ii 68]. Penitent Brothel feels he has lost his 'eternal portion at a minute's game' [*A Mad World*, iv i 5]; and in *Michaelmas Term*, the Father's verdict on his corrupted daughter is 'One minute, and eternally undone' [ii ii 30]. In *The Changeling*, Beatrice is speaking truer than she knows when she complains that De Flores 'has undone me endlessly', as is the Duchess in *The Revenger's Tragedy* when she informs Spurio that he has been 'By one false minute disinherited' [*R.T.*, i ii 168]. The lurking idea is that it is inheritance of God's spiritual kingdom his conception has deprived him of, not merely the dukedom. One of Donne's sermons supplies an apt footnote: 'Was not God's judgement executed speedily enough upon thy soul, when in the same instant that it was created and conceived and infused, it was put to a necessity of contracting original sin, and so submitted to the penalty of Adam's disobedience, the first minute?'[17]

The absence as well as the presence of certain features can be attributed to Middleton's Calvinism. Unlike the tragedies of Kyd, Fletcher, Ford, Marston, Shakespeare and Webster, his tragedies contain no major characters who lapse into outright insanity; but since to the Calvinist all mankind was psychologically diseased, dwelling on cases of conventional lunacy would merely obfuscate this fact. 'We thought them fools, when we ourselves were fools', Middleton remarks in *The Wisdom of Solomon*; 'We thought them mad, when we ourselves were mad' [v v 1–2]. Vindice repeats the idea: 'we are all mad people, and they / Whom we think are, are not; we mistake those: / 'Tis we are mad in sense, they but in clothes' [*R.T.*, iii v 80–2]. 'Thou art a mad beast', Lussurioso later tells him [*R.T.*, v i 52], in one of the play's thirteen uses of the word *mad*. Instead of overtly mad main characters, Middleton prefers peripheral lunatics in subordinate plots who spell out the interior moral insanity at large elsewhere. Examples are the madmen of 'the Bethlehem Monastery' in *The Honest Whore Part One*, curiously popping up in Italy; the inmates of Alibius's asylum in *The Changeling*; and, in the comedies, the demented lawyer Tangle in *The Phoenix* and the Passionate Madman in *The Nice Valour* (1615 / 16). No doubt Middleton, author of a play called *A Mad World, My Masters*, read with deep attention a sermon of 1615 by the Puritan Thomas Adams, entitled *Mystical Bedlam, or The World of Madmen*.

Middleton's Calvinism may also underlie his comparative lack of interest in revenge as an issue of complex debate. Given the absolute depravity of man's nature, all human behaviour, let alone vindictive impulses, yielded continual signs of inner corruption, and when Middleton writes that God is the 'judge how blood should be repaid' [*The Wisdom of Solomon*, xvii vii 2] he is thinking of the 'blood' that precipitates sin, not the spilled blood that activates the stage revenger. A measure of ambiguity does attach itself to Vindice, automatically: he has no recourse to legal justice, yet falls foul of such biblical injunctions as 'Vengeance is mine; I will repay, saith the Lord' [Romans, xii:19], and 'Cursed be he that smiteth his neighbour secretly' [Deuteronomy, xxvii:24]. But as far as any 'theme' of the legitimacy of retaliation is concerned, it is soon clear that Vindice's career will simply illustrate the truism voiced by Votarius in *The Second Maiden's Tragedy*: 'Revenge / Does no man good but to his greater harm [ii ii 146–7]. To discourage expectation of any more sophisticated analysis, Middleton robs the revenge element in *The Revenger's Tragedy* of much of its dramatic potential. The main crime has been committed before the play begins, and there is no process of detection and verification to be gone through, since the identity of the murderer is certainly known, as is that of the other criminals as they emerge. Moreover, the Duke and Lussurioso are entirely ignorant of the fact that they are being stalked by a vengeful antagonist until their dying moments, so no tension is supplied by the introduction of counterplots, as hunter and hunted as it were slowly circle one another looking for a moment of advantage, as in *Hamlet*. On top of all this, it is evident that Vindice's interventions are essentially redundant, for the ducal family is already riven by homicidal malice. In his pamphlet *The Peacemaker* (1618) Middleton advises any would-be revenger 'thou losest thy labour . . . in offering to do that which will be done without thee' [p. 337]. There he is recommending trust in God's retributive justice, but in *The Revenger's Tragedy* that seems already well in hand.

What galvanises Middleton's interest in place of such intrigue is the hidden spiritual identity proclaimed by Calvinism, the psychological subterfuges by which knowledge of it is suppressed, and its ultimate disclosure. 'God', the writer of Ecclesiastes declares, 'shall bring every work into judgement, with every secret thing, whether it be good, or whether it be evil' [xii:14]. Middleton endorses this in his satirical pamphlet *The Meeting of Gallants at an Ordinary* (1604): 'all things, be they never so lurking, break forth at the last'.[18] Middleton's plays are accordingly full of characters who are said to 'lose' or 'forget' themselves, out of an unconscious desire to evade any confrontation with their reprobate selves. 'You must be more forgetful', Goldstone tutors the disguised Fitzgrave in *Your Five Gallants* [II iii 78]; and Horsus in *Hengist* argues that 'Forgetfulness / Is the most pleasing virtue they can have, / That do spring up from nothing' [III i 39–41]. Vindice, too, resolves to 'forget my nature' as he turns himself into Piato, and ignores the warning latent in Hippolito's 'Brother, we lose ourselves' [*R.T.*, I iii 182; IV ii 200]. Like Lussurioso, who can 'forget myself in private' [I iii 39], Vindice prefers to believe 'man's happiest when he forgets himself' [IV iv 84], even as he deplores the 'forgetful feasts' consumed by the court [III v 91].

Middleton aggravates the doubts surrounding Vindice's true nature by hiding his name. For the first three acts the audience can know him only by his alias, Piato, meaning 'hidden', by which he is twice referred to before the killing of the Duke; then he throws off his disguise and the Duke exclaims 'Is it thou, villain?', and Vindice retorts ' 'Tis I, 'tis Vindice, 'tis I!' [*R.T.*, III v 167–8]. Other revengers make similar declarations having brought off their schemes. Marston's Pandulpho exclaims of the dead Piero, ''twas I, / 'Twas I sluiced out his life-blood' [*Antonio's Revenge*, v vi 7–8]; and Middleton's Fitzgrave, as he reveals himself to his victims, torments them with ''Twas I fram'd your device, do you see? 'twas I!' [*Your Five Gallants*, v ii 40]. Both dramatists may be recalling Hamlet's 'This is I, / Hamlet the Dane!' [*Hamlet*, v i 257–8]. But in *The Revenger's Tragedy* the coupling of the revenger's self-affirmation with the sudden disclosure of his real name implies that only now is his true identity revealed, in this moment of supreme vindictiveness. Nor is his alternative self of Piato so readily shrugged off, for Vindice remains 'in doubt whether I'm myself, or no' [IV iv 24]. What he eventually discovers, or what we discover about him, is that this false identity of treacherous pander was all along part of the true identity he had kept from sight, and from self-sight. His flippant boast about Piato's misdeeds, 'All this is I' [IV ii 131], is truer than he thinks.

One might suppose an existentialist conception here, as in Sartre's dictum 'Identity is a role we impersonate', but this would be wrong, as Sartre is suggesting that beneath the impersonations there is just a void. Middleton's position is more like that of Jonson in *Discoveries*:

I have considered our whole life is like a play, wherein every man, forgetful of himself, is in travail with expression of another. Nay, we so insist in imitating others, as we cannot, when it is necessary, return to ourselves; like children that imitate the vices of stammerers so long till at last they become such, and make the habit to another nature, as it is never forgotten.[19]

Yet this is not quite right either, for in Middleton's view one cannot develop an outward habit which proceeds to supplant one's original nature; the stable centre of self, created and donated by God, is permanently there, but cloaked in various forms of false consciousness. Planning to assume his role as Piato, Vindice claims, 'I have a habit that will fit it quaintly' [I i 102]; indeed he has, for *habit* may mean 'settled disposition to act in a certain way' (*OED*), as well as 'suit of clothes'. The irony of Vindice's role-playing is thus that he contrives to eradicate the doubleness of identity which for Middleton is the primary symptom of man's fallen nature. Normally, as he explains in *The Wisdom of Solomon*, 'the face' is 'the outward index of an outward deed', while 'The inward sins do keep an inward place' [IX xi 2–3]. In Vindice's case, however, his 'inward heart' and the 'outward shape' which he believes conceals it are 'cut out of one piece' [III v 9–10].

Middleton adopts various tactics to press home this view of human personality. One is the use of theatrical metaphors – for drama, too, involves the concealment of true identities beneath false ones, as each actor strives to lose himself in the role he is to play. Middleton is already fully aware of the analogy in *The Wisdom of Solomon*, where man is termed a 'tragic actor' and life a 'tragedy' of 'shadowed shows' [II iii 7; XI xiii 8; XIII xvii 10]. The idea recurs in other early non-dramatic works, such as *The Black Book*, where Lucifer 'ascends this dusty theatre of the world' [p. 7]. The plays themselves, in which the medium can become the message, are not only saturated in theatrical language (in *The Revenger's Tragedy*, for example, Junior Brother has 'play'd a rape', and Vindice calls his revenge an 'action' and the skull a 'property'), but regularly employ staged shows as vehicles of disclosure, whereby false identites are peeled away, discredited, or ironically confirmed to be true. *A Mad World, Your Five Gallants* and *Michaelmas Term* all end in this way – Quomodo admitting in the latter, having staged his own funeral (and with it the funeral of his respectable exterior), 'I am found what I am' [v iii 34]. The masques which conclude *The Revenger's Tragedy* and *Women Beware Women* have the same function. In the former, the visual inseparability of Vindice's masque from '*the other masque of intended murderers*' brings out their moral equivalence; and in the latter, Livia, Isabella and Hippolito act out parts which re-enact their own careers of deception and betrayal, as well as the careers of Bianca and the Duke, who are watching ('I have lost myself in this quite', the Duke complains). In *The Changeling*, there is the virginity test, in which Beatrice impersonates an innocent virgin – which is what she has been doing, in the unthinking belief that this constituted her true identity, all along.

Another tactic Middleton adopts is the use of the doppelgänger, the shadowy double which is the embodiment or custodian of a person's true self, and whose appearance causes confusion in others and spells death or disaster to its human equivalent. A notable example is the amazing introduction, in what is otherwise a realistic city comedy, of the succubus in *A Mad World*, who materialises before Penitent Brothel in the likeness of his adulterous partner Mistress Harebrain and capers about as a demented whore. Penitent Brothel, who, like us, has no way of telling at first that it is *not*

Mistress Harebrain, later points out the doubts about presumed identities that the visitation implies: 'What knows the lecher, when he clips his whore, / Whether it be the devil his parts adore?' [IV iv 57–8]. The chaste Alsemero in *The Changeling*, who would not dream of clipping a whore knowingly, voices the same anxiety when he discovers that he has for some time been married to one: 'oh cunning devils! / How should blind men know you from fair-fac'd saints?' [*Ch.*, v iii 108–9]. In this play, however, the relatively crude manoeuvre in *A Mad World* is abandoned in favour of two personalities, outwardly utterly unlike, which are gradually shown to be indistinguishable, indeed 'one' [III iv 140], as the action proceeds. 'I was / Lost in this small disturbance', Beatrice frets when De Flores has, she thinks inexplicably, annoyed her [II i 93–4]; she does not register the ulterior meaning of her false self dissolving whenever she is in the presence of what is in effect her true one.

The Revenger's Tragedy twice employs similar techniques of psychological or psycho-spiritual disclosure. One occasion is when Gratiana attempts to corrupt Castiza and Castiza pretends she is faced with a phantom, which she fears may be the 'inward' essence of her mother (see John Stachniewski's comments, in section 2 of Part Two, below). The other concerns the killing of the Duke and its often-remarked links with the Dance of Death. It is important to remember here that the English phrase is a mistranslation. The French term, besides Danse Macabre, is 'Danse des Morts', the dance of the dead; and each of the skeletons in illustrations of the dance – a famous set of which Middleton would have seen in the old St Paul's – is 'un mort', one of the dead, who has come to confront a member of the living with his or her own future. The point was stressed by the custom of making each skeleton, as far as was anatomically possible, the duplicate of the living person it had come to claim.[20] Thus the Duke, staring into the face of the skull, is confronting his own eternal destiny, and indeed his true self stretching back into the past, since sin had delivered him to death long ago. 'O, 't has poison'd me!', the Duke screams; 'Didst not know that till now?', Vindice rejoins [*R.T.*, III v 152–3]. If Gloriana's skull could speak, it might well repeat De Flores's announcement to Beatrice: 'peace and innocency has turn'd you out, / And made you one with me' [*Ch.*, III iv 139–40]. But while it looks forward to this deadly twinning, the Duke's death also looks back, in a manner characteristic of Middleton's complex retrievals, to his earliest work, *The Wisdom of Solomon*; for into this biblical poem Middleton inserted the myth of Narcissus, who died by kissing his own image: 'Narcissus fantasy did die to kiss, / O sugar'd kiss! died with a poison'd lip; . . . He died to kiss the shadow of his face' [XIII viii 1–5]. And once launched, the image can spread even into the comedies: 'Men only kiss their knaveries, and so die', Quomodo's servant pronounces on his master [*Michaelmas Term*, IV iii 10].

The foregoing discussion may have created the impression that I take *The Revenger's Tragedy* to be at the very centre of Middleton's achievement, all his other works radiating off it. In fact, any one of his dramatic and non-dramatic pieces could be so discussed, and this play viewed with everything else he wrote as an offshoot of it. The point is that *The Revenger's Tragedy* is not only by Middleton, it is typical of his work.

SOURCE: first published in this Casebook.

NOTES

1. E. H. C. Oliphant, 'The Authorship of *The Revenger's Tragedy*', *Studies in Philology*, XXIII (1926), pp. 157–68.

2. Cf. also VII xxx 1–6, and *The Ghost of Lucrece*, ed. J. Q. Adams (1937), lines 265–6.

3. Edited by Anne Lancashire (Manchester, 1978).

4. In *The Phoenix*, IV i 22, the evil Proditor tells Phoenix he is 'Next to a woman, but more close in secrets'.

5. *The Plague Pamphlets of Thomas Dekker*, ed. F. P. Wilson (Oxford, 1925), p. 99.

6. Jonson's Asper announces 'I go / To turn an actor': *Every Man out of His Humour*, Induction, 213–14.

7. Inga-Stina Ekeblad (Ewbank), 'On the Authorship of *The Revenger's Tragedy*', *English Studies*, XLI (1960), p. 237; see also R. A. Foakes's edition of the play, p. xlix.

8. Edited by A. C. Cawley and B. Gaines (Manchester, 1986).

9. Harebrain in *A Mad World* also doubts 'if modesty be in the world' [I ii 32], and the Courtesan in *A Trick* believes that putting profit before virtue is 'right the world' [I i 98]. With Vindice's resolve to be 'a right man' compare the title of *Women Beware Women* in the Stationers' Register: *A Right Woman, or Women Beware Women*.

10. Edited by F. Bowers, *The Dramatic Works of Thomas Dekker*, 4 vols (Cambridge, 1953–61), II.

11. In *The Wisdom of Solomon Paraphrased* sinners are said to argue in self-extenuation that 'God was our maker, and he made us good, / But our descent springs from another blood' [II viii 5–6]. Cf. Calvin, *Institutes*: 'The

reprobate wish to be considered excused in their sin on the grounds that they cannot avoid the necessity of sinning' [2.33.9].

12. P. Schaff, *The Creeds of the Evangelical Protestant Churches* (1877), p. 366.

13. *The Sermons of John Donne*, ed. G. R. Potter and E. M. Simpson, 10 vols. (Berkeley, 1953–62), II, p. 288 (spelling modernised).

14. Calvin, *Commentaries on Genesis*, tr. T. Tymme (1578), p. 251.

15. E.g. *The Revenger's Tragedy*, III v 186; *A Yorkshire Tragedy*, ii 122; *No Wit, No Help*, II ii 102; *Women Beware Women*, III iii 246–7; *The Changeling*, v iii 163–4.

16. As in Vindice's joke about the woman who 'Lets in her friend by water' [*R.T.*, II ii 40], where *water* puns on the sense 'semen'; cf. also 'Let in at water-gate' in *A Game at Chess* [II ii 43].

17. Donne, op. cit., I, p. 177.

18. *The Plague Pamphlets of Thomas Dekker*, pp. 131–2.

19. *Works of Ben Jonson*, ed. C. H. Herford and P. and E. Simpson, 11 vols. (Oxford, 1925–52), VIII, p. 597.

20. See Jane H. M. Taylor, 'Un Miroer Salutaire', in *Dies Illa: Death in the Middle Ages*, ed. Jane H. M. Taylor (Liverpool, 1984), p. 33, who notes that the skeletons in the Dance are the '*Doppelgänger* of the living'.

R. V. Holdsworth   *The Revenger's Tragedy* on the Stage   (1989)

DATE AND THEATRE COMPANY

The best date for *The Revenger's Tragedy*'s first performance is early 1606. The evidence is a reliance on *King Lear*. *The Revenger's Tragedy* contains not only a villainous bastard son who, like Edmund, plots against his father and stepbrother to avenge his bastardy, but some fleeting but definite verbal echoes of Shakespeare's play. *Lear* can be firmly assigned to the end of 1605 but was not in print before 1608, later than the first printing of *The Revenger's Tragedy*, so Middleton's recollections most probably stem from a stage performance. One would expect the remembered lines and phrases to pass fairly rapidly into his work, whether or not he jotted them down as he watched. Such a date puts Middleton's play in the same twelve-month period as *Lear*, *Volpone* and *Macbeth* – the best year that English theatre has ever seen.[1]

The odds are that, like these three plays, *The Revenger's Tragedy* was performed at the open-air Globe, at this time the only playhouse used by the King's Men, an adult company. Their ownership of the play is asserted by the quarto of 1607/8, which states that 'The Revengers Tragaedie . . . hath beene sundry times Acted, by the Kings Majesties Servants'. It is possible, nevertheless, that this is either wrong or not the whole story; that the play was written for a company of boy actors at a smaller, indoor, 'private' theatre, and acquired by the King's Men only later, if at all. There is first the question of style. Not merely the play's satirical tone, but its 'deliberately exploited artificiality and stylisation, its reliance on pageantry, choreography and burlesque pseudo-ritual, its simplified two-dimensional characterisation, all suggest the mannered technique of the writer for boy companies and private audiences.'[2] More specific stylistic links are the opening torchlit entry, a device copied from Marston's private-theatre plays, and the masque in Act v, scene iii. Of the nineteen plays containing masques first performed between 1599 and 1610, all but two (one of them *The Revenger's Tragedy*) were written for boy companies.[3]

There is also the question of *The Viper and Her Brood*. Is this lost tragedy, which Middleton delivered to the Children of the Queen's Revels in May 1606, *The Revenger's Tragedy* by another name? The title of the lost play, with its allusion to the viper's offspring supposedly devouring their mother at birth, would be apt. The two mothers in *The Revenger's Tragedy*, Gratiana and the Duchess, are vipers not only in that they commit acts of treachery, but in that they are betrayed, preyed on and threatened by their children. This link between them is made both visually (compare the stage-directions at the beginning of iv iii and iv iv) and verbally. Gratiana's 'are sons turn'd monsters?' [iv iv 4] recalls Supervacuo's hypocritical dismay at Lussurioso's incursion into his parents' bedroom, intending to kill his stepbrother and mother: 'In a son, O, monstrous!' [ii iii 72]. Literal echoes of the title of *The Viper and Her Brood* might be present, too, at i iv 62 and iv iv 130, where Junior Brother and Gratiana are likened to serpents, and above all in Vindice's final exit-line, 'We die after a nest of dukes', which seems to glance at the familiar phrase 'nest of snakes'. Even if *The Viper and Her Brood* was a different play, it has Middleton writing a private-theatre tragedy at the right date.

Still, a Globe staging, perhaps with Burbage playing Vindice, remains plausible, even though nothing in the action points specifically to the Globe's facilities.[4] *The Revenger's Tragedy* would not be

Middleton's only King's Men's play around this date, nor would his importation of private-theatre features into a public-theatre play be surprising, since the bulk of his dramatic work up to 1608 was for the Children of Paul's (see Appendix, below). One sees him making just such an insertion in his share of *Timon of Athens*, the only other public-theatre play between 1599 and 1610 to contain a masque. Indeed, the King's Men may have encouraged such features, for at this time they were deliberately shifting the complexion of their repertory towards that of the private theatres, performing *Sejanus* in 1603 and *Volpone* in 1605–6, and filching *The Malcontent* from the Blackfriars in 1604.[5] *The Revenger's Tragedy*, if it was not itself pirated, may have been commissioned as part of this strategy of stealing the thunder of the children's troupes.

THE FIRST PERFORMANCE

One can reconstruct various details of the original performance using the text and current knowledge of the Jacobean theatre. Few substantial props are needed. The throne or 'state', a large canopied chair on a dais, would have been thrust out from the rear for Lussurioso's coronation in v iii, and perhaps in I ii for the Duke to preside at Junior's trial. I iv requires a bier for the corpse of Antonio's wife, II iii a bed for the Duke and Duchess, and v iii a '*furnished table*' and chairs for the banqueters. None of the portable props – swords, daggers, torches, gold coins (Gratiana welcomes their 'comfortable shine' in II i, Vindice their 'bright, unusual shine' in IV ii), two prayer books, one skull, one head (male), a signet ring, a censer to raise the 'perfumed mist' in III v – would have taxed the resources of the stock room.

Occasionally one may infer the use of fixed features of the theatre. From his opening lines, when he reminds us that we are watching 'Four ex'llent characters', Vindice is continually sharpening his role as extra-dramatic commentator by puncturing the play's fictive façade, informing us in III v, for example, that he is engaged in 'tragic business' and that the skull is a 'property'. There is a visual version of this device at III v 2–4, where Vindice, relishing his imminent revenge, cries, 'O, 'tis able / To make a man spring up, and knock his forehead / Against yon silver ceiling'. Both the public and private theatres actually had such a ceiling, as the actor would have disconcertingly pointed out: this was the canopy or 'heavens' arching over the stage, painted to show the sky, sun, moon and stars. Middleton must have been pleased with the effect produced, for in the finale of *No Wit, No Help Like a Woman's* (1611) one finds Savourwit, or the actor preparing to exit from the part, making the same knowing allusion: 'I could spring up and knock my head / Against yon silver ceiling' [v i 455–6].

Use is also implied of the 'discovery space', the alcove, curtained when not needed, in the stage's rear wall. The corpse of Antonio's wife would have lain here, Antonio *'discovering'* (revealing) it by drawing aside the curtain while he and the *'certain lords'* remained on the main stage. In ii iii, after a typically bold indication of a location change (Lussurioso, Vindice and Hippolito simply *'Exit'* and *'Enter again'*), Lussurioso would have drawn the same curtain to reveal his parents, who are nowhere directed to enter, in bed; they would have leapt up and come forward to speak their lines.[6] The discovery space may also have represented the 'darken'd, blushless angle' [iii v 14] to which the Duke is lured for his amorous encounter, even though his torture and murder would need to be conducted nearer the audience; and it could then have served as the place where Vindice stows his corpse at the end of the scene, hiding it by closing the curtain. Since the discovery space is not needed again before v i, when the Duke's body is found, the audience could suppose it to be there throughout the intervening action, inches from detection, until Vindice reopens the curtain to reveal 'this room', 'that sad room' [25, 88], containing the corpse now dressed in Piato's clothes. That the rear alcove was used here is suggested by the deliberate harking back to the first 'discovery', that of Antonio's wife (also dead from poison), when Antonio enjoins his friends to 'be sad witnesses . . . behold, my lords, / A sight that strikes man out of me'. In v i, Lussurioso likewise exhorts the accompanying lords to 'Be witnesses of a strange spectacle . . . O sight! Look hither, see . . .'. A similar visual arrangement would assist the ironic counterpointing.

There is no compelling need for the Jacobean theatre's other main feature, the upper level at the rear of the stage. One might imagine Vindice here for the opening tableau, so that he and the skull can stare down on the ducal family as they *'pass over the stage'*, providing a symbolic equivalent of God's eternal eye; but at no point could he conveniently descend to play the rest of the scene. A Vindice on the main acting area whom the Duke and his train fail to see as they file by him would not have bothered a Jacobean audience, as a silent patrol by one or more characters while an unnoticed onlooker commented upon them was a much-used convention, regularly signalled by a direction to 'pass over the stage'. Middleton employs it again in *The Second Maiden's Tragedy*, II ii, *Women Beware Women*, IV iii and *The Changeling*, V ii. (Modern productions, less at home with this convention, sometimes maroon Vindice in a pool of light.) A more suitable occasion for the upper stage is III v 207–21, the little inset scene between Spurio and the Duchess which is watched by the revengers and their dying victim. Placing the couple here, with their attendant torchbearers and musicians, would give graphic edge to the Duke's question 'Is there a hell besides this?', for prostrate and staring up at them he would indeed resemble a damned soul being tortured in some subterranean depth. The whole spectacle would also anticipate the 'picture' Vindice later composes for Lussurioso: 'A usuring father to be boiling in hell, and his son and heir with a whore dancing over him' [IV ii 88–9].

Such a staging would have been enhanced, of course, if it was possible to make the lower level relatively dark. But was it? The question is of larger interest, for the idea of torchlit darkness, confounding the normal boundaries of night and day, is frequently invoked to suggest the furtive sexuality and unnaturalness of the court. (See especially I iv 26–7, II iii 44–5 and III v 18–19, quoted together in the preceding essay.) 'Men loved darkness rather than light', St John's Gospel remarks, 'because their deeds were evil. For every man that evil doeth hateth the light, neither cometh to light lest his deeds should be reproved' [iii: 19–20].[7] The action consolidates this symbolism by calling continually for night settings, in which torches provide the only illumination. 'Night' and 'midnight' are mentioned eighteen times, often to fix the time of events, and besides the opening procession practical business with a torch is an important element in the trapping and tormenting of the Duke [see III v 142, 148, 195].

If the play was produced at the unroofed Globe, where performances took place in the afternoon, could these lighting effects have been anything more than a matter of formal pretence? The standard view is no: 'variable lighting . . . was not available to the King's Men'.[8] However, new research has shown that the Globe's stage, thanks to its northeast orientation and its canopy (which was sometimes called 'the shadow'), was sufficiently shaded for much of the year to require illumination during the later acts of a play, and to permit practical effects to be obtained from artificial lighting.[9] There is thus no need to suppose that Middleton was still unthinkingly writing as a dramatist of the indoor theatres, where such effects, especially in the use of torchlight, were pioneered; he would have known that the King's Men could also achieve them in some measure.

Dwindling late-afternoon daylight would certainly have assisted the play's most spectacular lighting effect, the blazing star of v iii. This radiant natural phenomenon is God's devastating response to the night-loving, torchlit world of the court, and care is taken to establish its symbolic fitness. Burning with 'ill-knotted fire', it connects the finale with the 'Wild-fire at midnight' [ii ii 172] set in train by Vindice's opening manoeuvres, converting it from metaphor into fact, as it does the revengers' determination to 'let our hid flames break out as fire' [v ii 5]. It supplies, too, an ironically literal answer to Ambitioso's figurative question about the discovery of his father's corpse: 'Over what roof hangs this prodigious comet / In deadly fire?' [v i 105–6]. Blazing stars traditionally spelled the fall of rulers or disruptions of the state, and Middleton had so used them in *1 The Honest Whore*, i i and *The Phoenix*, v i; but here there is an additional allusion, prepared for by the play's insistent biblical language, to the promised revelation of truth at Doomsday, as in 1 Corinthians iv:5: 'Therefore judge nothing before the time, until the Lord come, who will lighten things that are hid in darkness, and make the counsels of the heart manifest'.[10] Judgement Day, the writer of Revelation predicts, will feature the falling of 'a great star from heaven, burning like a torch' [viii: 10]. Less apocalyptic versions of the same device, whereby actual illuminations embody or prefigure moral ones, occur in or near the endings of Middleton's later tragedies.[11] The last case of all, in the finale of *The Changeling*, is typical of Middleton's shift of interest towards the psychological interactions of character, for there the equivalent of *The Revenger's Tragedy*'s astral supervention is De Flores himself: 'yon meteor', Beatrice calls him, 'Mine honour fell with him'.

The Jacobean theatre's blazing star was a dazzlingly fiery affair, which is what the play requires. It consisted either of a firework on a line or flaming material suspended in an iron cage or cresset, and burned for up to a minute. (None of the modern productions I have seen achieved anything like enough candle-power, and at Stratford in 1966 it was not shown at all.) Quite when in v iii it should ignite is hard to tell. '*A blazing star appeareth*' heads the scene, but no one reacts until line 14, and the star is still alight at line 38, when Lussurioso defies it. Having it burn unnoticed for the first thirteen lines would symbolise the court's indifference to God's laws, as well as passing ironic judgement on the 'shine' of the new duke which his toadying nobles are busy praising, but their failure to spot something so visible to the audience would look very peculiar. It seems better to suppose an explosion of light at line 13, just as the First Noble mentions the masque and Lussurioso replies 'We are for pleasure', in order to mark God's (and our) foreknowledge that in calling for pleasure the new duke, like the old one, is calling for his own death.

A few other points in the action need discussion. In ii i editors fail to equip Vindice with the 'gifts' with which Lussurioso promised to 'furnish' him to assist Castiza's seduction [i iii 148–9]. More than a purse of money is involved, as Vindice offers 'a thousand angels', 'treasure' and 'jewels' [ii i 86, 160, 192]. As directors usually recognise, he should bring on a large chest (as Volpone does for his attempted seduction of Celia in *Volpone*, iii v: a scene which this one either imitates or inspired). In iii v how exactly is the poisoning of the Duke accomplished? The quarto directs Vindice to enter '*with the skull of his love dressed up in tires*', which implies that he holds the skull throughout, its long head-dress hiding the absence of a body. He thus acts as a ghoulish puppeteer, pressing the skull against his victim's face as he leans to kiss it, and the Duke's command 'conduct her' [139] perhaps prepares for this. Many directors, however, have preferred to make the Duke more independently responsible for his own poisoning by enabling Vindice and Hippolito to step aside as he advances to get acquainted with his new friend. At Stratford in 1966 Vindice laid the skull, shrouded in a black hood and cloak, on a tomb, and the Duke climbed on top of this apparently receptive figure. In the 1980 Liverpool production, in which Gratiana and Castiza were shown – as at Stratford – working in genteel poverty as seamstresses, dressmaker's dummies stood about on the stage, and Vindice set the skull on one of these.

One other question is whether thunder should sound at iv ii 199, where Vindice, enraged by Lussurioso's wickedness, demands, 'Is there no thunder left, or is't kept up / In stock for heavier vengeance?', then exclaims, 'There it goes!'. All editors add the direction '*Thunder sounds*', and modern productions, apart from the one at Stratford, when Ian Richardson banged a table, have complied. In fact no noise of any kind should occur. 'There it goes!' was a catch-phrase marking a flash of insight, equivalent to the modern 'That's it!', and Vindice is using it to introduce his hitting on the ruse of dressing the Duke's corpse in Piato's clothes.[12] Thunder does indeed sound in the finale, when the revengers kill Lussurioso and his courtiers (and there the quarto states '*It thunders*'); but like the blazing star this is to herald the fulfilment of God's judicial purposes and to strengthen the apocalyptic overtones of the play's close. The Bible often couples fire and thunder as signs of divine wrath, and Revelation insists, on eight occasions, that thunder will peal during Judgement Day.[13] To make God immediately responsive to Vindice's question would upstage these climactic portents, besides misleadingly implying that God is taking Vindice's side. When the 'big-voic'd crier' does at last give tongue, Vindice discovers that He is also thundering against him.

MODERN PRODUCTIONS

The first professional revival was as recent as 1965, at the Pitlochry Festival. Using an uncut and unelaborated text, the director, Brian Shelton, capitalised on the play's theatrical self-consciousness and homiletic harangues by urging the company to 'accept the physical presence of the audience as easily as does a music-hall comic – we play the show at them at point-blank range'. An Elizabethan-type projecting stage assisted this strategy, Vindice frequently 'stepping down towards the audience so as to instruct them on the meaning of the action'.[14]

The following year saw the most important production to date, directed by Trevor Nunn for the RSC at Stratford. Scheduled for eight performances, it achieved forty-eight, including a long run at the Aldwych in 1969, and has been much imitated since.[15] The set and costumes aptly blended opulence and deathliness:

The whole production was designed by Christopher Morley in terms of blacks and silvers, and the design was given a formal structure which centred on a huge silver circle on the black floor of the stage. This circle imposed a hierarchical order and formalised grouping on the court: the centre of the circle was the 'centre of the Court' (the Duke), and the Duke was costumed in bright glittering silver. As one moved further from this centre, the costumes and stage became less silver and more black.[16]

Some individual scenes were equally well handled. Especially powerful were Vindice's opening lines, during which the ducal family came downstage one by one to kneel and cross themselves as though in church, and Lussurioso's invasion of his mother's chamber, when he tore down the bed-curtains to reveal the Duke and Duchess in their nightclothes, both grovelling in terror, and the latter shrivelled and bald. All the reviewers admired Ian Richardson's Vindice, 'cool, witty, terrible in his guile and intent' (*The Guardian*, 28 Nov. 1969), while Alan Howard's bisexual Lussurioso, prompted by the hint of homosexual badinage at I iii 31–40, proved more controversial. *The Guardian* (6 Oct. 1966) praised his 'wonderful arrogant sneering pride', but *The Times* of the same day thought him 'more absurd than evil. Consequently one feels the court is being rid less of a contaminating presence than of a rather temperamental dandy; and the case for Vindice is thereby weakened'.

Other features of the RSC production of 1966/69 were, in my recollection, vulgarly spectacular and false to Middleton's intentions. The text's explosive opening was diminished by a long preliminary masque in which the courtiers in their short metallic capes wove about like birds of prey, finally forming a circle round Junior Brother as he raped Antonio's wife. Vindice's moralising sententiae and his set speeches of social, legal and sexual satire were heavily cut in favour of a relentless emphasis on spectacle. Lussurioso's interviews with Vindice, for example, were set respectively in a fencing school, a massage parlour and a torture chamber, and on each occasion sensational bits of side business distracted attention from the dialogue. In the closing masque, dressing everyone, spectators included, in skull visors made the Dance of Death symbolism seem crudely heavy-handed.

There were more active intrusions. One of several reshufflings of scenes was the running of a revamped I iv, in which Antonio is introduced and his friends swear to avenge his wife's death, onto the end of I i. Vindice, who is conspicuously absent in the text, became the leader of the revengers, and Antonio urged him to hold his hand and leave vengeance to God. The result was to make Vindice much less the isolated custodian of a long-forgotten crime (the murder of Gloriana), to instigate a debate about the ethics of revenge in which the play shows little interest (later additions kept the topic going), and to pre-empt the shock of the finale when Antonio condemns Vindice, since this Antonio's anti-revenge views –

boosted elsewhere in some non-textual appearances – made Vindice's fall predictable. Other additions, comprising over a hundred lines of pseudo-Jacobean verse written by John Barton, elaborated the sexual dalliance between the Duchess and Spurio, and dramatised the Duchess's banishment.

Later productions have interfered less, though along the same lines as Trevor Nunn's. In 1974 the Abbey Theatre, New York, also tried to impose revenge as a governing theme by having a figure personifying Vengeance silently shepherd events throughout.[17] At Oregon in 1984 there was a similar effort to amplify the role of Antonio. In this production, the play was made to begin at I iv, followed by the trial in I ii, before Vindice came on with the skull. The scene with Junior's head [III vi] was watched from above by Antonio, who then announced that justice had been done. At the end, the Fourth Noble was not marched off to execution but was abruptly despatched by Vindice, a change which helped to vindicate Antonio's repudiation of the protagonist.[18] Not that the purgative Stratford ending has always been accepted. At the Oxford Playhouse in 1978 the corpses of the Duke and Duchess stood ominously beside Antonio in the closing tableau; and in the production at Magdalen College, Oxford, in 1985 'one realised that the old society had only been replaced by one equally unscrupulous and corrupt'.[19]

Two recent productions merit fuller description. The Liverpool Playhouse Company, directed by Peter Lichtenfels, performed the play in 1980. This was a straight and effective rendering, true to the play's homiletic spirit and its grotesque mixings of humour and horror, and marred only by some tentative acting in the supporting parts. (None of the three women, in particular, was convincing; the play's 'humour' psychology clearly called for a more forthright, less nuanced approach.) Apart from Vindice's satiric tirades, the most memorable moments were the scenes of savagely funny reversal: Lussurioso rushing in to his parents' chamber to find not his half-brother but his father in bed with his mother; Supervacuo and Ambitioso discovering whose head is really in the executioner's bag; and the Duke amorously courting the bony lady with the grave look. Here and elsewhere the director exactly caught Middleton's technique, employed also in his city comedies, of juxtaposing real anguish with farcical absurdity; while the extra element of ghoulishness was brought out by an amplified heart-beat, introduced at the tensest moments (for example, as the Duke slowly stepped forward, arms thrown wide, to kiss the skull).

Middleton's characteristic detachment was well served by the costumes and set. The stage, hung with purple and backed with tinsel, was vast and bare, so dwarfing the characters that at times they resembled miniature puppets. Masks, white make-up and lead-coloured lipstick aided this impression, as did an enormous silver throne, wheeled from the back for the court scenes, which was carved in the shape of a skeleton wearing a bishop's mitre and carrying a sceptre. The throne's occupant perched in the lap of this monstrous effigy, and looked about three inches tall. The same distortion of scale was emphasised, less successfully, in the closing masques. The first was danced, if that is the word, by four colossal papier-mâché puppets twenty feet high, one of them a skeleton. These teetered about the stage in an unassuming way until the assassins, hiding under their skirts, darted out to polish off the court. In the second, each masquer sported a huge golden head, equipped with a proboscis-like nose. The director no doubt intended to combine suggestions of the Danse Macabre with a *Volpone*-like distortion of men to beasts, but the effect was more like a Disneyland extravaganza.

The best performances were of Spurio and Vindice. The former's vivid account of his conception 'in impudent wine and lust' and his gleeful cynicism ('Old dad dead?') gave his villainy an edge of attractiveness which set him apart from his more mechanically monstrous family. Vindice directed his sardonic invectives straight at the audience, and switched about between his three identities with great success. As himself he was deliberately low-key, as though only able to become fully alive by adopting disguises and deceiving people; as the pander Piato he was slimy and insinuating, all leering grins and twitching eyebrows; and as the supposed (and actual) malcontented brother whom Hippolito brings to court, he became dourly graceless and glum. Despite his rapid sequence of roles, the actor was able to convey a sense of the real Vindice's growing callousness, as he extends his revenge to the entire ducal family. There was a telling moment in v i when, 'mad to lose such a sweet opportunity' of killing Lussurioso over the body of his father, he pettishly took out his disappointment on the corpse, pushing and thumping it as though it were a punch-bag.

There was only one marked departure from the text. Perhaps because of a misunderstanding of the sense of '*discovering*' in the stage-direction heading I iv, we saw Antonio's wife kill herself, Antonio and the other lords coming on to find the body. In fact Antonio already knows of her death, and his long speech has the formal quality of a funeral oration. As an immediate response to the death, which it had to become here, the speech seemed very wooden. A less strained piece of interpretation involving Antonio was the open verdict of the finale, where his sincere-sounding denunciation of Vindice and Hippolito ('Such an old man as he; / You that would murder him would murder me') was spoken as he protectively cradled the crown. It was impossible to tell whether he was genuinely revolted, and unaware of the old Duke's villainy, or getting down to the Machiavellian business of eliminating all potential opponents.

Students of Manchester University Students' Union, directed by Charlotte Bogard, staged the play in 1986. This production caught the right note of sardonic gusto and was (like the play) gripping without being moving. The set was a black-tiled patch of floor dominated by a large crucifix of rough white stone which hung down from a chain. The audience hemmed in the tiny acting area on all sides, enabling Vindice to step effortlessly through the play's fictional wall and include them in the proceedings. He treated them as potential clients for Gloriana ('Who now bids twenty pound a night? . . . All are hush'd'), buttonholed particular groups for his moral and mortuary tirades ('There are few *here* that would not blush outright'), and gave his reference to 'this luxurious circle' [III v. 22] the same ambiguity as Middleton intended in 1606, when the phrase fitted not only the Duke's unsunned lodge but the theatre's stage and auditorium. Costumes as well as set echoed the play's black-and-white moral and religious pigeon-holing. All the courtiers except Spurio (a swaggering tough in black leathers) wore black evening dress, as did the courtly Hippolito (who 'holds by th' duchess' skirt') and the readily corrupted Gratiana. Vindice's apparent distance from, but real kinship with, the vice typified by the court was signalled by his more casual black jumper and jeans. Only the incorruptible Castiza appeared in white – unless one counts Gloriana, who, black-cloaked and hatted for her assignation with the Duke, was revealed first to us and then to him as a polished white skull.

There was some textual tinkering. A preliminary dumb show, lit

with strobe lighting, presented two courtiers being ambushed and
stabbed while a chanted chorus of 'Revenge!' rose from a whisper
to a shout. Since the play's own opening lets us know very clearly
what we are in for, this seemed merely indulgent. Three characters
disappeared: Dondolo, Sordido and Antonio. The loss of the first
two – whose names Middleton re-uses in *More Dissemblers Besides
Women* and *Women Beware Women* – did not show, but with the
removal of Antonio, and with him all of I iv, the readiness of his
supporters to join Vindice in the revengers' masque became very
abrupt. The aim was perhaps to darken the play by omitting any
hint of a right-thinking political opposition. A pessimistic note was
certainly striven for in the finale, where an unnamed court lady,
speaking some of Antonio's lines, appeared from nowhere to inherit
the dukedom. Her tone was menacing and cynical, and she was not
allowed to retain Antonio's pious closing prayer. Instead Vindice
ended the play with a flippant and perfunctory 'Adieu'.

The production went at a headlong pace, appropriate to a play
obsessed with the fleeting 'minute' of existence, yet found time to
accentuate the starkest moments of horror and farce. A single bass
note, throbbingly repeated, accompanied the Duke's discovery of
the skull beneath the hat; in v iii it made a muted return during
the dialogue which leads up to Vindice's casual self-betrayal. More
antics with a head, this time Junior Brother's, follow the business
of the Duke's murder, affording a debunking parallel to Vindice's
abuse of the head of Gloriana. The director signalled the link by
having the Officer who brings on the head duplicate some of
Vindice's gestures in the previous scene, and by making Ambitioso's
stricken amazement a comic version of the Duke's. (His spluttered
demand, 'Whose head's that then?', was the evening's funniest
line.) A later case of parallelism, which brings out the moral
questionableness of Vindice's second killing-bout, is the visual
resemblance, 'e'en to an undistinguish'd hair almost', of his revenge
masque to that of Ambitioso, Supervacuo and Spurio which it pre-
empts. At Liverpool this equation was destroyed, but not in the
Manchester production. Thanks to strobe lighting, the same plain
black masks and identical choreography, the two sets of revengers
were virtually impossible to tell apart.

Lussurioso and Vindice were memorably portrayed. The former,
until he became duke, was a brutal upper-class bully, who constantly
banged the floor and anyone within reach with a heavy walking

cane; on his coronation he gave way to dithering paranoia, and was reduced to jelly by the blazing star. The ease with which Vindice duped him was due to his eagerness to seduce not only Vindice's sister but also Vindice: in their first encounter his announcement that Vindice was 'e'en shap'd to my purpose' acquired a literal meaning as he droolingly kneaded Vindice's leg; in their second, echoing Nunn's Stratford production, Vindice took over from a masseuse, and wound up writhing on the floor with his all but naked employer.

Vindice slid steadily into an insanity which his temporary excursions into alternative personalities seemed his only means of alleviating. As Piato he was a cockney wide-boy in a shiny suit; as Hippolito's boorish, melancholy brother he became a comic northerner with a woollen hat pulled down over his ears. But a progressive loss of control, already hinted at in the bitter, agitated style of his opening speech, was evident between these performances. After each of his perorations on death and sex he blinked uncertainly, as though coming out of a trance. While killing the Duke he developed a compulsive cackle, and to this were cumulatively added staring eyes, a stutter and a facial twitch. Final proof of schizophrenic collapse was supplied brilliantly at the very end, when Vindice quotes a 'knavish sentence' which he claims 'Piato brought forth' two scenes earlier. Underlining the loss of grip displayed here (since the sentence was in fact spoken by a 'Third Noble', and Vindice was present as himself, not as Piato), this Vindice falteringly experimented with a variety of accents, as his discrete personalities jostled for control. This gave a grimly literal twist to his earlier angry cry when rebuking Gratiana: 'O, I'm in doubt whether I'm myself, or no!' [IV iv 24]. Throughout the play he achieved a mood of calm only once, in the silk-worm speech, when he propped the skull-topped dummy in a chair, knelt before it, and addressed it in hushed, awe-struck tones. In spite or perhaps because of the near hysteria so evident elsewhere, this was the Manchester production's most disturbing moment.

Source: first published in this Casebook, incorporating theatre reviews by the author in *Research Opportunities in Renaissance Drama*, XXIII (1980) and XXIX (1986).

NOTES

1. On the date of *Lear* see Gary Taylor, 'A New Source and an Old Date

for *King Lear*', *Review of English Studies*, xxxiii (1982), pp. 396–413, and, for the *Lear* echoes, R. V. Holdsworth, 'Middleton and William Perkins: A Biblical Echo in *The Revenger's Tragedy*', *Notes and Queries*, ccxxx (1985), p. 63, n. 13. The probable reference in *The Revenger's Tragedy*, ii ii 171 to the Gunpowder Plot of 5 November 1605 fits this dating.

2. MacD. P. Jackson, *Studies in Attribution: Middleton and Shakespeare* (Salzburg, 1979), pp. 173–4.

3. Sarah P. Sutherland, *Masques in Jacobean Tragedy* (New York, 1983), p. 23.

4. In 'A Note on *The Revenger's Tragedy*', *Notes and Queries*, cc (1955), pp. 98–9, Inga-Stina Ekeblad (Ewbank) contends that the blazing star in v iii corroborates a Globe staging because, 'of all the Jacobean playhouses', the Globe was noted for this property, but this is simply incorrect. Of the seven plays of the period which call for blazing stars, only *The Revenger's Tragedy* has any claim to have been intended for the Globe. See Jackson, op. cit., p. 171.

5. See Alfred Harbage, *Shakespeare and the Rival Traditions* (New York, 1952), pp. 88–9, 303–4.

6. This is preferable to supposing that a curtained bed was 'put out' from the rear, as could be done (and was done at Stratford in 1966), since the Duke remains on stage throughout this long scene, and the setting unobtrusively changes from the Duchess's bedchamber to 'the court'.

7. Cf. also Isaiah v:20–1: 'Woe unto them that speak good of evil and evil of good, which put darkness for light and light for darkness'; and Job v:13–14: 'the wicked . . . meet with darkness in the daytime, and grope at noonday as in the night'. Quotation here and below is from the Geneva Bible, which Middleton would have used in 1606.

8. Alan C. Dessen, *Elizabethan Stage Conventions and Modern Interpreters* (1984), p. 70.

9. See Keith Brown, 'More Light, More Light', *Essays in Criticism*, xxxiv (1984), pp. 1–13, 283–4.

10. Cf. also 1 Corinthians iii:13, and Ephesians v:13.

11. E.g., the '*great light*' which accompanies the Lady's spirit in *The Second Maiden's Tragedy* [iv iv 42 s.d.]; the fire which consumes Roxena on stage in *Hengist* [v ii 100ff.]; the lights which the Cardinal puts to admonitory use in *Women Beware Women* [iv i 180, 208–9, 264–5], and the lights and fire in the closing masque [v ii 72 s.d.]; and the shining of the morning-star in *The Changeling* [v i 25].

12. See Daniel J. Jacobson, '"There It Goes" – or Does It?', *English Language Notes*, xiii (1975–76), pp. 6–10, who notes a further instance of the phrase in Middleton in *The Family of Love*. There are others in *A Mad World, My Masters* [v ii 174], *A Yorkshire Tragedy* [ii 158] and *The Widow* [i i 178].

13. E.g., 2 Samuel xxii:13–14; Psalms xviii:12–13; Isaiah xxix:6; Revelation iv:5. Cf. the references to thunder in *The Second Maiden's Tragedy* [v i 167], *Hengist* [iv ii 93] and *Women Beware Women* [ii ii 353; iv iii 3].

14. Michael Scott, *Renaissance Drama and a Modern Audience* (1982), pp. 40–1.

15. For a detailed study, see Stanley Wells, '*The Revenger's Tragedy*

Revived', in G. R. Hibbard (ed.), *Elizabethan Theatre*: VI (1978), pp. 105–33. There are photographs of the production in David Addenbrooke, *The Royal Shakespeare Company* (1974), p. 126, and Sally Beauman, *The Royal Shakespeare Company* (1982), p. 245.

16. Addenbrooke, *The Royal Shakespeare Company*, p. 145.

17. See David J. Bradshaw's review, *Research Opportunities in Renaissance Drama*, XVII (1974), pp. 64–5.

18. See Alan C. Dessen, *Research Opportunities in Renaissance Drama*, XXVII (1984), pp. 138–40.

19. M. T. Burnett, *Marlowe Society of America Newsletter*, V, no. 1 (1985), p. 10.

PART TWO

Women Beware Women and *The Changeling*

1. CRITICAL COMMENT, 1657–1935

Nathaniel Richards (1657)

Upon the tragedy of my familiar acquaintance, Thomas Middleton

Women Beware Women: 'tis a true text
Never to be forgot. Drabs of state, vexed,
Have plots, poisons, mischiefs that seldom miss,
To murder virtue with a venom kiss.
Witness this worthy tragedy, expressed
By him that well deserved among the best
Of poets in his time. He knew the rage,
Madness of women crossed, and for the stage
Fitted their humours – hell-bred malice, strife
Acted in state, presented to the life.
I that have seen't can say, having just cause,
Never came tragedy off with more applause.[1]

SOURCE: Thomas Middleton, *Two New Plays* [*More Dissemblers Besides Women* and *Women Beware Women*] (1657), sig. A4ʳ; spelling and punctuation modernised.

NOTE

1. [Ed.] *text*: maxim, motto, especially one which encapsulates the subject of a sermon or exposition; *Drabs of state*: court whores; *humours*: moods, typical qualities of character; *in state*: amid great pomp and solemnity.

Nathaniel Richards (fl. 1630–60), poet and dramatist, was probably some twenty-five years younger than Middleton. Since he echoes both *Women Beware Women* and *The Changeling* many times in works written before either reached print, he may have possessed manuscripts of the plays given to him by Middleton, and may himself have secured the plays' publication. (They were published by the same publisher four years apart in the 1650s.) 'Drabs of state' is taken from *The Revenger's Tragedy*: 'A drab of state, a cloth o' silver slut' [IV iv 70] – a line Richards repeats in full in *The Tragedy of Messalina* and in part elsewhere. 'Venom kiss' may have been prompted by the frequency of such kisses in Middleton: cf. *The Revenger's Tragedy*, III v,

The Second Maiden's Tragedy, v ii and *Women Beware Women*, v ii; though in each of these cases the venom is kissed from the lips of a corpse, and cannot be said to 'murder virtue'.

William Hazlitt   (1820)

In [Middleton's] *Women Beware Women*, there is a rich marrowy vein of internal sentiment, with fine occasional insight into human nature, and cool cutting irony of expression. He is lamentably deficient in the plot and denouement of the story. It is like the rough draught of a tragedy, with a number of fine things thrown in, and the best made use of first; but it tends to no fixed goal, and the interest decreases, instead of increasing, as we read on, for want of previous arrangement and an eye to the whole. We have fine studies of heads, a piece of richly-coloured drapery, 'a foot, an hand, an eye from Nature drawn, that's worth a history'; but the groups are ill disposed, nor are the figures proportioned to each other or the size of the canvas. The author's power is *in* the subject, not *over* it; or he is in possession of excellent materials, which he husbands very ill. . . . The characters of Livia, of Bianca, of Leantio and his Mother, in the play of which I am speaking, are all admirably drawn. The art and malice of Livia shew equal want of principle and acquaintance with the world; and the scene in which she holds the mother in suspense, while she betrays the daughter into the power of the profligate Duke, is a master-piece of dramatic skill. The proneness of Bianca to tread the primrose path of pleasure, after she has made the first false step, and her sudden transition from unblemished virtue to the most abandoned vice, in which she is notably seconded by her mother-in-law's ready submission to the temptations of wealth and power, form a true and striking picture. . . . The moral of this tragedy is rendered more impressive from the manly, independent character of Leantio in the first instance, and the manner in which he dwells, in a sort of doting abstraction, on his own comforts, in being possessed of a beautiful and faithful wife.

Source: extracts from *Lectures Chiefly on the Dramatic Literature of the Age of Elizabeth* (1820); reprinted from Hazlitt's *Works*, ed. P. P. Howe, 21 vols (1930–34), vi, pp. 214–16.

James Russell Lowell (1843)

In the opening of [*The Changeling*], Beatrice thus strongly expresses
her aversion to De Flores:

> 'tis my infirmity,
> Nor can I other reason render you,
> Than his or hers, of some particular thing
> They must abandon as a deadly poison,
> Which to a thousand other tastes were wholesome;
> Such to mine eyes is that same fellow there,
> The same that report speaks of the basilisk.

It was a fine thought in our author thus to give a dim foreshadowing
of that bloody eclipse of her better nature which Beatrice was to
suffer from De Flores. It is always an unacknowledged sense of our
own weaknesses that gives birth to those vague feelings and
presentiments which warn us of an approaching calamity, and when
the blow has fallen, we soothe our wounded self-respect by calling
it Fate. We cheat our sterner reason into a belief that some higher
power has interfered to bring about that blight in us whose steady
growth always circles outward from some hidden meanness in our
own souls. ... Beatrice would make us believe that she has a
natural antipathy to De Flores. But antipathies are only so many
proofs of something wanting in ourselves, whereby we are hindered
of that perfect sympathy with all things, for which we were created,
and without which that life, which should be as harmonious as the
soft consent of love, becomes harsh and jarring. The thought of De
Flores is to Beatrice what the air-drawn dagger was to Macbeth;
she foresees in her own heart the crime yet uncommitted, and
trembles at the weapon even while she stretches her quivering hand
to grasp it. A terrible fascination seems to draw us on to the doing
of ill deeds, the foreconsciousness whereof, graciously implanted in
our natures by God as a safeguard, we misconstrue into the
promptings of our evil demon. ...

In the scene we next quote, the bloody dawning of the thought of
Piracquo's murder in the soul of Beatrice, blots out luridly the
tender morning-star of love which still trembles there, making us
feel yet more thrillingly the swiftly nearing horrors which it betokens.

[Quotes II ii 8–40] . . . Thus she works herself up to a pitch of horror at the fancied guilt of Alsemero, and with half-conscious cunning renders her own plot, (which she now for the first time acknowledges to herself) less full of loathsomeness. She continues, aside:

> And now I think on one: I was to blame,
> I ha' marr'd so good a market with my scorn;
> 'T had been done questionless; the ugliest creature
> Creation fram'd for some use, yet to see
> I could not mark so much where it should be!

How full of doubt and trembling hesitation is the broken structure of the verse, too, and how true to nature the lie in the last line and a half, which she will persist in telling herself!

ALS.   Lady –

But she does not hear him; she is too fearfully intent with watching a murder even now adoing in her own heart. . . . [Quotes II ii 87–94.] She strives to persuade herself that De Flores is not so hideous to her after all, like a child talking aloud in the dark to relieve its terrors. . . .

[In III iv] how finely is the contemptuous coolness of De Flores, the villain by calculation, set off by the shrinking dread of Beatrice, whose guilt is the child of a ravished intercourse between her passions and her affections. The sight of the ring carries her and us back to the sweet days of her innocency, and the picture is complete. ''Tis the first token my father made me send him', she sighs, remembering the calm purity from which she has fallen, and yet, at the same time, with the true cunning of a guiltiness which only half repents, strives to palliate the sin of whose terrible consciousness she must evermore be the cringing bondslave, by thinking of her father's tyranny. . . . In another scene between Beatrice and De Flores [v i], she is made to say something which is full of touching pathos. She suspects her maid of having betrayed her to her husband. De Flores asks,

>   who'd trust
>   A waiting-woman?
> BEA.   I must trust somebody.

How truly is here expressed the wilderness of bleak loneliness into which guilt drives those it possesses.

SOURCE: extracts from 'The Plays of Thomas Middleton', *The Pioneer*, vol. I (January 1843), pp. 35–7.

Hermann Ulrici   (1876)

On *Women Beware Women*

Women Beware Women is a play full of immorality and adultery, murders and slaughter, the reflection of common morality in a completely demoralised age. The tragic muse is here no longer the earnest, exalted goddess absorbed in deep thought and moved by inward sympathy, but the Fury of crime who visits the demoralised world in order to destroy it, and herself with it. The moral forces are indeed partly represented by the Lord Cardinal, but they only externally affect the dramatic characters, without actually influencing their actions, and scarcely find time enough to express a few religious commonplaces about eternal punishment in hell and such things. We cannot sympathise with any of the persons represented, because they are mere fools and wretches, who rush past so rapidly and in so unmotived a manner, from crime to crime, or, like Bianca, fall so rapidly from the height of pure and noble womanhood into the lowest immorality, that they do not seem like real human beings, but empty, hideous masks.

The composition corresponds with the subject, and is evidently incapable of controlling the multitude of events and actions, hence is somewhat restless and irregular and appears defective, forced and obscure. The catastrophe especially, is so unintelligible, that one cannot say with certainty how the six-fold murder, with which the piece closes, is brought about. And yet the piece is one of Middleton's best works and, as Hazlitt says, is distinguished by 'a rich marrowy vein of internal sentiment, and cool cutting irony of expression' [see Hazlitt extract, above]; still the language suffers from a certain dryness and poverty, and hence may perhaps be adequate for describing what takes place externally, but not for delineating the violent emotions, affections and passions which arise in the piece.

SOURCE: extract from *Shakespeare's Dramatic Art*, revised edition, 2 vols. (1876), vol. I, p. 285.

A. C. Swinburne   (1886)

On *Women Beware Women*

The opening or exposition of the play is quite masterly: and the scene in which the forsaken husband is seduced into consolation by the temptress of his wife is worthy of all praise for the straightforward ingenuity and the serious delicacy by which the action is rendered credible and the situation endurable. But I fear that few or none will be found to disagree with my opinion that no such approbation or tolerance can be reasonably extended so as to cover or condone the offences of either the underplot or the upshot of the play. The one is repulsive beyond redemption by elegance of style, the other is preposterous beyond extenuation on the score of logical or poetical justice. Those who object on principle to solution by massacre must object in consistency to the conclusions of *Hamlet* and *King Lear*: nor are the results of Webster's tragic invention more questionable or less inevitable than the results of Shakespeare's: but the dragnet of murder which gathers in the characters at the close of this play is as promiscuous in its sweep as that cast by Cyril Tourneur over the internecine shoal of sharks who are hauled in and ripped open at the close of *The Revenger's Tragedy*. Had Middleton been content with the admirable subject of his main action, he might have given us a simple and unimpeachable masterpiece: and even as it is he has left us a noble and memorable work. It is true that the irredeemable infamy of the leading characters degrades and deforms the nature of the interest excited: the good and gentle old mother whose affectionate simplicity is so gracefully and attractively painted passes out of the story and drops out of the list of actors just when some redeeming figure is most needed to assuage the dreariness of disgust with which we follow the fortunes of so meanly criminal a crew: and the splendid eloquence of the only other respectable person in the play is not of itself sufficient to make a living figure, rather than the mere mouthpiece for indignant emotion, of so subordinate and inactive a character as the Cardinal. The lower comedy of the play is identical in motive with that which defaces the master-work of Ford: more stupid and offensive it hardly could be. But the high comedy of the scene between Livia and the Widow is as fine as the best work in that kind left us by the best poets and humourists of the Shakespearean age; it is not indeed unworthy of the comparison with Chaucer's which it suggested to the all but impeccable judgement of Charles Lamb.[1]

On *The Changeling*

Even Webster's men seem but splendid sketches, as Tourneur's seem but shadowy or fiery outlines, beside the perfect and living figure of De Flores. The man is so horribly human, so fearfully and wonderfully natural, in his single-hearted brutality of devotion, his absolute absorption of soul and body by one consuming force of passionately cynical desire, that we must go to Shakespeare for an equally original and an equally unquestionable revelation of indubitable truth. And in no play by Beaumont and Fletcher is the concord between the two partners more singularly complete in unity of spirit and of style than throughout the tragic part of this play. The underplot from which it most unluckily and absurdly derives its title is very stupid, rather coarse, and almost vulgar: but the two great parts of Beatrice and De Flores are equally consistent, coherent and sustained, in the scenes obviously written by Middleton and in the scenes obviously written by Rowley. . . . To both poets alike must unqualified and equal praise be given for the subtle simplicity of skill with which they make us appreciate the fatal and foreordained affinity between the ill-favoured, rough-mannered, broken-down gentleman, and the headstrong unscrupulous unobservant girl whose very abhorrence of him serves only to fling her down from her high station of haughty beauty into the very clutch of his ravenous and pitiless passion. Her cry of horror and astonishment at first perception of the price to be paid for a service she had thought to purchase with mere money is so wonderfully real in its artless and ingenuous sincerity that Shakespeare himself could hardly have bettered it:

> Why, 'tis impossible thou canst be so wicked,
> Or shelter such a cunning cruelty,
> To make his death the murderer of my honour!

That note of incredulous amazement that the man whom she has just instigated to the commission of murder 'can be so wicked' as to have served her ends for any end of his own beyond the pay of a professional assassin is a touch worthy of the greatest dramatist that ever lived. The perfect simplicity of expression is as notable as the perfect innocence of her surprise; the candid astonishment of a nature absolutely incapable of seeing more than one thing or holding more than one thought at a time. That she, the first criminal, should be honestly shocked as well as physically horrified by revelation of the real motive which impelled her accomplice into crime, gives a lurid streak of tragic humour to the lifelike interest of the scene.

SOURCE: extracts from 'Thomas Middleton', *The Nineteenth Century*, XIX (1886), pp. 149, 151–3; reprinted in Swinburne's *The Age of Shakespeare* (1908).

NOTE

1. [Ed.] Among the extracts from *Women Beware Women* reprinted by Lamb in his *Specimens of English Dramatic Poets* (1808) is II ii 138–226, in which Livia artfully induces the Mother first to admit to Bianca's existence and then to send for her. Lamb comments: 'This is one of those scenes which has the air of being an immediate transcript from life. Livia the "good neighbour" is as real a creature as one of Chaucer's characters. She is such another jolly Housewife as the Wife of Bath.'

William Archer   (1923)

The theme [of *The Changeling*] is undoubtedly very tragic; but the treatment affords an excellent example of the way in which the minor Elizabethans neglected verisimilitude, ignored psychology, and concentrated their whole effort on the elements of lust and horror.

Middleton found the outlines of the story in John Reynolds's *God's Revenge against Murther* ... [and] saw, very justly, that this story demanded concentration for dramatic purposes. The part played by the gallant young De Flores, who, out of devotion to Beatrice, commits a murder in order that she may marry another man, is utterly feeble and even inexplicable. She does ultimately become his mistress, but only because she happens to have quarrelled with her husband. Middleton saw that the drama lay in her putting herself, for love of one man, into the power of another; and so far he was right – this is an intensely dramatic theme. But what does he do? He makes De Flores, instead of a gallant young gentleman, a hideously ugly and ruffianly retainer of Beatrice's father, who follows her about like a dog, only to be flouted and insulted by her on every possible occasion. She knows that he must feel bitter resentment of the ostentatious contempt and loathing with which she constantly treats him; and yet this is the man with whom she plots a murder, imagining that he will be content with a money reward! Such imbecility is not in nature – at any rate not in the nature of Beatrice-Joanna, who, though utterly unscrupulous, is a clever woman. A dramatist of any skill, who wanted to handle this situation, would arrange things so that Beatrice-Joanna could reasonably expect her hired assassin to be content with his money-wage. He might, for instance, be a needy adventurer whom she had befriended, and whom she had no reason to suspect of any hungry passion for herself; or he might be a moonstruck youth, whom she knew to be hopelessly infatuated with her, and believed to be capable of doing murder simply for a smile and a kiss of the hand. In one way or another, in short, the assassin ought to be a plausible instrument for her purpose, not one whose feeling towards her she knew to be a combination of lust and hatred. And this was necessary not only from the psychological but also from the purely theatrical point of view. One of the great effects of the play ought to have lain in her amazement and consternation when the murderer, instead of humbly accepting his wages, demanded of her the one recompense she most abhorred to give him. This scene Middleton does not fail to present; but it is discounted by our sense of the sheer silliness of Beatrice-Joanna's action. Her simplicity is actually comic, . . . [and] her emotions are naïve to the point of ludicrousness.

But the scene leaves us face to face with a situation full of dramatic possibilities. Here is a woman so intensely in love with a man, that she will murder an inconvenient obstacle to their union, who suddenly finds a pistol held to her head, so to speak, with the demand that she shall surrender herself to a brutal ruffian whom

her soul abhors. What is she to do? There are two courses open to
her, either of which would lead to fine dramatic developments. She
might deny all complicity in the murder of Piracquo, and declare
that De Flores is simply attempting to blackmail her. Given the
character of Beatrice-Joanna as presented in the play, this seems
her most probable and hopeful course. De Flores has no proof
whatever that she incited him to the murder, and she could argue
with much plausibility that he was merely taking revenge for her
abominable treatment of him. She might even say to her tormentor,
like the Duke of Wellington. 'Publish and be d——d', pointing out
to him that he would simply be putting his own neck in the noose.
But of course it would have been very easy for the dramatist to
exclude this line of action by giving De Flores some material proof
of her complicity; and in any case she might feel herself lacking in
the effrontery necessary to brazen the thing out. The second course
would then offer itself – and this would be at once the simplest and
the most fruitful, perhaps, in truly dramatic possibilities. She might
go to her intended husband, confess the crime to which her love for
him had driven her, and implore him to protect her from the brute
who was threatening her. How Alsemero would take the confession
would, of course, depend upon his character. There are several
possible turns which the action might take, all very interesting and
effective. We need not speculate further upon these might-have-
beens; it is enough to point out that any number of branching ways
were open to the dramatist, had he taken the trouble to think the
thing out.

Then a third and horribly cynical course of action would have
been possible. Beatrice-Joanna might have said to De Flores: 'Yes,
I will take you for my secret lover; but you must be so moderate in
your claims as not to make my marriage impossible.' Then the
catastrophe would have come about from De Flores's inevitable
failure to act up to this compact. He would have become importunate,
overbearing and foolhardy, so that Alsemero would have discovered
the intrigue and taken his revenge.

The course which Middleton in fact adopts is something like that
which I have just indicated; but he modulates into the key of a
mediaeval Novella, and concentrates on the physiological rather
than the psychological aspect of the situation. I cannot here discuss
the crude childishness of the means adopted by Beatrice-Joanna to
escape detection. It is enough to say that she employs drugs known

only to the pharmacopoeia of fantasy, and that the audience is regaled with that favourite mediaeval titbit – a dark bedchamber, in which one woman is substituted for another. In this case the savour of the situation is heightened by the fact that we see Beatrice-Joanna waiting and fuming outside the door of the room in which her waiting-woman, Diaphanta, has taken her place. The play winds up with a series of grisly episodes which do not even show any ingenuity of invention.

Here, then, we have a drama which is full of good material, spoilt partly by sheer lack of thought, partly by a wilful and quite unnecessary dragging to the front of the physical incidents of depravity, with the obvious design of tickling the sensual imagination of the audience. To the Elizabethan public, an ounce of sexual suggestion was worth a pound of psychological analysis or moral casuistry. *The Changeling* is, in fact, a good play gone wrong: it rattles at the joints, and falls to pieces at a touch for lack of thoughtful and rational adjustment. And in this respect it is absolutely typical. The plays of the period which will stand even the least exacting tests of external plausibility or internal consistency are few indeed. What distinguishes *The Changeling* from the general ruck of Elizabethan melodramas is that it more narrowly misses being a good play.[1] We feel that Middleton was a real dramatist, who, in another environment, would have been capable of working up to higher standards.

SOURCE: extracts from *The Old Drama and the New* (1923), pp. 96–100.

NOTE

1. I have said nothing of the distasteful and tedious under-plot, usually ascribed to Rowley.

T. S. Eliot   (1927)

[Middleton] was one of the most voluminous, and one of the best, dramatic writers of his time. But it is easy to understand why he is not better known or more popular. It is difficult to imagine his 'personality'. . . . Middleton, who collaborated shamelessly, who is hardly separated from Rowley, Middleton who wrote plays so diverse as *Women Beware Women* and *A Game at Chess* and *The Roaring Girl*, Middleton remains merely a collective name for a number of plays – some of which, like *The Spanish Gipsy*, are patently by other people.[1]

If we write about Middleton's plays we must write about Middleton's plays, and not about Middleton's personality. Many of these plays are still in doubt. Of all the Elizabethan dramatists Middleton seems the most impersonal, the most indifferent to personal fame or perpetuity, the readiest, except Rowley, to accept collaboration. Also he is the most various. His greatest tragedies and his greatest comedies are as if written by two different men. . . . Between the tragedies and the comedies of Shakespeare, and certainly between the tragedies and the comedies of Jonson, we can establish a relation; we can see, for Shakespeare or Jonson, that each had in the end a personal point of view which can be called neither comic nor tragic. But with Middleton we can establish no such relation. He remains merely a name, a voice, the author of certain plays, which are all of them great plays. He has no point of view, is neither sentimental nor cynical; he is neither resigned, nor disillusioned, nor romantic; he has no message. He is merely the name which associates six or seven great plays.

For there is no doubt about *The Changeling*. Like all of the plays attributed to Middleton, it is long-winded and tiresome; the characters talk too much, and then suddenly stop talking and act; they are real and impelled irresistibly by the fundamental motions of humanity to good or evil. This mixture of tedious discourse and sudden reality is everywhere in the work of Middleton, in his comedy also. In *The Roaring Girl* we read with toil through a mass of cheap conventional intrigue, and suddenly realise that we are, and have been for some time without knowing it, observing a real and unique human being. In reading *The Changeling* we may think, till almost the end of the play, that we have been concerned merely with a fantastic Elizabethan morality, and then discover that we are looking on at a dispassionate exposure of fundamental passions of any time and any place. The usual opinion remains the just judgement: *The Changeling* is Middleton's greatest play. The morality of the convention seems to us absurd. To many intelligent readers this play has only an historical interest, and serves only to illustrate the moral taboos of the Elizabethans. The heroine is a young woman who, in order to dispose of a fiancé to whom she is indifferent, so that she may marry the man she loves, accepts the offer of an adventurer to murder the affianced, at the price (as she finds in due course) of becoming the murderer's mistress. Such a plot is, to a modern mind, absurd; and the consequent tragedy seems a fuss about nothing. But *The Changeling* is not merely contingent for its effect upon our acceptance of Elizabethan good form or convention; it is, in fact, no more dependent upon the convention of its epoch than a play like *A Doll's House*. Underneath the convention there is the stratum of truth permanent in human nature. The tragedy of *The Changeling* is an eternal tragedy, as permanent as *Œdipus* or *Antony and Cleopatra*; it is the tragedy of the not naturally bad but ✗irresponsible and undeveloped nature, caught in the consequences of its own action. In every age and in every civilization there are instances of the same thing: the unmoral nature, suddenly trapped in the inexorable toils of morality – of morality not made by man but by Nature – and forced to take the consequences of an act which it had planned light-heartedly. Beatrice is not a moral creature; she becomes moral only by becoming damned. Our conventions are not the same as those which Middleton assumed for his play. But the possibility of that frightful discovery of morality remains permanent.

The words in which Middleton expresses his tragedy are as great as the tragedy. The process through which Beatrice, having decided that De Flores is the instrument for her purpose, passes from aversion to habituation, remains a permanent commentary on human nature. The directness and precision of De Flores are masterly, as is also the virtuousness of Beatrice on first realising his motives – [quotes III iv 120–5] – a passage which ends with the really great lines of De Flores, lines of which Shakespeare or Sophocles might have been proud: 'Can you weep fate from its determin'd purpose? / So soon may you weep me.' But what constitutes the essence of the tragedy is something which has not been sufficiently remarked; it is the *habituation* of Beatrice to her sin; it becomes no longer merely sin but custom. Such is the essence of the tragedy of *Macbeth* – the habituation to crime. And in the end Beatrice, having been so long the enforced conspirator of De Flores, becomes (and this is permanently true to human nature) more *his* partner, *his* mate, than the mate and partner of the man for the love of whom she consented to the crime. Her lover disappears not only from the scene but from her own imagination. When she says of De Flores, 'A wondrous necessary man, my lord', her praise is more than half sincere; and at the end she belongs far more to De Flores – towards whom, at the beginning, she felt strong physical repulsion – than to her lover Alsemero. . . . The tragedy of Beatrice is not that she has lost Alsemero, for whose possession she played; it is that she has won De Flores. Such tragedies are not limited to Elizabethan times: they happen every day and perpetually. The greatest tragedies are occupied with great and permanent moral conflicts: the great tragedies of Æschylus, of Sophocles, of Corneille, of Racine, of Shakespeare have the same burden. In poetry, in dramatic technique, *The Changeling* is inferior to the best plays of Webster. But in the moral essence of tragedy it is safe to say that in this play Middleton is surpassed by one Elizabethan alone, and that is Shakespeare. In some respects in which Elizabethan tragedy can be compared to French or to Greek tragedy *The Changeling* stands above every tragic play of its time, except those of Shakespeare.

The genius which blazed in *The Changeling* was fitful but not accidental. The best tragedy after *The Changeling* is *Women Beware Women*. The thesis of the play, as the title indicates, is more arbitrary and less fundamental. The play itself, although less disfigured by ribaldry or clowning, is more tedious. Middleton sinks himself in conventional moralizing of the epoch; so that, if we are impatient, we decide that he gives merely a document of Elizabethan humbug – and then suddenly a personage will blaze out in genuine fire of vituperation. The wickedness of the personages in *Women Beware Women* is conventional wickedness of the stage of the time; yet slowly the exasperation of Bianca, the wife who married beneath her, beneath the ambitions to which she was entitled, emerges from the negative; slowly the real human passions emerge from the mesh of interest in which they begin. And here again Middleton, in writing what appears on the surface a conventional picture-palace Italian melodrama of the time, has caught permanent human feelings. . . . There is hardly anything truer in Elizabethan drama than Bianca's gradual self-will and self-importance in consequence of her courtship by the Duke [quotes iii i 42–5]. In spite of all the long-winded speeches, in spite of all the conventional Italianate horrors, Bianca remains, like Beatrice in *The Changeling*, a real woman; as real, indeed, as any woman of Elizabethan tragedy. Bianca is a woman of the type who is purely moved by vanity. . . .

Middleton was a great observer of human nature, without fear, without sentiment, without prejudice. And Middleton in the end – after criticism has subtracted all that Rowley, all that Dekker, all that others contributed – is a great example of great English drama. He has no message; he is merely a great recorder. Incidentally, in flashes and when the dramatic need comes, he is a great poet, a great master of versification:

> I am that of your blood was taken from you
> For your better health; look no more upon't,
> But cast it to the ground regardlessly:
> Let the common sewer take it from distinction.
> Beneath the stars, upon yon meteor
> Ever hung my fate, 'mongst things corruptible;
> I ne'er could pluck it from him: my loathing
> Was prophet to the rest, but ne'er believed.[2]

The man who wrote these lines remains inscrutable, solitary, unadmired; welcoming collaboration, indifferent to fame; dying no one knows when[3] and no one knows how; attracting, in three hundred years, no personal admiration. Yet he wrote one tragedy which more than any play except those of Shakespeare has a profound and permanent moral value and horror; and one comedy [*The Roaring Girl*] which more than any Elizabethan comedy realises a free and noble womanhood.

SOURCE: extracts from 'Thomas Middleton', *Selected Essays* (1934), pp. 161–9, a slightly revised form of the essay first published in *The Times Literary Supplement* (30 June 1927), pp. 445–6.

NOTES

1. Mr H. Dugdale Sykes has written authoritatively on this subject [in *Sidelights on Elizabethan Drama* (1924), pp. 183–99].

2. [Ed.] *The Changeling* [v iii 150–7]. In the first line of this passage, 'I am that of your blood. . .', Eliot prints 'I that am. . .', a reading derived from Havelock Ellis's Mermaid text of 1887 where the line is thus emended (or misprinted). The alteration might be defended on the ground that it makes explicit the idea that Beatrice is a changeling, but such an association here would be strained, since in folklore it is usually the beautiful or healthy child which is taken by the fairies, and the substituted one which is malevolent or deformed. The original reading, retained by modern editors, anyway makes good sense, involving an image from medicinal blood-letting used elsewhere by Middleton; e.g., *Hengist, King of Kent*: 'Changing pure blood for some that's mix'd and soil'd' [III ii 107], and 'For my blood's health' [IV iii 95]. It is Ellis's version of the line which Eliot echoes in his poem 'Gerontion' ('I that was near your heart was removed therefrom. . .').

3. [Ed.] Middleton was buried in the parish church (St Mary's) of Newington Butts in South London on July 4 1627. The church was demolished in 1876 and the corpses reinterred in a common grave.

William Empson   (1935)

Swinburne said of *The Changeling* that 'the underplot from which it most absurdly and unluckily derives its title is very stupid, rather coarse, and almost vulgar,' after which it is no use saying, as he does, that it is Middleton and Rowley's greatest play, 'a work which should suffice to make either name immortal'; the thing might have good passages but would be a bad play. [See Swinburne extract, above − Ed.] And however disagreeable the comic part may be it is of no use to ignore it; it is woven into the tragic part very thoroughly. Not that this interferes with the accepted view that the comic part is by Rowley and most of the tragic part by Middleton; the sort of unity required depends on the order of the scenes, which they would presumably draw up together, and on ironies which they could work out separately.

The chief reason why modern critics have passed over the comic part is that it forces one to take the unembarrassed Elizabethan view of lunatics, and though still alive in the villages this seems mere brutality to the cultivated. They were hearty jokes, to be treated like animals, and yet were possessed by, or actually were, fairies or evil spirits; they had some positive extra-human quality; they might say things profoundly true. No doubt it was crude to keep a lunatic as a pet, but we may call Shakespeare and Velasquez in evidence that the interest was not as trivial as it was brutal; and though no other Elizabethan could write the part of the madman-critic as Shakespeare could, so that their lunatics are less pleasant than his, this was chiefly for lack of his surrealist literary technique; they could assume the same attitude to lunatics in the audience as he could. People nowadays can swallow the idea in terms of painting or metaphor but to feel it at first hand about a realistic stage lunatic is too much. Certainly if the chorus of imbeciles here was merely convenient or merely funny the effect would be disgusting; but the madhouse dominates every scene; every irony refers back to it; that is why the play is so much nearer Webster than either of its parts.

Though their tones are different the two plots are very alike; in both the heroine has been married for social convenience to a man she does not love, so that there is a case for her if she cuckolds him.[1] In the comic story she gets enough fun out of her lovers to keep up her spirits without being unfaithful to him even in detail; no doubt this is coarse and flat enough, but the contrast is not pointless. Beside the tragic characters she is sane; living among madmen she sees the need to be. This in itself compares the madmen to the tragic sinners, and a close parallel is used to drive it home. The idea of the changeling, a child stolen into the fairies' world, a fairy child replaced for it, makes you feel that the shock of seeing into a mad mind is dangerous; it may snatch you to itself. This shock is in all the discoveries of the play. When Antonio, disguised as a lunatic, makes love to Isabella, she breaks after three lines of his rhetoric into hearty laughter: 'You are a fine fool indeed . . . a parlous fool'; he is a changeling the other way round, she finds, but that is the same thing; he may snatch her into his world. It is in the next scene, so that we are forced to compare them, that we have the discovery the critics have praised so justly in isolation:

> Why, 'tis impossible thou canst be so wicked,
> Or shelter such a cunning cruelty,
> To make his death the murderer of my honour!

The real changeling from which the play 'derives its title' is De Flores.

One need not look at all the jokes about the jealous madhouse keeper; they simply repeat that love is a madness. There is a more striking parallel between De Flores and the subordinate keeper Lollio, who has some claim to be counted among the fools. He demands 'his share' from Isabella as a price for keeping his mouth shut about Antonio, just as De Flores does from Beatrice. This is not irony but preparation ('device prior to irony'); coming in the scene after De Flores commits the murder and before he demands his reward it acts as a proof of Isabella's wisdom and a hint of the future of Beatrice. Isabella threatens to make Antonio cut Lollio's throat, which does not impress him; when the tragic scene they foreshadow is over we find them smacking the threats at each other as casually as ever. I don't say that this is delicate, but it is a relief; Isabella is a very impressive creature; and the assumption in the tragic part that Alsemero will take his maid's virginity without discovering she is not his wife is more really brutal than anything in the asylum scenes.

The two stories get their connection of plot from the two lovers of Isabella, who leave Beatrice's court to be disguised as madmen and are brought back with other madmen to amuse it in the masque at her wedding. This was not merely a fine show on the stage but the chief source of the ideas of the play. The antimasque at a great wedding, considered as subhuman, stood for the insanity of disorder to show marriage as necessary, considered as the mob, ritually mocked the couple (for being or for not being faithful, innocent, etc.), both to appease those who might otherwise mock and to show that the marriage was too strong to be hurt by mockery. We have been shown the chief thing the madmen of the play stand for, when Isabella seemed likely to take Antonio seriously.

> LOL.   Cuckoo, cuckoo!
> [Enter] Madmen above, some as birds, others as beasts.
> ANT.   What are these?
> ISA.   Of fear enough to part us.

Fear parted Beatrice from Alsemero, the husband won falsely; the madmen brought in to be mocked form, for her as for Isabella, an appalling chorus of mockers, and assimilate her to themselves. The richness of the thought here does not come from isolated thinking but from a still hearty custom; to an audience which took the feelings about a marriage masque and a changeling for granted the ideas would arise directly from the two plots.

So the effect of the vulgar asylum scenes is to surround the characters with a herd of lunatics, howling outside in the night, one step into whose company is irretrievable; looking back to the stock form, this herd is the 'people' of which the tragic characters are 'heroes.' Beatrice too becomes a changeling; 'I that am of your blood was taken from you', she tells her father.[2] Morally a child such as the fairies can steal, and fearing De Flores as a goblin, she puts him to a practical use to escape him; he could then steal her; she must realise his way of feeling and be dragged into his world. It is the untruth of the appeal that makes it so terrible, and the hint of the changeling idea given by the other plot that makes us accept it. As a finale this connection is at last made obvious; the venomous courage of De Flores is united to the howling of the madmen.

BEA.   Alsemero, I am a stranger to your bed,
        Your bed was cozen'd on the nuptial night,
        For which your false bride died.

ALS   Diaphanta!

DE F. Yes; and the while I coupled with your mate
        At barley-brake; now we are left in hell.

VER.   We are all there, it circumscribes here.

We have heard about barley-brake before. 'Catch there, catch the last couple in hell!' scream the lunatics in the darkness at the back of the stage, when Antonio discloses his plot to Isabella; the two parts are united, and they are all there together.

SOURCE: extract from *Some Versions of Pastoral* (1935), pp. 48–52.

NOTES

1. [Ed.] In fact Beatrice-Joanna is not married to Alonzo, though she is pledged to do so by her father, and it is hard to deduce from the text that Isabella's marriage to Alibius has been forced on her, or that she does not love him.

2. [Ed.] The correct form of this line is 'I am that. . .'; see the preceding extract from Eliot, note 2. Thus restored it serves Empson's point less well, though one might still agree that the play's title is meant to include Beatrice.

2. MODERN STUDIES

Una Ellis-Fermor   'Middleton's Tragedies'   (1936)

When Middleton, perhaps as a result of association with Rowley, turned to tragedy through the intermediate stages of such tragi-comedies as *A Fair Quarrel*, the experience of a long period of comedy writing remained with him. The peculiar quality of Middleton's tragedy, the grimness, the plainness, the absence alike of romance, pathos, passion or heroism, derives thus directly from the long training in matter-of-fact and unemotional observation, culminating as it does in the wide but precise satire of *A Chaste Maid*. It is not merely, then, that his range of character and episode has been widened, that his theatre technique has become familiar to the point of oblivion, though both of these advantages undoubtedly came to him, as to Shakespeare, through a long period of successful comedy preceding his tragic work; above all, he understands, in the later half of his career, that those very elements that at one time seemed to point only to a comic universe may now be present in the midst of tragic events, not in detached and significant contrast only, but intimately associated, not only as parts of the plot, but as indispensable constituents of the total mood. Some of his contemporaries (Chapman, for example, and Ben Jonson) demonstrate in alternate plays their capacity for tragic and for comic work. Some, the tragi-comedy writers, Fletcher, Beaumont and Massinger (occasionally also Chapman), blend the comic with the near-tragic so closely that though 'it wants deaths, which is enough to make it no tragedy, yet [it] brings some near it, which is enough to make it no comedy'[1]. But Middleton's process, like Shakespeare's, goes as far beyond the second as the second goes beyond the first. He shows the sternest tragic issues intimately blended with comic ones, with characters that are themselves hardly capable of tragic passion, that yet play an indispensable part, not only in the direct disposal of events, but indirectly through their effect upon the central characters, and contribute vitally to the colouring of the final impression. The countryman who brings the asps to Cleopatra, the porter of Macbeth's castle, Emilia in *Othello*, the grave-diggers and Osric in *Hamlet*, not only come from a comic world, but bring it with them, unsubdued, when they enter tragedy and modify thereby the mood, the conduct, even, it may be, the very nature of the tragic figures. This principle of extending and modifying tragedy by the intimate association of comedy, Middleton carried, I think, perhaps further than Shakespeare. For in Middleton's tragedies, the levelling effect of the one mood upon the other goes so far as to obscure the tragic effect at first glance. The constant, not the occasional, presence of the coarse, the impercipient, the shallow and the callous renders the whole more cynical, diminishes, not the sufferings of the main figures, but the dignity of the sufferings. Had *Troilus and Cressida* been focused upon the death of the two lovers it would have achieved something like the balance of tragic and comic mood in Middleton, though not, even so, Middleton's synthesis. The significant thing is that, even had it been so altered, Thersites's summary would still be valid: 'All the argument is a whore and a cuckold.' A grey light results from this even balancing of tragic and comic; the colours subdue each other and the mood is neither heroic nor genial, pathetic nor gay, but something in which each impulse strives with its opposite and comes to equilibrium in frustrated denial. But the resulting atmosphere has a stillness and clarity in which we see with startling sharpness the details of the processes at work upon the minds. . . .

In *Women Beware Women* much of the tragic effect is derived from the relating of the tragic action with a figure as broadly based and as surely drawn as anything in his best comic work. The character of Livia, as original in conception as that of the Roaring Girl and of far more mature and economical workmanship, plays in the first half of the play a part such as even Shakespeare would hardly have given her in tragedy. Her astuteness and her impercipience, her bluff comradely affection for her brother and her accompanying coarse moral obliquity, her level-headed business sense and her equally business-like sensuality are just such a blend of qualities as make us exclaim at sight upon the truth of the portrait. We might have met her in Augustan Rome or modern London. But it is a genius of liberal comprehension which can set such a character at the centre of Bianca's tragedy, can not only make her the agent of the younger woman's seduction but make these very qualities in her an enveloping atmosphere which infects with moral perversion (from which she herself is free) a nature at once finer and more capable of degradation than herself. This is a true and intimate blending of the tragic and the comic elements of both of which Middleton was master, a perception of the complex interplay of environment on character like those which gave Emilia to Desdemona for counsellor and companion or Pandare to Crisseyde. . . .

Middleton shows that knowledge of the hardening of the spirit under certain forms of shock or misery that is his peculiar province in tragedy and that Ford after him shows also in his treatment of Giovanni (though he develops it to rather different ends, in all his subsequent plays). Middleton in *The Changeling* and in *Women Beware Women* (and, to the extent at least of the figure of Francisca, in *The Witch*) reveals in some three or four unforgettable studies the process by which a nature may be dislocated by a sudden jar or shock of evil fate or contaminated and poisoned by a slow chemical process of infiltration. Leantio, Bianca and Francisca are cases of the first and Beatrice of the second. In every case there is enough indication that the nature is drawn on a generous scale; it is the promise of a fine flowering that is destroyed. Middleton seems to have grasped the principle (as did few of his contemporaries) that the more generously a nature is endowed, especially perhaps a woman's, the more bitter is its corruption if it is thwarted or maimed in the full course of its development. Not that he cannot imagine also those more placid and limited beings who accept with patience the cutting off of their natural mode of expression. But he knew as only Shakespeare else, and studied at a length which Shakespeare never attempted, the destruction of a nature by the simple process of administering the shock or poison of fate and leaving it to work out its own disintegration. . . .

[After Bianca's seduction] the rest of the play is a lucid but rapid exposition of the descent of both characters, Leantio and Bianca. In the quick action of a five-act play the contrast is sharpened bitterly between the opening scene and the final clash between husband and wife in the beginning of the fourth act. The same experiment is applied to both and both follow the same broad lines of reaction. Bianca passes from a still, brooding, almost an enchanted meekness of devotion, through the shock of her betrayal, into an awakening which (as Middleton indicates also in *The Changeling*), though more accurately aware of the actual world, may be less clear-sighted in ultimate reality, and is certainly less happy. Her love for the Duke redeems her at the end, but the taunts she gives the husband she has cuckolded almost take us unawares unless we have followed closely the hardening and coarsening of her spirit. Leantio follows a similar course, from the blind, intoxicated devotion of the first act, a mood that hints disaster in the breathlessness of its passion, to the shock of Livia's proof that his idol is a whore.

> As if a punishment of after-life
> Were fallen upon man here; so new it is
> To flesh and blood, so strange, so insupportable.
>
> [III iii 246–8]

When the shock has passed it is an easy step to the cynical acceptance of Livia's patronage and the flaunting in Bianca's face of a prosperity as great as her similar relation with the Duke has brought to her. The sureness of Middleton's touch on Leantio's mood here is beyond comment; it is a mixture of lingering passion, jealousy and the flaunting vanity with which Leantio tries to cover the simultaneous injuries to his affection, to his manhood and to his self-esteem:

> there read,
> Vex, gnaw; thou shalt find there I am not love-starved.
> The world was never yet so cold, or pitiless,
> But there was ever still more charity found out
> Than at one proud fool's door; and 'twere hard 'faith
> If I could not pass that. Read to thy shame there;
> A cheerful and a beauteous benefactor too,
> As e'er erected the good works of love.   [IV i 65–72]

It is, finally, essential to the mood of this play that irony, a sense of the bitter repercussions of event, of the fantastic hypocrisy of society's pretensions and the rotten absurdity of its codes, should run through the commentary, touched in at intervals by a single line or phrase or by the relation of scene and scene. Hippolito, whom she knows to be guilty of incest, presents himself before Livia, having killed her lover in redemption of her honour. To his amazement, the sound common sense of Livia will have none of this prattle of honour nor listen to his excellent reasons. 'The reason!' she cries. 'That's a jest hell falls a-laughing at.' The later 'jests' of Middleton, particularly those deep, underlying tricks of fortune that tangle the blind agents and bring their spirits to disintegration, are indeed such – the jests 'hell falls a-laughing at'. Certainly, in these later plays, the reader feels no temptation to join the laughter.

The Changeling, although this is joint work with Rowley, has something of the same balance of qualities and a corresponding central theme. The avowedly comic sub-plot could, as with the plays of Ford a little later, be detached without much damage and the resulting tragedy would stand as one of the most compact and pitiless in this drama. The tragic material of Middleton contains, unlike that of Marston and Tourneur, elements of great beauty and the subsequent action, unlike that of Webster, Shakespeare or Ford, disintegrates these elements by the spiritual evil set at work within them.[2] The first scene of *The Changeling* sets the atmosphere and defines the nature of the beauty which is in hazard. . . . Alsemero, coming out of the temple in which he has seen Beatrice, fittingly defines it in his first speech, and suggests at the same time the sense, equally essential to Middleton's tragic characters, of 'the unwar wo or harm that comth bihinde':

> 'Twas in the temple where I first beheld her,
> And now again the same; what omen yet
> Follows of that? None but imaginary;
> Why should my hopes or fate be timorous?
> The place is holy, so is my intent:
> I love her beauties to the holy purpose,
> And that, methinks, admits comparison
> With man's first creation, the place blest,
> And is his right home back, if he achieve it.

From this point the play plunges headlong to its action: Beatrice's equally instantaneous love for Alsemero, her father's insistence on the marriage with Alonzo, her insane alliance with the hated De Flores in order to break out of the net and her entanglement in an association far more fatal alike to her fortunes and to her spirit. Middleton wastes no time, as indeed he could not, having so vast a track of experience to cover. His power over plain, brief statements, the records of swiftly succeeding phases of experience and perception, is never more continuously revealed than in Beatrice's speeches throughout the play:

> . . . For five days past
> To be recall'd! Sure, mine eyes were mistaken,
> This was the man was meant me; that he should come
> So near his time, and miss it!   [i i 83–6]

Slowly this sense of contaminated beauty thickens the atmosphere[3] and at the same time, by swiftly moving indications, the mind of the reader is drawn unconsciously to focus on Beatrice and De Flores, bringing them together in ominous isolation before the second act is over:

> BEA. I never see this fellow, but I think
> Of some harm towards me, danger's in my mind still
> . . .
> The next good mood I find my father in,
> I'll get him quite discarded. [II i 89–93]

And in the course of the next scene the acceleration is completed. It opens with a brief passage between her and Alsemero where she passes from mournful regret that Alonzo stands between them, to horror at his offer to challenge him, from that to a half-unconscious acknowledgement that Alonzo's removal is indeed what she desires, from that again to a sudden realisation that De Flores's proffered service can well be used for this purpose. It is in the very suddenness of these snipe-like darts of her mind that Middleton reveals its weakness. Beatrice has a process of thought like that of Othello, whose judgements are rather pictures suddenly presented to it and, once presented, blocking out all other views. She rebukes Alsemero for offering to venture his own life and then, aside:

> here was a course
> Found to bring sorrow on her way to death:
> The tears would ne'er ha' dried, till dust had chok'd 'em.
> Blood-guiltiness becomes a fouler visage –
> And now I think on one: I was to blame,
> I ha' marr'd so good market with my scorn;
> 'T had been done questionless; the ugliest creature
> Creation fram'd for some use.
> . . .
> Why, men of art make much of poison,
> Keep one to expel another; where was my art? [II ii 37–47]

It is the 'art' of a clever child that has learnt a rule out of a book and the pert self-satisfaction is a child's too. When De Flores enters she is still a child playing with a complicated machine of whose mechanism or capacities she knows nothing, concerned only to release the catch that will start it working and delighted when, in accordance with the text-book's instructions, it begins to move. Only when De Flores speaks do we realise that she is not a child, but a woman sleep-walking. Without a sign of realising what she is doing, she accepts his offer to kill Alonzo. His most sharply-pointed references to his reward slip past her consciousness, serving only to measure the depth of her sleep. Indeed, in De Flores himself, the delirium of love (as in his earlier dialogue in II i) invests his figure too with the movements of a sleep-walker so that he believes he can read her mind and prophesy its capitulation. And so both figures move through the scene, she without sense of the reality about her or within her, he crippled by his blindness to her nature and to her unawareness.

From this the main action moves swiftly to the next meeting after the murder has been done, prefixed only by the brief speech of terrible irony in which Beatrice's love for Alsemero builds happily on the assumption of Alonzo's death. There is an essential innocence in this; the quality of her limitation is to realise nothing that is not pictured in her mind. The moment De Flores shows her the dead man's finger she sees the murder as an actual thing. From that moment uneasiness stirs her. The sinister undertones of De Flores's speeches as they skirt the question of reward for his deed are not clear to her as they are to the audience, but she knows her danger subconsciously before she can define it:

> I'm in a labyrinth;
> What will content him? I would fain be rid of him.
> I'll double the sum, sir.   [III iv 71–3]

It is in vain that she attempts to persuade herself that if she does not see, hear, remember or admit it, it will virtually cease to exist (and how profound is Middleton's knowledge of this kind of woman); De Flores pushes her resolutely to the realisation from which her life of a spoilt child has hitherto shielded her. From this point onward every line of De Flores is an immovable logical statement, each statement revealing a merciless fact in that world of reality she has wandered into, sleep-walking. Every line in her part is now the simple utterance of reality; the plain speech that is all a swiftly travelling mind can spare for recording the landmarks in its new and changing observation. The lines themselves harden and grow metallic as the strokes of logic harden her mind.

'Settle you / In what the act has made you . . . Y'are the deed's creature' [III iv 134–7]. It is the business of the rest of the play to show the stages by which her hold upon Alsemero and a life of sane happiness is prised away by her complicity with De Flores and its series of unforeseen but inevitable consequences. Step by step she is driven further from Alsemero and identified more and more completely with De Flores, who becomes 'a wondrous necessary man'. In the central scene [III iv] Middleton has carried Beatrice, as he does Bianca in the corresponding scenes of *Women Beware Women*, from ignorance to experience, from a romantic sleep-walking to an awakening in the midst of horrors. The poison that she had used 'to expel another' has proved too strong for her 'art', which proves in its turn to be no art at all, but the dream of a precocious child.✳ Between the pert cleverness of those early lines and the end of this scene a world of reality has intervened and the experience of years has been lived through with a rapidity that leaves the mind stupid, terrified and a prey to its own guilt:

> BEA. Let me go poor unto my bed with honour,
> And I am rich in all things.
> . . .
> Can you weep fate from its determin'd purpose?
> So soon may you weep me. [III iv 158–63]

She does not see to the end at once and, indeed, until the end, fights with tenacity and strategy to save something of her happiness. Her mind has toughened. Even in becoming coarser in fibre it has become more enduring, more energetic. Only as she moves step by step among the events her deeds have raised does she realise their control and only at the end does she perceive something of their effect upon her:

> Beneath the stars, upon yon meteor
> Ever hung my fate, 'mongst things corruptible;
> I ne'er could pluck it from him: my loathing
> Was prophet to the rest, but ne'er believed. [v iii 154–7]

From the direction inevitably taken by these analyses it will be seen that Middleton's capacity for tragedy is inseparable from his other supreme gift, his discernment of the minds of women; in this no dramatist of the period except Shakespeare is his equal at once for variety and for penetration.

. . . The interplay of tragedy and comedy makes the chief excellence of his work as a whole. In comedy he early developed the ironic detachment which only a potential tragic sense can give, and into tragedy he carried the habit of clear, single-minded observation learnt during almost a lifetime's practice in naturalistic comedy. No mist of sentiment confuses the delicate outlines in which he sparingly defines the processes by which a mind gropes, discovers, recoils from and is engulfed in the events with which it has entangled itself. No rush of passionate identification of himself with its fate drives athwart his judgement or opens up vistas of perception into worlds beyond normal experience. All his concern is with its experience in contact with a present actuality, and however deep or however rare be that experience he finds in it nothing which passes comprehension, never resigns into the hands of a circumambient mystery that soul upon which he has focussed so steady and so dry a light. His sight is clear, his draughtsmanship of a fineness and rapidity that can cover in a single scene the growth that would seem to ask a whole play for its delineation. In these superlative scenes he, like his successor and pupil Ford, writes without faltering and without flaw; each speech and often each sentence is the imperishable record of a stage in that progress which he is following step by step. What results is as clear of pathos as it is of colour or incidental poetry. It terrifies by the scientific clarity with which it reveals the operation of natural laws about the inevitable destruction of those who unawares have broken them. It stirs what is perhaps pity (lying, if so, too deep for instant or immediate expression), but what is left at the end is above all else the sense of passionless and ineluctable law, smooth, unhurried, lucid in its processes, dwarfing the men it overwhelms to something below the status of tragedy as they are dwarfed by those other great operations of nature, flood and earthquake and pestilence. We attend, as we rarely do in Jacobean drama, the destruction of a soul, not the gigantic triumph of the human spirit in uttermost physical catastrophe. No one in these plays cries 'I am Duchess of Malfi still'. No one speaks over the dead or dying those tributes which Shakespeare, Webster, Ford put in the mouths of the bystanders, often even of the very foes who have destroyed them. Their lives are indeed 'a black charnel' but they do not redeem themselves in death; their deaths are of a piece with their lives and become them no better. It is in this pitiless abstemiousness that Middleton stands alone in Jacobean tragedy, suggesting again and again to the reader of a later age that here was in germ the Ibsen of the seventeenth century. Faithful to his observation and to the record of underlying psychological laws which it revealed to him, he is untouched by the heroic, the romantic and the pathetic mood, to the very belittling of those human figures which his contemporaries, even to Ben Jonson himself in tragedy, exalt.

Source: extracts from *The Jacobean Drama* (1936); revised edition (1958), pp. 138–52.

NOTES

1. John Fletcher, 'To the Reader', prefixed to *The Faithful Shepherdess* (printed 1609).
2. The likeness between the themes of *Macbeth* and *The Changeling* is often noted. But *Macbeth* is the only play in which Shakespeare makes a study of spiritual degeneration in any degree similar to Middleton's.
3. The frustration of happiness which is the outward form of the contamination of the principle of beauty in this play is, at first glance, like that which besieges the characters in *The Broken Heart*. But suffering in Ford's plays ennobles and matures the mind, in Middleton's it, as often as not, degrades it.

N. W. Bawcutt   'The Double Plot of *The Changeling*'   (1958)

The sub-plot of *The Changeling* has been dismissed very briefly by the great majority of critics. T. S. Eliot, for example, speaks of its 'nauseousness',[1] and uses the play as an illustration of Sidney's dictum:

So falleth it out, that having indeed no right Comedy, in that comical part of our Tragedy we have nothing but scurrility, unworthy of any chaste ears, or some extreme show of doltishness, indeed fit to lift up a loud laughter, and nothing else.[2]

Una Ellis-Fermor even considers that the sub-plot might have been omitted from the play without serious loss.[3] It is, of course, much inferior to the main plot, and parts of it, especially in I ii, are crude and trivial. But the sub-plot as a whole is far from being worthless, and some at least of the objections that have been made to it spring from misconceptions of its nature and purpose.

The sub-plot may best be defined as a comedy of sexual intrigue which has its setting in a mad-house. It is neither mere 'comic relief' nor a travesty of madness which twentieth-century taste is bound to find offensive. In a variety of ways it echoes or reflects the main plot, as several modern critics have pointed out,[4] and at the end of the play the connection between the two plots is clearly and deliberately stated. No doubt there is an element of buffoonery in the sub-plot which appears to have been one of the main reasons for the play's popularity; but we are not forced to accept the contemporary judgement if we can find convincing evidence for a more intelligent appreciation.

The use of madness in the sub-plot can be seen in its true light only if we remember that virtually all the mad speeches are given to two characters, Antonio and Franciscus, who are not genuine madmen at all. The contemporary audience probably recognised almost immediately that Antonio and Franciscus were would-be lovers in disguise, and a good deal of what appears to be gibberish consists of ambiguous references to their purpose in entering the mad-house.[5] This aspect of the sub-plot is emphasised in IV iii, where Isabella herself pretends to be a madwoman and completely deceives Antonio. The humour is not at the expense of real madness, which Isabella does not seem to find very amusing; it is directed at the absurdity of the lovers in disguise, at the 'madness' of love itself and the fantastic behaviour it provokes.

In its treatment of sexual intrigue the sub-plot is linked to the main plot in a variety of ways. There are, of course, several cross-references between the two plots, and in v ii and especially in v iii characters from both parts are brought together. There are also similarities of plot. As William Empson points out,[6] Isabella corresponds to Beatrice, both women being key figures in their respective parts of the play. Each is surrounded by a set of would-be lovers, and has to make her choice among them, the choice being between an illicit love and duty, in Isabella's case to her husband and in Beatrice's to her father and the man she has promised to marry. The theme of blackmail, of rewards demanded for services given, is equally important in both parts. In III iii Lollio overhears Antonio revealing his love to Isabella, and with that knowledge attempts to coerce her as De Flores in III iv successfully coerces Beatrice. But Isabella is too strong for him, and counters him, as M. C. Bradbrook shows,[7] by threatening to have Antonio treat him in exactly the way De Flores treated Alonzo:

> . . . be silent, mute,
> Mute as a statue, or his injunction
> For me enjoying, shall be to cut thy throat . . .   [iii iii 240–2]

A variant of the same theme occurs twice later in the sub-plot, first
with Antonio [iv iii 145–57] and then with Franciscus [iv iii 188–
202]; each gallant is told by Lollio that he can earn Isabella's love
by ridding her of the unwelcome attentions of his rival. All these
incidents parallel in some way the relationship of Beatrice, Alonzo,
and De Flores.

The imagery of the sub-plot provides a further link with the main
plot. Some of the themes that recur in the latter – sight and outward
appearance, and the transformation of appearances – are equally
important in the sub-plot, particularly in Antonio's speeches:

> This shape of folly shrouds your dearest love,
> The truest servant to your powerful beauties,
> Whose magic had this force thus to transform me.
>   [iii iii 119–21]

The theme is most fully expressed in iv iii, where Antonio's inability
to see through Isabella's disguise parallels the 'blindness' of the
characters in the main plot:

> Have I put on this habit of a frantic,
> With love as full of fury to beguile
> The nimble eye of watchful jealousy,
> And am I thus rewarded?   [*Reveals herself.*]
>
> ANT. Ha! Dearest beauty!
> ISA.   No, I have no beauty now,
> Nor never had, but what was in my garments.
> You a quick-sighted lover? Come not near me!
> Keep your caparisons, y'are aptly clad;
> I came a feigner to return stark mad.   [iv iii 127–35]

There are other, though less important, similarities: Antonio's
'deformity' at iii iii 186 anticipates v iii 32; both Beatrice and
Isabella use metaphors derived from the legend of the labyrinth, at
iii iv 71 and iv iii 106–8; and De Flores's reference to plucking
'sweets' at ii i 46 is echoed by Antonio's:

> Shall I alone
> Walk through the orchard of the Hesperides,
> And cowardly not dare to pull an apple?   [iii iii 173–5]

The main plot itself provides certain links. As Miss Bradbrook points out,[8] Tomazo's comment on his brother, 'Why, here is love's tame madness . . .' [II i 154], reminds us of the sub-plot, and when Alsemero hears Beatrice confess the murder of Alonzo, he locks her into the closet with the comment, 'I'll be your keeper yet' [v iii 87], much as Lollio has to lock up the madmen when they become out of control.

All these parallels, however, point to a very real difference in tone and intention between the two plots. Though the sub-plot contains potentially tragic material, and such a speech as Isabella's in III iii:

> . . . would a woman stray,
> She need not gad abroad to seek her sin,
> It would be brought home one ways or other . . .
> [III iii 213–15]

would not be out of place in the main plot, all the situations which parallel the main plot are turned to comic effect, and certain points in the sub-plot almost suggest a deliberate parody of the main plot. When Franciscus, at IV iii 188–99, is told of the rival he must meet, he cries 'He's dead already', which seems to echo De Flores's 'His end's upon him' [II ii 134]; but whereas De Flores's speech is eagerly accepted by Beatrice, and a tragic situation begins to develop, in the sub-plot any possibility of tragedy is cut short by Lollio's naive common-sense: 'Will you tell me that, and I parted but now with him?' [IV iii 193]. Similarly, Lollio's attempt to ape De Flores in III iii is an almost pathetic failure, and it is as though one character after another in the sub-plot tries to expand into a heroic figure, a sinner of tragic dimensions, only to be abruptly deflated. As Isabella puts it:

> When you are weary, you may leave the school,
> For all this while you have but play'd the fool.   [III iii 145–6]

Antonio wishes to be the gallant and seducer, the master of intrigue, but succeeds only in making a fool of himself, both literally and metaphorically.

At two points in the sub-plot there are passages which appear to be satirical commentary on the main plot. The dialogue on honour between Lollio and Antonio at IV iii 90–9 bears the same relationship to the somewhat brittle 'honour' of Beatrice as Falstaff's speech on honour in *Henry IV, Part I* does to that of Hotspur. In the same scene Alibius's fear that the madmen in the wedding entertainment may alarm the ladies present, who are 'nice things, thou know'st', and Lollio's reply:

You need not fear, sir; so long as we are there with our commanding pizzles, they'll be as tame as the ladies themselves.   [iv iii 61–3]

both reflect ironically on the behaviour of Beatrice and Diaphanta.

A further difference between the two plots might be summed up by saying that what is implied in the main plot becomes literal in the sub-plot. The deceptive appearances which are suggested by imagery in the main plot become actual disguises in the sub-plot, and the madness of love which is no more than hinted at in the main plot moves much closer to real madness in the sub-plot. The first of these two ideas is developed explicitly near the end of the play:

VER. Beseech you hear me; these two have been disguis'd
 E'er since the deed was done.
ALS.   I have two other
 That were more close disguis'd than you two could be,
 E'er since the deed was done.   [v iii 126–9]

In the main plot, the woman's outward appearance is deceptive because it provides no index to the true nature of her character, and this theme is developed metaphorically at some length. In the sub-plot, the whole matter is put much more simply and literally:

. . . I have no beauty now,
Nor never had, but what was in my garments. [iv iii 131–2]

In the one case, the lover is unable to judge the woman's character because of her beauty, in the other he cannot even see that beauty for what it is. Indeed, one of the functions of the sub-plot is to enable the audience to grasp the essential themes of the main plot – the madness of love, the deceptiveness of appearances, the transformations men and women undergo through love – by isolating and enlarging them to the point of literalness, and some effect of this sort is probably felt even by those critics who dismiss the sub-plot as valueless.

The total effect of all these different kinds of relationship between the two halves of the play is not easily assessed. Possibly a deliberate and symbolic contrast is intended by the dramatists. Two sets of characters are portrayed, one group living in a world of normal human relationships, the other in a fantastic environment of madness which might be expected to have a damaging effect upon conduct. Yet the first group behaves with a real and terrible madness that leads to the death of four people, while in the world of apparent madness sanity always manages to assert itself, so that no real damage is done. Beatrice becomes entangled in her own intrigues and is destroyed; Isabella retains her sanity and integrity through her own strength of character. It may be, as Empson suggests, that her surroundings force Isabella to see the problem more clearly than Beatrice; Antonio's attempt to seduce her is interrupted by the sudden appearance of madmen dressed as birds and beasts, a symbolic presentation of the bestiality that is released when human actions cease to be governed by reason and sanity.

The final connection of the two parts comes in the last scene of the play. As Empson points out, De Flores's reference to 'barley-brake' [v iii 162–3] echoes the madmen's cries at III iii 165, but the most important link occurs some lines later, after Alsemero has made his speech beginning: 'What an opacous body had that moon . . .' [v iii 196ff]. Alsemero sums up the events of the main plot, and then, one after the other, each in terms of the transformation imagery we have come to recognise as characteristic of the play, the leading figures of the sub-plot acknowledge their mistakes, and Alibius pledges himself to wiser conduct in future. All that has happened is now seen in its true light. The two halves of the play have followed a similar pattern: sexual passion has led to a series of complicated intrigues which have now worked themselves out, in the one part in tragic disaster, in the other in ludicrous failure on the part of the intriguers. The normal tenor of life has been interrupted by a sudden crisis; at the end of the play the crisis is resolved, and normality finally reasserts itself.

SOURCE: extract from Introduction to the Revels Plays edition of *The Changeling* (1958), pp. lxii–lxviii.

NOTES

[Reorganised and renumbered from the original – Ed.]

1. T. S. Eliot, *The Use of Poetry and the Use of Criticism* (1933), p. 41.
2. Sidney, *An Apology for Poetry*, in G. Gregory Smith (ed.), *Elizabethan Critical Essays* (Oxford, 1904), vol. I, p. 199.
3. [Ed.] See Ellis-Fermor's essay, above, in this selection.
4. [Ed.] See Introduction to this Casebook, note 22.

5. This makes unnecessary a preliminary scene in which they plot their entry into the mad-house.

6. [Ed.] See Empson's comments, above, in this selection.

7. M. C. Bradbrook, *Themes and Conventions of Elizabethan Tragedy* (1935), p. 221.

8. Ibid., p. 217.

Christopher Ricks   The Moral and Poetic Structure of *The Changeling*   (1960)

To think of *The Changeling* is to think at once of the two great scenes between Beatrice and De Flores [ii ii & iii iv]. In the first, she tempts him into murdering Alonzo; in the second, he returns to claim his reward, her body. The greatness of the play is usually said to lie in its psychological power; and there have been various answers to the objections made by William Archer, that Beatrice was uncharacteristically imbecile in not understanding what De Flores was after.[1] This essay begins with the poetic method of *The Changeling*, but its aim is also to unravel the question of the psychological realism, to comment on the nature of the sub-plot, and to arrive at the moral and poetic structure of the play.

Mr T. S. Eliot emphatically reminded us of how 'Middleton shows his interest – more than any of his contemporaries – in innuendo and double meanings'.[2] Miss M. C. Bradbrook reached a similar conclusion: 'he does not rely upon explicit statement or direct speech but upon implication'.[3] The task of the editor is to see that the implications do not escape the modern reader, and even Mr N. W. Bawcutt's thorough edition leaves too many unmentioned.[4] Middleton and Rowley had treated the same theme of seduction by blackmail in *A Fair Quarrel*; when the Physician begins his attack on Jane, he says, 'Tush, our meanings are better understood / Than shifted to the tongue' [iii ii 82–3]. The 'meanings' of *The Changeling* have not received enough attention.

Beatrice sums up the play at an elementary and moralistic level when she says, 'Murder I see is follow'd by more sins' [iii iv 164]. One sin is inextricable from another. But how does Middleton convert his moral commonplace into a drama, into an enactment rather than a *sententia*? The device with which he expresses his dramatic and psychological insights is amazing in its simplicity: he uses the same word for both sins – one might say, he puns. The verbal structure of the play does not exist in its own right, and it gains its importance solely from its dramatic and thematic relevance. Yet I must first try to show what that verbal structure is, in temporary disregard of the larger points.

The verbal basis of the play is a group of words each of which has two meanings, one of them sexual; at the beginning of the play, the two meanings are distinct; by its end, they have become inextricable. There are five of these major words, the most important being one that has apparently gone unmentioned by the editors, *service*. After a close study of their part in the play, I shall pass to a related group of words of a more general kind, words which have both a general moral application and a particular sexual one – the most obvious instances being *honour* and *honesty*.

But what difference does it make that *The Changeling* was a collaboration? Not very much; because the structure which I shall trace is based mainly on the scenes written by Middleton – II i to III ii, III iv to IV ii and V i, ii (to accept Mr Bawcutt's division on p. xxxix). In fact I take his point that the play is 'an unusually close collaboration', and I would like to think that the famous 'barley-brake' repetition is not a solitary example; but it is not necessary to the thesis for me to press for close verbal collaboration. Roughly, Middleton wrote the main plot, and Rowley the sub-plot; this study is almost entirely of the main plot. And the function which I suggest for the sub-plot, its use of innuendo, need depend on no more than a strategic decision by the playwrights.

Middleton, as is abundantly plain from the comedies, was a master of innuendo, especially sexual innuendo. I must anticipate my remarks on the sub-plot to say that one of its important functions is to bring such a tone into the play. The sub-plot is full of obscene and witty puns; often they are the same as are used more quietly in the main plot; and always they alert us to a fascination with innuendo, making it possible for us to pick it up in the main plot without poetic grossness or buffoonery. Moreover, this does not depend solely on the sub-plot; before we reach it, we see that the lovers' meeting of Beatrice and Alsemero is parodied by the brisk lust of Jasperino and Diaphanta. Jasperino hears the greetings of the lovers, and himself makes the comment of parody when he sees Diaphanta:

> I meant to be a venturer in this voyage.
> Yonder's another vessel, I'll board her.   [I i 90–1][5]

For a while the stage is held by the interchanges of Beatrice and Alsemero, until 'they talk apart' and we hear instead the witty obscenities of the other pair [I i 137–51]. That the master woos courteously, and the servant coarsely, is perhaps a frequent contrast; but here it has a strong dramatic point – we can be shown both the smooth façade of Beatrice's virtue, and the crude facts of her lust.

Of the words whose double meanings are the foundation of the play, the most obvious is *blood*. It is used (as in *Othello*) to mean both lust and murder. It is not only De Flores who lusts; Beatrice's lustful change from Alonzo to Alsemero begins the tragic cycle. In its first use in the play, *blood* means lust, in the obscenely witty dialogue between Jasperino and Diaphanta. But when De Flores, leaving Beatrice, exclaims:

> Oh my blood!
> Methinks I feel her in mine arms already,

the satisfaction of his lust will depend on his promise to murder Alonzo; and he claims his great reward because he took 'the life blood of man!'. So his threatening demand is simply reciprocal, with a brutal sense of justice: 'Justice invites your blood to understand me'. Beatrice's outraged refusal he meets with contempt: 'A woman dipp'd in blood, and talk of modesty'[6] – the one sort of blood entails the other. So Beatrice must yield. The lust of Diaphanta when she is substituted for Beatrice on the bridal night nearly causes discovery; for Diaphanta 'cannot rule her blood to keep her promise' [v i 7] – and so she too pays with her blood. The final scene exposes their guilt, and Alsemero compresses into one image the meanings of lust and murder:

> Blood and beauty first unlawfully
> Fir'd their devotion, and quench'd the right one.
> [v iii 74–5]

For Beatrice and De Flores had crossed 'this dangerous bridge of blood' [v iii 81]; and so the inexorable laws which are caught in the unity of the word insist not only that Beatrice's lust must cause murder and be trapped by De Flores's lust, but also that they both must pay with *their* blood.

Middleton had already expressed the theme which he expands

here in a passage in *The Old Law* [IV ii 264–6], very different in tone though it is; Cleanthes rebukes Eugenia in a street-brawl:

> Thy thirst of blood proclaims thee now a strumpet.
> EUG.   'Tis dainty, next to procreation fitting;
> I'd either be destroying men or getting.

And Webster made Vittoria lay bare the justice of the word: 'O my greatest sin lay in my blood. / Now my blood pays for't' [*The White Devil*, v vi 240–1].

The importance of Middleton's use of such words as *blood* is that they sum up the moral and poetic theme of the play. Beatrice ignores and defies the moral order when it suits her; but then she invokes its protection against De Flores. Beatrice wants simply to have her cake and eat it, but for that you need two cakes; and what are, at first, two meanings, are inexorably one word. For

> lust
> Is perjured, murd'rous, bloody, full of blame,
> Savage, extreme, rude, cruel, not to trust.[7]

The pattern is the same with all these major words. My point is not necessarily that they are *puns*. There are occasions when the character who speaks them is not intending a double meaning – that is, when the playwright puns, not the character (as when Shakespeare makes Hastings, in *Richard III*, say naïvely, 'The Boar will use us kindly'). And there are occasions, too, when a word is deliberately used in a simple single sense – yet one which would not have the same meaning in another play, since its simplicity is a conscious state of not being complex. When a word has been often played upon in the play, not to play upon it may be a deliberate act, may be to create a power of contrast which the word merely in a dictionary could not possess.

Repeating the theme of *blood*, *will* means both lust[8] and self-will (in particular, that of Beatrice which causes Alonzo's murder). So in the first scene, De Flores deplores her behaviour to him: 'She knows no cause for't, but a peevish will'. Beatrice's father, Vermandero, rejoices at the approaching marriage with Alonzo (but she already desires Alsemero):

> VERM.   He shall be bound to me,
> As fast as this tie can hold him; I'll want
> My will else.
> BEA.   [*aside*] I shall want mine if you do it.

But De Flores too has both selfish purpose and lust, and his vow ends the scene: 'Though I get nothing else, I'll have my will' [I i 107, 218–20, 237].

The next two words can be taken together. Both *act* and *deed* are most often used to refer to the murder of Alonzo, but they are also used where there is a clear sexual meaning. *Act* is of course used countless times by Shakespeare[9] for the sexual act, and Middleton uses it so in *A Chaste Maid in Cheapside* [II i 32], and in *A Fair Quarrel* [II ii 149] (an important passage because the seduction parallels that in *The Changeling*[10]). *Deed* is likewise frequent in Shakespeare,[11] and Middleton and Rowley have characteristically serious puns in *A Fair Quarrel* when the Physician blackmails Jane about her baby:

> PHYS. Pray you, mistake me not; indeed I love you.
> JANE   Indeed? what deed?
> PHYS. The deed that you have done.
> JANE   I cannot believe you.
> PHYS. Believe the deed then!   [III ii 98–100][12]

That last exclamation rings with the cynicism of De Flores.

By means of the double meaning of *act* and *deed*, De Flores's reward is inescapably associated with his crime. For De Flores himself, with a cool cynicism, has a sexual meaning for his first use of *act*:

> 'Tis half an act of pleasure
> To hear her talk thus to me.   [II ii 86–7]

Beatrice questions his ardour, and he links his crime and his reward with *act*:

> If you knew
> How sweet it were to me to be employed
> In any act of yours . . .   [II ii 120–2]

The suggestion is reinforced by *employed*; it had twice been used punningly in the sub-plot [I ii 33–8],[13] and earlier in this scene [II ii 92–7] Beatrice had offered De Flores 'employment', an offer met by him with solicitously suggestive puns. So there is to be a terrible irony in Beatrice's final account of why she used De Flores as a murderer:

> That thing of hate, worthy in my esteem
> Of no better employment, and him most worthy
> To be so employ'd.   [v iii 67–9]

Beatrice's misunderstanding of De Flores, as I shall suggest, is part of a simple egotism which does not understand puns. Accordingly, she is offended at his importunity, but mentions the *deed*:

> BEA.   I would not hear so much offence again
> For such another deed.
> DE F.   Soft, lady, soft;
> The last is not yet paid for! Oh, this act
> Has put me into spirit!   [III iv 104–7]

Murder is the deed, the act; but De Flores thinks of his reward, and reinforces it with 'has put me into spirit'; which has a sexual meaning common in Middleton and in Shakespeare.[14] Once again Beatrice must accept both deeds, both acts:

>   settle you
> In what the act has made you . . .
> Y'are the deed's creature.   [III iv 134–7]

For Beatrice had rejoiced at the idea of the 'deed'; De Flores had returned with a more sardonic rejoicing ('My thoughts are at a banquet for the deed'); and one result is another 'deed', the murder of Diaphanta (who dies because of her extreme lust).[15] And so in the final choric comment, the murder of Alonzo is for us associated with those other deeds which had to follow:

> VERM.   . . . these two have been disguis'd
> E'er since the deed was done.
> ALS.   I have two other
> That were more close disguis'd than your two could be,
> E'er since the deed was done.   [v iii 126–9]

The most important of all these words is *service*, and the fact that its sexual meaning has gone unmentioned has meant a serious omission from our reading of the play. The lover is the servant of Love and of his lady; but the cruder sexual sense, linked as it is with the farmyard sense, is also very frequent in Shakespeare[16] and in Middleton. In *The Roaring Girl*, Moll questions Trapdoor: 'What parts are there in you for a gentlewoman's service?'; and he answers both the meanings: 'Of two kinds, right worshipful; moveable and immoveable – moveable to run of errands, and immoveable to stand when you have occasion to use me'.[17] *Service*, then, for Middleton and his audience could mean copulation as well as the duty of a servant. There is an exact parallel with the other words; De Flores's service to Beatrice is the murder of Alonzo, and she cannot have

the one kind of service without the other. So the word comes again
and again. It is best to study first of all the method of the two crucial
scenes between Beatrice and De Flores.

Beatrice's decision to use him is tragically expressed through a
phrase which is given its clear sexual aptness in the sub-plot[18]; she
hates De Flores, but

> Cannot I keep that secret,
> And serve my turn upon him?   [II ii 68–9]

(He is to serve his turn upon her.) She begins her wheedling by
saying that

> Hardness becomes the visage of a man well,
> It argues service, resolution, manhood,
> If cause were of employment.   [II ii 92–4]

De Flores, we must remember, does not yet know what is being
proposed, and so he makes the wrong supposition; he selects his
own meaning of *service*, reinforced as it is by *manhood* and by
employment. Therefore he replies, significantly repeating *service*, and
supporting his meaning by *use*[19] (taken up from his aside in line 91)
and *mounts*[20]:

> 'Twould be soon seen,
> If e'er your ladyship had cause to use it.
> I would but wish the honour of a service
> So happy as that mounts to.   [II ii 94–8]

But Beatrice thinks only of *her* meaning, and exclaims, 'We shall try
you – / Oh my De Flores!', an exclamation tragically capable of
misunderstanding.[21] The misunderstandings continue; when
Beatrice talks of *creation*, De Flores thinks of 'procreation'[22]:

> BEA.   Would creation –
> DE F. Ay, well said, that's it.
> BEA.   Had form'd me man.
> DE F. Nay, that's not it.   [II ii 107–9]

'Not it', both because she has got off the subject (procreation, he
thought), and because he hardly thinks she ought to have been
formed a man. Then he offers her his manhood; they again exchange
the word *service*; and after a mention of *blood*, De Flores talks
cunningly of 'employment' and 'act':

> DE F. Without change to your sex, you have your wishes.
> Claim so much man in me.

BEA.   In thee, De Flores?
      There's small cause for that.
DE F.   Put it not from me,
      It's a service that I kneel for to you.
BEA. You are too violent to mean faithfully;
      There's horror in my service, blood and danger,
      Can those be things to sue for?
DE F.   If you knew
      How sweet it were to me to be employed
      In any act of yours . . .   [II ii 114–22]

'Claim so much man in me': again the dilemma of Beatrice. She
can claim De Flores's manhood or reject it, but if she wants his
courage, she must have his lust. She offers to reward him, praising
him for being *forward* (a word which has both a general sense of
'brave' and a particular sexual application – I shall return to it);
and De Flores understands her mention of *service* in his own way, as
is clear from the play on *ravishes*:

BEA. As thou art forward and thy service dangerous,
      Thy reward shall be precious. . . .
DE F. [I] know it will be precious, the thought ravishes. [II ii 129–32]

So there is tragic incomprehension in Beatrice's cry, 'Then I throw
all my fears upon thy service' [II ii 140].

   In the next act, De Flores returns and introduces the crime and
its reward:

              All things are answerable, time, circumstance,
              Your wishes, and my service.   [III iv 22–3]

But Beatrice hangs back, and De Flores menaces her with the word:

              That were strange, lady; 'tis not possible
              My service should draw such a cause from you.
              Offended? Could you think so? That were much
              For one of my performance, and so warm
              Yet in my service.   [III iv 53–7]

For De Flores's *performance* has entitled him to another kind of
performance,[23] and she must accept that he is 'so warm[24] yet in my
service'. Beatrice does accept the situation, and a great part of the
tragedy is that finally she welcomes it, and can say of De Flores,
'How heartily he serves me! . . . The east is not more beauteous
than his service' [v i 70–2].

   The word, then, was used with great skill and power in the two most important scenes; it should be possible now to study it in the other scenes. Act II begins with a five-line episode which is apparently of no dramatic value; Beatrice sends Jasperino with an unnecessary letter to Alsemero. Why did Middleton bother to retain this episode from his source, now made unnecessary by his changes? Its point is to show the straightfoward simplicity of *service*; Jasperino's attitude is very different from De Flores's:

> BEA. Oh sir, I'm ready now for that fair service,
> Which makes the name of friend sit glorious on you
> . . .
>
> JASP. The joy I shall return rewards my service. [II i 1–5]

De Flores, too, is as yet bound to 'true service', and he comes to Beatrice with the humble plea that 'true service merits mercy' [II i 63]. Ironically, it is Alsemero who first uses 'service' to mean the death of Alonzo: 'one good service / Would strike off both your fears'. Beatrice does not understand him, and asks, 'What might that service be so strangely happy?' [II ii 21–6]. The service which will be rendered by De Flores is indeed 'strangely happy'; and he is soon to beg 'a service so happy' [II ii 96]. Possibly, too, the extraordinary power which Middleton develops in the word is responsible for another little scene which seems (like the sending of the letter) to lack dramatic point. Why does Middleton retain from his source the unnecessary scene where Beatrice sends for Diaphanta in order to show Alsemero out? I suggest that in the wording of Beatrice's command there is an adumbration of the later sexual relationship between Diaphanta and the unwitting Alsemero. We already associate lust with Diaphanta from her exchanges with Jasperino, and she has had some cryptically significant words when earlier she brings in Alsemero [II ii 1–5]. Beatrice's command is to

> Perfect your service, and conduct this gentleman
> The private way you brought him. [II ii 54–5]

Diaphanta is indeed to perfect her service with Alsemero – and both *private* and *way*[25] hint at it.

This last conjecture is perhaps over-ingenious, but one cannot doubt the importance of the double meaning of *service* at the height of the play, in the interchanges between Beatrice and De Flores. *Service*, like *blood, will, act* and *deed*, presents two meanings (one sexual) which the tragedy shows to be inextricable.

Related to the group of major words are those words of a more general kind, where there is both a general and a sexual application. I have mentioned *forward*. Beatrice is glad that De Flores is forward (brave), so she must accept that he is forward (lustful). In fact she had originally rebuked his amorous helpfulness when she dropped her glove: 'Mischief on your officious forwardness!' [I i 227]. She is tragically trapped when she exclaims as he tries to kiss her, 'He's bold, and I am blam'd for't!' [III iv 97]. Yes, she is blamed for it, because she wanted him to be bold – though not sexually. It is futile for her to complain now, and to say that his 'language is so bold and vicious' [III iv 123].

In the same way Middleton exploits the apparent clash between the general meanings of *modesty, honour* and *honesty*, and their particular sexual applications. Beatrice's indignation is answered by De Flores:

> BEA. I cannot see which way I can forgive it
> With any modesty.
> DE F.   Push, you forget yourself!
> A woman dipp'd in blood, and talk of modesty?   [III iv 124–6]

As a result, there is a pathetic censoriousness in Beatrice's saying to Diaphanta, 'I fear thou art not modest' [IV i 64]; and she herself is to be rebuked by Alsemero when he knows her guilt:

> ALS. Are you honest?
> BEA. Ha, ha, ha! That's a broad question, my lord.
> ALS. But that's not a modest answer, my lady.   [v iii 20–2][26]

The similar use of *honour* and *honesty* is perhaps not subtle, but it is undeniably powerful, just because it too enacts the same tragic dilemma as the other words – all the main plot pulls in the same direction. So Beatrice pleads with De Flores, desperately late:

> Let me go poor unto my bed with honour,
> And I am rich in all things.   [III iv 158–9]

In a later scene, the words are hammered home [IV i 88, 90, 95, 98, 118]; and finally Beatrice, terrified for her *honour* [v i 4] because of Diaphanta's lustful thoughtlessness, is once again 'forc'd to love' De Flores, but in a different sense:

> I'm forc'd to love thee now,
> 'Cause thou provid'st so carefully for my honour.   [v i 47–8]

It is only at the very end that Beatrice can see the simple truth:

'Mine honour fell with him, and now my life'; and even De Flores can say that 'her honour's prize / Was my reward' [v iii 158, 167–8].

My claim, then, is that Middleton establishes the moral and poetic themes (superbly united) of *The Changeling* through his handling of these words, that the play is what Empson sees in *Othello*, a critique on a pun[27] – or rather, is built on such a critique. Before turning to some linguistic implications, I wish to suggest the importance of such a view for the two main critical problems of the play, the sub-plot and the psychological realism.

That there are some curiously minor connections between the sub-plot and the main plot has been shown by Empson in *Some Versions of Pastoral*; yet a major connection still seems lacking, and I must admit that the thesis which I have put forward cannot establish one. But it does point to one clear function of the sub-plot: its use of innuendo, which makes possible the effects subtly gained in the main plot. The sub-plot is full of obscene wit; see, for example, the scene which opens it (the interchange between Alibius and Lollio), or the dialogue between Lollio and Pedro about Antonio [i ii 1–75, 115–40]. Often the same words are played with, or the sexual applications chosen: employment, honour, serve, serve the turn, forward, bold; always it is clear that this is a play full of innuendo. But the crude buffoonery of the sub-plot (the meanings are forced on us) makes possible the seriousness of the main plot. The episode of the glove (which is not in Middleton's source) is an example. Beatrice, in a spasm of fury that De Flores has picked up the glove she dropped, throws off the other glove; and De Flores's comment suggests the sexual significance – he knows that she would rather have him flayed 'than I should thrust my fingers / Into her sockets here' [i i 233–4].[28] And the significance is immediately stressed in the exchange which follows, between Alibius and Lollio; Alibius must not leave his wife, he must wear his ring: 'If it but lie by, one or other will be thrusting into't' [i ii 30–1].

But how does such a theory affect the psychological realism? William Archer's objections are extremely forceful. *The Changeling* is for him an example of the way in which the Elizabethans 'neglected verisimilitude, ignored psychology'. Beatrice did not understand what De Flores was driving at, and 'such imbecility is not in nature – at any rate not in the nature of Beatrice-Joanna, who, though utterly unscrupulous, is a clever woman'. The scene of her consternation at De Flores's blackmail 'is discounted by our sense of the sheer silliness of Beatrice-Joanna's action', though it 'would indeed be admirable if the relation of the speakers had been so adjusted as to render Beatrice's surprise and horror credible'. The answers to these objections have diverged. E. E. Stoll[29] brilliantly uses them to support his theory that great tragedy is not really psychological at all; he says in fact that Archer's objections are true, but that they are exactly the reason for the play's greatness. 'Passion, not character', he insists; Beatrice's incomprehension *is* 'psychologically improbable', but then so is great tragedy, with 'the character somewhat in contrast to conduct instead of being its source'.

Those who do not accept Stoll's premises may find a different answer in Mr Bawcutt's Introduction (p. liv): 'Beatrice is not a particularly intelligent woman', she is 'a poor judge of characters' and is clumsy; after all, 'until he becomes brutally plain, she completely fails to understand De Flores'. Yet elsewhere Beatrice *does* seem to be clever and cunning. Surely we can save her cleverness by suggesting that her failure is an egotistic single-mindedness, a tragic failure to see puns. Obsessed by her own wishes and meanings, she does not see that De Flores has other wishes and other meanings – but that does not make her unintelligent. The tragedy springs from the fact that hers is 'a nature', in Swinburne's admirable phrase,[30] 'absolutely incapable of seeing more than one thing or holding more than one thought at a time'.

Perhaps, too, the recurring words throw some light on the question of Beatrice's relation with De Flores. How far are we to take her initial loathing for him as sexual in origin? Certainly from the start of the play, she is far from indifferent to him; her thoughts return again and again to him, with obvious fascination; and there is more than mere dislike in the violent episode of the glove, which Middleton added to the original story. She herself is to say that 'My loathing / Was prophet to the rest, but ne'er believ'd' [v iii 156–7]. And in support of such a view, one might perhaps instance those pregnant interchanges with De Flores, where for all her simple cunning and, in the later scene, outraged modesty, she picks again and again the words which are tragically capable of a double meaning. Miss Mahood has made a related point:

Shakespeare also makes his characters speak unconscious puns, which reveal their inmost feelings exactly in the way that people's wishes are exposed by a slip of the tongue or of the pen. By selecting a word with a secondary meaning, the speaker allows himself – or more frequently, herself – the opportunity to say something which caution or modesty withholds from direct expression.[31]

Finally, I shall try to suggest some of the linguistic and critical implications of the verbal structure. In the first place, we are not, I think, faced with Complex Words. There is no dramatic and moral exploration of a complex linguistic situation, as there is, say, with *Nature* in *King Lear*. On the contrary, what makes the verbal structure dramatically viable is precisely its combination of fundamental simplicity with local subtlety. The basic device is strong and simple; the numberless particular uses of it can be confidently sophisticated just because of that larger simplicity. Moreover, they are thoroughly *actable*; the possibilities are obvious as soon as one sees not only that Beatrice misunderstands De Flores, but why she does so.

The next point is that the verbal structure so exactly provides the moral structure of the play. The morality against which Beatrice is broken is the morality of Nature, it is an inexorable fact – a fact as plain as that *blood* is one word, not two. There is the same ruthless justice in Hamlet's pun as he forces Claudius to drink what had been poisoned by the union pearl: 'Drink off this potion. Is thy union here?' And Miss Mahood makes a good point in adducing the methods of Elizabethan preachers:

A simple piece of poetic parallelism is developed into two topics on the assumption that where there are two words there are two things. If a word has several meanings they are shown, through the serious punning which so exasperated a later generation, to bear a kind of transcendental relationship to one another.[32]

The perfect combination of word, situation, and moral in the main plot of *The Changeling* hardly needs elaboration; and the result is consequently more convincing than *Fool* in *King Lear*, of which Mr Empson says:

If you assume that a key word, or better no doubt a whole pattern of related key words, is the proper thing to follow in considering a poetic drama, you get a noticeably different result in this play from the result of the Victorian assumption that the characters ought to be followed separately.[33]

I do not share the general assumption as to 'the proper thing to follow'; but in *The Changeling* the words seem one of the proper things to follow, and there is not 'a noticeably different result'. On the contrary, the words corroborate the traditional view of the play, of its characters, its dilemma, and its morality. The characters and the key words act the same tragedy. Miss Mahood has given a convincing tribute to Shakespeare's word play, and there is nothing far-fetched in applying her words to a great Jacobean tragedy:

The vital wordplay in Shakespeare's writings is that between the characters and their creator, between the primary meanings of words in the context of a person's speech and their secondary meanings as part of the play's underlying pattern of thought. The chief function of the pun is to connect subject and object, inner force with outer form, the poetic vision with the characters in action that are its theatrical embodiment.[34]

SOURCE: essay on 'The Moral and Poetic Structure of *The Changeling*', in *Essays in Criticism*, x (1960), pp. 290–306.

NOTES

[Reorganised and renumbered from the original – Ed.]

1. [Ed.] See Archer's comments above.

2. [Ed.] See Eliot's essay, above, in this selection.

3. M. C. Bradbrook, *Themes and Conventions of Elizabethan Tragedy* (1935), p. 239.

4. *The Changeling*, Revels Plays (1958). E.g. the glossary gives '*treadings*: movements, actions'; the context [I ii 39] indicates a sexual pun. Perhaps a note is needed on 'every man's case' [I ii 37], in view of H. Kökeritz, *Shakespeare's Pronunciation* (New Haven, 1953), p. 119. [*Case* puns on the sense 'vagina', as in *A Fair Quarrel*, v i 315–16 – Ed.]

5. Diaphanta's night with Alsemero is to be described as a 'sweet voyage' [IV ii 123].

6. I i 145; II ii 146–7; III iv 66, 100, 126.

7. Shakespeare, Sonnet 129.

8. See *The Phoenix*, II iii 84, 'You do allude all to incestuous will', and often in Shakespeare (e.g. *All's Well*, IV iii 16).

9. E.g. *Troilus and Cressida*, III ii 83–8; *The Merchant of Venice*, I iii 83.

10. [Ed.] On the indebtedness of *The Changeling* to the scene of attempted sexual blackmail in *A Fair Quarrel* see E. Engelberg, 'A Middleton-Rowley Dispute', *Notes and Queries*, CXCVIII (1953), pp. 330–2.

11. E.g. *Love's Labour's Lost*, III i 198; *The Merchant of Venice*, I iii 85.

12. Cf. also *The Family of Love*, v iii 368; *Women Beware Women*, II i 64. And compare the sub-plot of *The Changeling*, III iii 5, 'You shall be doing, if it please you'.

13. Cf. *King John*, I i 98, 'how he employ'd my mother'.

14. *The Old Law*, III ii 60; *The Family of Love*, v i 12; *King Lear*, IV ii 23; and Sonnet 129. [Middleton also plays on the sexual sense of *spirit* in *The Revenger's Tragedy*, I iii 92 – Ed.]

15. II ii 141; III iv 18; v i 54.

16. See *OED*, 'serve', v.[1] 8.d, 52. E.g. *Measure for Measure*, III ii 120; *All's Well*, IV v 24–37.

17. *The Roaring Girl*, II i 371–4. Also *Blurt, Master Constable*, II ii 109–10, 133; *A Mad World, My Masters*, IV iii 12–13; *The Old Law*, II ii 176; *Women Beware Women*, IV i 48–50.

18. I ii 127–36 ('If it be lower than that it might serve turn . . . then I think 'twill serve his turn'). Compare *Antony and Cleopatra*, II v 58–9, and *Cymbeline*, II v 142.

19. See the quotation from *The Roaring Girl* above; *A Mad World*, III iii 88–90; *Women Beware Women*, II ii 442; *A Game at Chess*, v iii 25. [Cf. *The Revenger's Tragedy*, II ii 99, 'Her tongue has turn'd my sister into use' – Ed.]

20. See *OED*, 'mount', v.10. Also *A Fair Quarrel*, II ii 137; *A Chaste Maid in Cheapside*, v iv 111.

21. *A Fair Quarrel*, v i 80–2, 'have you tried her? . . . She has been tried'; *The Roaring Girl*, II i 334–9; *The Second Maiden's Tragedy*, ed. Anne Lancashire, Revels Plays (Manchester, 1978), II ii 61–3.

22. As in *Measure for Measure*, III ii 105.

23. See the unmistakable meaning of *Michaelmas Term*, III iv 11–12 ('an old lecher . . . Whose mind stands stiff, but his performance down'), and compare *2 Henry IV*, II iv 261; *Troilus and Cressida*, III ii 83–4. [Note also *The Revenger's Tragedy*, I i 34–6, 'old men lustful . . . Outbid like their limited performances', and I ii 74–5, 'an old-cool duke . . . slack in tongue as in performance' – Ed.]

24. See *OED*, 'warm', a.13. Compare Diaphanta [IV i 125]: 'I shall be cool by that time'.

25. Compare *The Family of Love*, v i 112; *Hamlet*, II ii 234; *Measure for Measure*, v i 275; also *The Merry Wives*, IV ii 212; *Pericles*, IV vi 15–19. [Cf. *The Revenger's Tragedy*, I ii 117–23: 'Madam, your grace so private . . . It is as easy way unto a duchess / As to a hatted dame' – Ed.]

26. Compare the repetition of *modest* at IV ii 119, 125, 128.

27. William Empson, *The Structure of Complex Words* (1951), p. 230.

28. Compare Jonson's *The Gypsies Metamorphosed*, 194–5, 'And sounding the socketts / Of *Simper-the-Cocketts*' (C. H. Herford and P. and E. Simpson, eds., *Ben Jonson*, 11 vols. (Oxford, 1925–52), VII, p. 571); and *OED*, 'socket', sb. 4.a. Also the episode of the glove in Shakespeare's *The Rape of Lucrece*, when a needle pricks Tarquin: 'As who should say, "This glove to wanton tricks / Is not inur'd"' (lines 320–1).

29. E. E. Stoll, 'Heroes and Villains', *Review of English Studies*, XVIII (1942), p. 259.

30. A. C. Swinburne, *The Age of Shakespeare* (1908), p. 181.

31. M. M. Mahood, *Shakespeare's Wordplay* (1957), p. 34.

32. Ibid., p. 170.

33. Empson, op. cit., p. 155.

34. Mahood, op. cit., p. 41.

Christopher Ricks   Word-play in *Women Beware*
Women   (1961)   *Women*

Middleton's *Women Beware Women* is very obviously a play about the
corruption of life and love by money. This is at once clear in the
fundamental terms of the action and characters. Leantio elopes with
Bianca, in defiance of her higher social position: the Duke lusts for
her and so (with the aid of Livia and Guardiano, who are eager for
riches and advancement) he bribes her into becoming his mistress.
Livia becomes enamoured of Leantio, and seduces him with money,
clothes, and promises; but Leantio is killed by her brother Hippolito,
whose sense of family honour is outraged, and who has been falsely
told by the Duke that a great marriage has been planned for Livia.
In her fury, Livia reveals the incestuous affair (which she had herself
furthered) between her brother and his niece Isabella – the affair
which is masked by the arranged marriage of Isabella to the rich
half-witted Ward.

  The action and characters, then, are explicit about the power of
money. And the imagery reinforces the theme; there are innumerable
references to treasure, precious stones, silver: all the familiar bric-à-
brac of romantic love takes on a disconcertingly materialist tone.
Miss Bradbrook sees that such images are obvious enough, and so
passes quickly over them: 'The metaphors of wealth need hardly be
considered; their functions will be evident. Affection is the wealth
of the good. Bianca, while she is chaste, is Leantio's "treasure", his
"jewel", his "life's wealth". He in turn is Livia's "riches".'[1] But the
subtleties of Middleton's word-play are rather less obvious. As Mr
T. S. Eliot pointed out, 'in this play Middleton shows his interest –
more than any of his contemporaries – in innuendo and double
meanings'.[2] The following pages are an attempt to show that the
words enact the same tragic dilemma as the action, characters and
images.

  Middleton's aim is to connect the world of money with the world
of love, and to demonstrate how they interpenetrate, so that love
becomes mercenary lust. Of the words which connect the two worlds,
the most important is *business*. It stands, clearly enough, for the
workaday world of money; but it also often has a sexual application

which is commonly found in the seventeenth century.[3] *Business* epitomises the conflicts of the play. The first use of it is one that, by careful syntax, leaves its meaning poised between the alternatives: Leantio in the first scene tells his mother not to worry about the elopement:

> I'll prove an excellent husband, here's my hand;
> Lay in provision, follow my business roundly,
> And make you a grandmother in forty weeks. [i i 107–9]

But Leantio's resolution is never firm, and fifty lines later he has already swung into feeling that worldly business can be ignored for the pleasure of Bianca's company:

> Though my own care and my rich master's trust
> Lay their commands both on my factorship,
> This day and night I'll know no other business
> But her and her dear welcome. [i i 151–4]

Yet Leantio simply cannot afford to keep Bianca without working; and so he must leave early the next morning. He manages to tear himself away – though not without a twinge when Bianca appears at the window, so that he cries out:

> Farewell all business, I desire no more
> Than I see yonder. [i iii 16–17]

His tragedy (one which he has himself chosen by eloping) is that the only way for him to keep what he sees yonder is to earn money; while earning it, he loses her.

For the Duke is struck by her beauty; she is (as the bawd's accomplice, Guardiano, then tells us)

> a creature
> Able to draw a state from serious business,
> And make it their best piece to do her service. [ii ii 16–18]

Here the double meaning of *business* is emphasised by *do her service* – a phrase to return to. Livia's role in the seduction means that she must first persuade the Mother to bring Bianca to the house. Livia has full scope for her innuendoes; and so when she wheedles the Mother into admitting that she has left a gentlewoman at home, and sending for her, it is not surprising that Livia should play cruelly with *business*, and with Leantio's absence. With dazzling hypocrisy she complains that the Mother is such an unfriendly neighbour:

> I sit here
> Sometime whole days together without company,
> When business draws this gentleman [Guardiano] from home.
> [II ii 145–7]

But surely, she asks, the Mother has nothing to do at home?

> you have great business sure
> To sit alone at home . . .
> What business can you have, if you be sure
> Y'have locked the doors?   [II ii 181–2, 193–4]

Therefore when Bianca appears, Livia enjoys comparing the game of chess (with which she will occupy the Mother) with the seduction that awaits Bianca: she brings out, for her own and Guardiano's pleasure, the meaning of *business* with *employed*, another important word that includes the same double meaning:

> Look you, lady, here's our business.
> Are we not well employed think you?   [II ii 262–3]

And the irony of this is strengthened when the Duke echoes the word as he seduces Bianca:

> I can command,
> Think upon that. Yet if thou truly knewest
> The infinite pleasure my affection takes
> In gentle, fair entreatings, when love's businesses
> Are carried courteously 'twixt heart and heart,
> You'd make more haste to please me.   [II ii 362–7]

When Leantio returns to his house, it is to meet a new and ruthless Bianca, and the ruthlessness is clearer if we remember that he has been away on business in order to maintain her:

> No matter for a kiss, sir; let it pass,
> 'Tis but a toy, we'll not so much as mind it;
> Let's talk of other business, and forget it.   [III ii 69–71]

But the Duke has no intention of forgetting *his* business; and he sends a messenger to ask for the gentlewoman. Leantio does not realise to whom his business is: 'Y'are welcome, sir; to whom your business, pray?' And Leantio is forced to lie – there is no gentlewoman in the house:

> It is the most erroneous business
> That e'er your honest pains was abus'd with.   [III ii 107–8]

The Duke, though, is denounced by his brother the Cardinal, and there is a neat echo of that early description of Bianca ('She's a creature able to draw a state from serious business') as the Cardinal approaches: 'There's serious business / Fixed in his look' [IV i 181–2]. But since the word encompasses the world of the play, it is also appropriate to the secondary plot. Livia dupes Isabella into becoming Hippolito's mistress by suggesting that he is not really her uncle; since Isabella's father was not really Fabritio but the Marquis of Coria:

> That was he. But all the business
> So carefully and so discreetly carried
> That fame receiv'd no spot by't, not a blemish.   [II i 149–51]

The idiotic Ward, however, has no need of employment or even activity; his world consists solely of games, and the marriage is to become part of it. Once again the meaning of *business* is stressed, this time by the obscene innuendo in *shittlecock* (one which Isabella takes advantage of, when she later sinks to the Ward's level). The Ward asks 'What's the next business after shittlecock now?', and Guardiano replies: 'Tomorrow you shall see the gentlewoman / Must be your wife' [II ii 80–2].

By means of such a word, Middleton is able to fuse the two forces in the play, so that his purpose is active in small details as well as in such larger effects as the death of Isabella in the shower of gold. Moreover, he does not leave *business* to do all the work. He sees the aptness, for example, of the double meaning of *employ*:[4] it too is excellently fitted to the world in which people can be bought and hired and used like things. Middleton underlines his effect by using the word four times in one scene – the game of chess. So Livia says (with fraudulent politeness) that she will welcome Bianca:

> When is courtesy
> In better practice, than when 'tis employed
> In entertaining strangers?   [II ii 220–2]

And eight lines later, Guardiano stresses the double application, when Livia reminds him of the part he has to play in the seduction:

> True, I know it, lady, and if I be out
> May the Duke banish me from all employments,
> Wanton, or serious.   [II ii 230–2]

Livia enjoys her visitors' ignorance; and she points to the chess-board to draw attention sardonically to the *business* in which they are *employed*. It is the Duke who caps the word-play as he grapples with Bianca (and the mercenary context at the same time invigorates the usually empty word *spent*):

> Pish, strive not, sweet;
> This strength were excellent employed in love now,
> But here 'tis spent amiss.   [II ii 327–9]

The important point about such word-play is that it is certainly not a concession to bawdy groundlings. It has a serious relevance to the moral analysis in the play, and Middleton creates a pattern which encourages one phrase to influence another. Words such as *work* and *labour* reinforce *employment* when they are applied to lustful intrigue or to any other manipulation of people. So Leantio finds that the Duke knows Bianca, and asks 'How comes this work about?' [III ii 128]; later he discovers that the seduction is the result of 'some close bawd's working' [III iii 267]. But that very bawd, Livia, is talking to him at that moment, and becomes his mistress; and so, when the unwitting Leantio praises her to Bianca, the lines have a far from cheerful undertone:

> A cheerful and a beauteous benefactor too,
> As e'er erected the good works of love.   [IV i 71–2]

The good works of love which Livia had erected had hardly brought happiness to Leantio.

Livia's hopes of catching Leantio had made her decide she must work for him – with cosmetics:

> I am not yet so old but he may think of me;
> My own fault, I have been idle a long time,
> But I'll begin the week, and paint tomorrow,
> So follow my true labour day by day –
> I never thrived so well as when I used it.   [III iii 138–42]

But once again 'true labour' is simply an instrument of lust; Livia deplores having been *idle* just as Leantio had once complained that a honeymoon was like a holiday, making 'your poor heads idle' [I iii 7]; and Bianca learns from Isabella's sordid marriage that 'Our Florentine damsels are not brought up idly' [III iii 131]. Even *leisure* is always contaminated by its setting; so when the Duke offers the resisting Bianca a moment's leisure, it is with a firm reminder of how to use it: 'I am not here in vain; have but the leisure / To think on that' [II ii 334–5]. Indeed, the Duke makes the same association in his mind when he jokes with Bianca about Isabella's fortune in marrying the Ward:

> There is no doubt, Bianca, she'll find leisure
> To make that good enough; he's rich and simple.
>
> [III iii 208–9]

Insisting still on the same moral interconnections is the repetition of the word *use*. This often has a sexual application in Middleton (and elsewhere), and in this play it is particularly apt. Bianca tries to defend herself against the Duke by insisting that

> His weight is deadly, who commits with strumpets
> After they have been abased, and made for use. [II ii 435–6]

'Abased, and made for use': it is an excellent summing up of the denial of love which dehumanises the characters. But Bianca's sense of honour is short-lived, as Livia predicts – 'Are you so bitter? 'Tis but want of use' [II ii 470]. Nor is the denial of humanity which characterises mercenary lust simply the fault of the man, since the woman sells herself even in marriage. Bianca petulantly points out that

> Wives do not give away themselves to husbands,
> To the end to be quite cast away; they look
> To be the better used, and tendered rather. [III i 47–9]

The Duke thinks that all can be put right if he marries Bianca, but the Cardinal is firm:

> holy ceremonies
> Were made for sacred uses, not for sinful.
> . . .
> Is it enough to use adulterous thefts,
> And then take sanctuary in marriage? [IV iii 3–4, 36–7]

With its variant of *abused* or *abuser*, the word *use* rings through the play, indicting the forces which reduce people to things.

That indictment is also made with a word which Middleton used with great brilliance in *The Changeling*. *Service* can mean both the work of those whom one pays, and the homage of the lover (the servant of Venus and of his mistress). The lover's meaning, though, can have the darker undertone of the crude sexual sense of *service* (which survives in the farmyard). When in *The Changeling* De Flores returns (after committing murder for Beatrice) to claim her body as his reward, her moral dilemma is superbly caught in the word itself.

She wanted De Flores's *service*; well then, she must have his *service*. The word plays a less crucial but similar part in *Women Beware Women*, where it is clearly applicable to the selling of love, the hiring of various kinds of prostitute. Livia, for instance, tries to tell her brother that an incestuous love is really so uneconomical. She brings out the aptness of her illustration with a brisk pun on *husbandry* – it's a waste (to stay in the family when there's such riches of women available), and it's a bad way of marrying; and she follows this with *servants*, which both keeps to the economic image and brings in lovers. Livia insists that Hippolito's love

> Is allowed a stranger; and where bounty
> Is made the great man's honour, 'tis ill husbandry
> To spare, and servants shall have small thanks for't.
>
> [II i 12–14]

Miss Bradbrook has pointed out how the images of gluttony are applied to lust;[5] and Isabella thinks of her relationship with Hippolito in terms, coarsely gluttonous, which direct our attention to the implications of *service*:

> She that comes once to be a housekeeper
> Must not look every day to fare well, sir,
> Like a young waiting-gentlewoman in service:
> For she feeds commonly as her lady does,
> No good bit passes her, but she gets a taste on't.   [II i 217–21]

Guardiano knew that Bianca was

> Able to draw a state from serious business,
> And make it their best piece to do her service.   [II ii 17–18]

And when he plays the bawd, his offer to show Bianca round Livia's house is cruelly ambiguous:

>   All my intentions
> Are servants to such mistresses.
> . . .
> If you but give acceptance to my service
> You do the greatest grace and honour to me.
>
> [II ii 259–60, 284–5]

Similarly, there is a crude and mercenary relationship (mistress and servant in an economic sense) behind the urbane protestations of Leantio to Livia – '[Speak] with me, lady? you shall, I am at your service' [III iii 66]. At least, that is how the revengeful Duke views it, when he scorns any romantic pretences in the affair, and urges Hippolito to cut it short:

> her ignorant pleasures,
> Only by lust instructed, have received
> Into their services an impudent boaster.   [IV i 148–50]

Perhaps the most brilliant instance of the power which Middleton can develop in such words comes when Leantio is sneering at Bianca as they both stand in their new finery. It is a real case of *double entendre*, since the obscene innuendo does not take precedence over the straightforward battle for social prestige; they each make perfect, and perfectly separable, sense – since they coexist as manifestations of inseparable weaknesses, lust and pride. Behind the smooth retorts are the crude facts, just as behind the new clothes are the new acts of prostitution, for both of them. Leantio makes a leg, a mocking bow:

> LEAN. A bow i'th' ham to your greatness;
>   You must have now three legs, I take it, must you not?
> BIAN. Then must I take another, I shall want else
>   The service I should have; you have but two there.
>   [IV i 47–50]

The urbane obscenity of that is masterly.

But by an excellent irony, the contrast to the world of work, business, and service is not one that shows a fine flowering of the spirit in its freedom from the mercenary. On the contrary: if the Duke need not worry about money or advancement, he uses this freedom simply as a means of forcing servitude on others. The only other character in the play who need take no thought for money is the wealthy Ward: his life is given to childish jokes and childish games. On the one hand, business; on the other, the vacuous pleasures of the Ward. His games fit the play not only because of their aptness for innuendo,[6] but also because sensual pleasure is itself a *game* or a *sport*. Leantio has to cut short his nuptial pleasures, since he must work to maintain Bianca; and Middleton brilliantly integrates the themes as Leantio complains at having to leave:

> 'Tis e'en a second hell to part from pleasure
> When man has got a smack on't. As many holidays
> Coming together makes your poor heads idle
> A great while after, and are said to stick
> Fast in their fingers' ends, e'en so does game
> In a new-married couple: for the time
> It spoils all thrift, and indeed lies abed

> To invent all the new ways for great expenses.   [ɪ iii 5–12]

What is deft here is the incorporation of *game* (sexual pleasure) into
the simile as the counterpart of holidays as against work. And
Middleton follows this up by linking the two reasons for lying in
bed, thriftless idleness and sensual pleasure (which are connected
in Leantio's dilemma) – the double reference is stressed by 'indeed'.
Then the effect is capped by an acutely relevant pun on *expenses* –
applied both to economy and to love (as it is in Shakespeare's
description of lust as 'the expense of spirit in a waste of shame'):

> It spoils all thrift, and indeed lies abed
> To invent all the new ways for great expenses.

But 'game in a new-married couple' turns all too soon into the
sinister game of chess, where the seduction is enacted on the board.
The unwitting Mother and the taunting Livia repeat the word again
and again, until 'the game's e'en at the best now' [ɪɪ ii 410] (and
the point is hammered home by lines 288, 293, 295, 298, 301, 416).

As is usual when Middleton is at his best, there is a searching
interplay between character, action, imagery and word-play. So
Livia, when she seduces Leantio, offers him not only money and
servants, but also

> Your race-horses, or any various pleasure
> Exercised youth delights in; but to me
> Only, sir, wear your heart of constant stuff.   [ɪɪɪ iii 371–3]

As the sequence of thought makes clear, all is in return for his body,
his 'exercised youth'. In the world of *Women Beware Women*, the sports
of the rich are as squalid as their employments – and both can also
stand as emblems of that 'lust and forgetfulness' which envelops the
characters.

One of Middleton's key words stands slightly apart from the
pattern so far traced – a pattern that links the mercenary and the
lustful in words like *business, work* and *service*, or in their equally
sordid opposites, *games* and *sports*. In using the word *pride*, Middleton
is more concerned to stress the inseparable links between social
vanity and adultery. Bianca is not merely lustful; she is also fond of
position, power and luxury. Through the word *pride*, Middleton can
establish that these failings go hand in hand. The sexual meaning
of pride was an extremely common one;[7] and Middleton's method
of insisting that the word itself can provide the initial moral analysis

is to use it in contexts which at least suggest the sexual meaning. The first instance keeps the word finely balanced between the alternatives. Leantio exults in his possession of Bianca:

> Oh fair-eyed Florence,
> Didst thou but know what a most matchless jewel
> Thou now art mistress of, a pride would take thee,
> Able to shoot destruction through the bloods
> Of all thy youthful sons.   [I i 161–5]

Here the exultation is more than mere pride; it is also a boast about his sexual prowess, as is clear in the sequence *pride—bloods—youthful sons*. Middleton relies on the context (as well as on the happenings of the play) to insist on this crucial connection between the two sins; as when Leantio sneers at 'base lust, / With all her powders, paintings, and best pride' [III ii 11–12].

Bianca's sins are linked with the cause of all sins when the Mother confesses herself unable to understand what has come over Bianca during the petulant interval between her seduction and the return of Leantio:

> Unless it be the same gave Lucifer
> A tumbling cast: that's pride.   [III ii 44–5]

The Mother speaks truer than she knows, as *pride* insists – supported as it is by *tumbling*. (The low meaning is clear when the Ward later complains about Isabella's unchastity: 'This is she brought up so courtly, can sing, and dance – and tumble too, methinks' [IV ii 105–6].)

The pressure exerted by the context is always insisting on the double guilt of Bianca's pride. The Duke, for instance, sneers at the Ward: 'I thought he would have married her by attorney, / And lain with her so too.' Bianca replies

> Nay, my kind lord,
> There's very seldom any found so foolish
> To give away his part there.   [III iii 222–4]

And at once the cheated Leantio sees the torturing applicability of her words:

> Bitter scoff!
> Yet I must do't – with what a cruel pride
> The glory of her sin strikes by my afflictions!   [III iii 225–7]

In the same way, there is more than social vanity at issue when

Leantio and Bianca, both in the new finery that rewards their prostitution, meet at the window; and Bianca jibes 'How now? what silk-worm's this, i' th' name of pride?' [IV i 46]. Leantio is later to condemn her 'blind pride' [IV i 100] – in a passage which, with its references to the *monuments*, reminds us of the fatal tour of Livia's house: 'Show her the Monument too – and that's a thing / Everyone sees not' [II ii 277–8]. Bianca herself admits her complicated guilt in her words as she commits suicide:

> Pride, greatness, honours, beauty, youth, ambition,
> You must all down together, there's no help for't.
>
> [v ii 218–19]

What makes such sustained word-play really impressive is the way in which Middleton uses it to confirm the dramatic and moral analysis which he is simultaneously enacting through the other media at his disposal – action, character and image. We do not arrive at a different reading of the play if we examine his handling of words; instead, we arrive at an understanding of how firmly realised his purpose was – at work, too, in the smallest details of the play. (At any rate, in the first four acts; the massacre at the end is pitifully unconvincing.) But it would be misleading to give the impression that Middleton's mastery of words is entirely a matter of using the pun. Often the words are perfectly straightforward, and nothing but the skill of their use is unusual.

The nature of the match between Isabella and the Ward is brought out by consistently using the verb to *tender*; the mercenariness is clear, for example, when Guardiano says:

> Let her be sent tomorrow before noon,
> And handsomely tricked up; for 'bout that time
> I mean to bring her in, and tender her to him.   [II ii 58–60][8]

Even so apparently insignificant a word as *gentlewoman* is turned to Middleton's purposes. The Mother had asked suspiciously when she first saw Bianca: 'What's this gentlewoman?' [I i 11]; and Middleton insists on Bianca's social status by referring to her again and again in this way. Moreover, Isabella too is always the *gentlewoman* (that is why the Ward wants to marry her). The word comes about thirty times in the play, and each time we are reminded of the nature of the match which Bianca and Isabella make. The constant use of *gentlewoman* makes it possible for Middleton to give us the moments of disillusionment and collapse for both Bianca and

Isabella with the strength of the unexpected word. The climax of the Duke's seduction of Bianca is a superb change from *gentlewoman* (and in any case she is no longer marrying *beneath* her, 'a poor, base start-up'):

> And can you be so much your beauty's enemy,
> To kiss away a month or two in wedlock,
> And weep whole years in wants for ever after?
> Come, play the wise wench, and provide for ever.
>
> [II ii 379–82]

The word *wench*, with its collapse from the pinnacle, is also the degradation of Isabella, when Livia in her rage reveals how she was tricked into the intrigue with Hippolito: 'Look upon me, wench! / 'Twas I betrayed thy honour subtly to him' [IV ii 72–3]. So that the Ward gives up all hopes, and wishes, of marrying a gentlewoman ('I'll never marry wife again that has so many qualities'); and his retainer agrees: 'Well, give me a wench but with one good quality, to lie with none but her husband' [IV ii 106–12].

The pressure of this cruelly consistent world is such that the most ordinary phrases are invigorated. So Leantio says how much luckier than he are those men who spend their money but do not spend their care on women:

> Nay, what a quietness has he 'bove mine
> That wears his youth out in a strumpet's arms,
> And never spends more care upon a woman
> Than at the time of lust.   [III ii 205–8]

'Spends more care': the metaphorical life in the verb, dulled in the usual way, is renewed. It is a characteristically bold irony which repeats the phrase in order to stress the prostitution when Leantio himself is bought by Livia:

> Couldst thou love such a one, that, blow all fortunes,
> Would never see thee want?
> Nay more, maintain thee to thine enemy's envy?
> And shalt not spend a care for't.   [III iii 301–4]

The same new life is active in innumerable commonplace words like *reward, debt, pay*. In the first line of the play, Leantio's Mother greets him: 'Thy sight was never yet more precious to me.' A way of speaking – but one that should answer to truth, and does (for once) in the Mother's love for her son.

Often word-play shades into imagery. Leantio's love for Bianca

is by no means mercenary, but it is stupidly imprudent; he is shown
as having a coarseness of mind which is allied to complacency. That
it bodes ill for the future of their love is clear from the words which
come to his lips when Bianca urges him to stay ('But this one night,
I prithee'):

> Alas, I'm in for twenty if I stay,
> And then for forty more: I have such luck to flesh
> I never bought a horse but he bore double.   [I iii 49–52]

The brutality of the analogy, clearest in *flesh* and in the hidden pun
on *ride*, sharpens our dissatisfaction with Leantio. And his sighing
complacency rebounds on himself, since he did not buy Bianca, he
stole her; and she will be bought by the Duke and so indeed *bear
double*. She says to the Duke when he tries to seduce her: 'I have a
husband.'

> DUKE.   That's a single comfort;
>   Take a friend to him.
> BIAN.   That's a double mischief.   [II ii 347–8]

  To marshal such instances can unfortunately make the handling
of words seem aridly schematic. But *Women Beware Women* has a
subtle and varied pattern, and the struggle within the individual
words is the struggle within the characters and within the society.
Such word-play is by no means always strictly a matter of a pun.
Sometimes it is that the characters tragically do not know the
limitations of their words (and so of their power) whereas the
dramatist does. *Tender* is such a verb, and so is *provide* – applicable
to some parts of life, and mistakenly thought by Middleton's
characters to be applicable to all. So Leantio promises to 'Lay in
provision' [I i 108]; but the Duke can out-promise him: 'Come, play
the wise wench, and provide for ever' [II ii 382]. So Bianca in her
false superiority can see that Isabella is well provided for in one
way in marrying the Ward – but not in another:

> She's ill bestead, unless sh'as dealt the wiselier
> And laid in more provision for her youth;
> Fools will not keep in summer.   [III iii 116–18]

As we know, this is indeed what Isabella has done, and the Ward is
merely one who 'provides / All for another's table' [III iv 38–9]. By
a magnificently moral irony, the Duke promises to provide Bianca
with one of the few things that are beyond his capabilities, beyond

the capabilities of a word used so mercenarily; she murmurs, after Leantio has threatened her, 'I love peace, sir': and the Duke emptily promises:

> And so do all that love; take you no care for't,
> It shall be still provided to your hand.   [IV i 125–6]

It does not matter whether or not such effects are called word-play; it does matter that we should appreciate that Middleton in such lines achieves the same sort of moral analysis as Mr Robert Frost in his crisp and desperate poem 'Provide, Provide'. The important words in *Women Beware Women* are both dramatically and morally relevant. And Middleton, as Miss Bradbrook has said, 'does not rely upon explicit statement or direct speech but upon implication; nor upon a gorgeous and elaborate vocabulary, but upon a pregnant simplicity which is perhaps more difficult to achieve, and is certainly found more seldom'.[9]

SOURCE: 'Word-play in *Women Beware Women*', essay in *Review of English Studies*, XII (1961), pp. 238–50.

NOTES

[Reorganised and renumbered from the original – Ed.]

1. M. C. Bradbrook, *Themes and Conventions of Elizabethan Tragedy* (1935), p. 238.
2. [Ed.] See Eliot's essay, above, in this selection.
3. See *OED*, 'business', sb. 19.b, and 'busy', a. 1.e.
4. [Ed.] See Ricks's 1960 essay on *The Changeling*, note 13 – above, in this selection.
5. Bradbrook, op. cit., p. 236.
6. The obscene puns at III iv 89–95 include not only the various games, but also the word *game* itself.
7. See *OED*, 'pride', sb.[1] 11, where one of the instances is 'As salt as wolves in pride' (*Othello*, III iii 404).
8. Cf. also I ii 6, II ii 101, III i 49, III iii 101, III iv 4, IV ii 114.
9. Bradbrook, op. cit., p. 239.

Edward Engelberg   Tragic Blindness in *The Changeling* and *Women Beware Women*   (1962)

The theme of man's tragic blindness pervades Western literature: blindness to the true nature of self and world deprives man of the spiritual perception necessary for a full apprehension of the universe. Always the tragic struggle is to gain *in*-sight, to wrest from the helplessness of the dark some final vision which illuminates the inner self as it receives – and understands – the harvested wisdom of life. Inwardly, the blinded hero ascends a scale of increasing values as he moves from observation to experience, from what Goethe subtly distinguished as 'Erlebnis' to the deeper 'Erfahrung'. Light was God's first gift and, as ancient mythology reminds us, one of the most coveted. Prometheus was guilty on two counts: he stole the secret of illumination, a mere case of larceny; but he thereby endangered the higher sight of the gods, thus creating the possibility of human wisdom.

To lose one's sight is easy: it is to lose one's way; but darkness brings chaos. Milton's Samson knows it:

> Since light so necessary is to life,
> And almost life itself, if it be true
> That light is in the soul,
> She all in every part, why was the sight
> To such a tender ball as the eye confined?
>
> [*Samson Agonistes*, 90–4]

As the chorus remarks some lines later, to be blind is to be in a 'Prison within prison / Inseparably dark' [153–4] – which, of course, also suits the particular symbolic position of Samson's actual bondage. Yet *Samson Agonistes* is tragedy because the stress is ultimately on the ensuing struggle to see, to regain sight. In this sense Shakespeare, too, dealt conventionally with tragic blindness in *Lear*. The purgative and restorative ritual that Lear undergoes in Act IV is centred on sleep: he has literally cried his eyes out – his old eyes. And sleep restores him to better sight, just as suffering makes Gloucester finally see.

Traditionally, the hero's awareness of his blindness and the accompanying contest with Necessity – the willing to see once again beyond it – is what the tragic poet works toward. In the plays about to be examined, there is no such compensation. Middleton is unique because he is interested neither in the loss of sight nor in its restoration, but rather in the stumbling of his blinded characters, in the steady decline of unsteady people. Victims of vertigo, they plunge to depths where no light can reach them. Because there is no reward, however temporary, for suffering, we feel that the blindness does not matter or, worse still, that it is the only thing that does matter. It is a terrible vision of life. And its terror lies in the nightmarish defencelessness of the blinded characters who are so quickly, so mercilessly, ambushed by their afflictions.

T. S. Eliot set a fashion when he wrote that Middleton 'has no point of view . . . has no message. He is merely the name which associates six or seven great plays.'[1] Two recent studies of Middleton have attempted to persuade us – and, I think, convincingly – that Middleton's artistry links the plays thematically, so that something like a 'point of view' emerges after all.[2] Indeed, in *The Changeling* and *Women Beware Women*, it is in his figurative language, inconspicuous though it often may appear, that Middleton's consistency is made most evident. His 'view', his central perception of human nature in these plays, is embodied in the dominant metaphor of sight – or the lack of it.[3] In each play, blindness shuts out the consequences of impulsive acts, and, with what amounts to an *idée fixe*, the chief characters then seek to impose their wills on an unbending and indifferent world, victimising those equally as blind.[4] Perception is partial and distorted, and so reality is tragically misapprehended.

The main action of *The Changeling* ensues from Beatrice's defective sight, her impulsive responses to the world which she can see but never visualise. When the play opens, Beatrice and Alsemero are destined for separate lives; but a first sight of each other embarks them jointly on a course that will bring disaster to each.[5] Even De Flores is aware that Beatrice's hatred of him, as well as his uncontrollable lust for her, is motivated by visual responses:

> I can as well be hang'd as refrain seeing her
> . . .
> To come into her sight
> . . .
> At no hand can [she] abide the sight of me,
> As if danger or ill luck hung in my looks.
> She turns her blessed eye upon me now

> . . .
> I must see her still!   [II i 28–78]

And Beatrice, her mood violently altered in the presence of De Flores, explains to Alsemero that De Flores is to her like poison, like the basilisk – whose eyes strike death with a single look – a simile Middleton employs frequently. When she sees him, her revulsion is expressed as much in terms of sight as was De Flores's desire:

> what cause was there in this
> To bring thee to my sight? . . .
> I never see this fellow, but I think
> Of some harm towards me.   [II i 72–3, 89–90]

No one knows better than Beatrice that she sees the world as she chooses. When De Flores accepts her suggestion that he kill her intended husband to free her so that she may pursue her sudden infatuation with Alsemero, she at once 'sees' him differently: 'How lovely now / Dost thou appear to me!' [II ii 135–6].

Earlier, Beatrice is similarly deluded (or is deluding herself) when she becomes convinced that her first-sight passion for Alsemero is perceived through 'the eyes of judgment': 'clearly . . . A true deserver like a diamond sparkles, / In darkness you may see him . . . With intellectual eyesight' [II i 13–19]. But her 'intellectual eyesight' is only a crude mask for actions more impulsive than those prompted by her first, presumably rasher, sight of Alonzo. And how 'clearly' she will 'see' in 'darkness' will soon become ironically apparent.

In this play the eye also reveals character. Alonzo does not acknowledge his brother's sharper sight when the latter warns him to beware of Beatrice: 'In troth I see small welcome in her eye' [II i 106]. With an ignorance that suits his own surface perceptions, he pleads, 'Where's the oversight?' [II i 127]. Beatrice fares no better. Throughout the second and third acts, the eye governs the very idiom of her emotions. She lives and dies, is in ecstasy or despair, in terms of what passes her line of vision; she becomes virtually enslaved to her sight. When she suggests Alonzo's murder, she wishes to remove her 'loathings' (Alonzo has now taken the place of De Flores) 'For ever from my sight' [II ii 113], while the presence of Alsemero prompts, 'I have within mine eye all my desires' [II ii 8]. Informed of Alonzo's death, she cries out, 'joys start at mine eyes' [III iv 25], for she has long been waiting for 'that eye [to] be darkened that offends me' [III iv 14]. With this eye's 'eclipse', she believes her problems are solved, whereas, of course, they are just beginning. For De Flores will have his reward: 'I live in pain now: that shooting eye / Will burn my heart to cinders' [III iv 152–3].

In *Women Beware Women* the eye-motif is also established at the start of the main action. Leantio has come home with a 'jewel', Bianca, which he plants in his mother's house, 'cased up from all men's eyes' [I i 170]. His failure to keep her 'cased up' serves as the impetus of the tragedy. While he is absent on travels, his mother and Bianca witness the Duke's annual parade through the streets of Florence. Indeed, the mother assures Bianca – though quite innocently – 'I would not ... / That you had lost the sight!' [I iii 88–9]. Meanwhile, the sub-plot, involving Isabella, her uncle Hippolito and his sister Livia, centres on the incestuous attachment of Hippolito for his niece and the proposed marriage of Isabella to the foolish Ward in order to camouflage her promiscuity.

The eye is really made the agent of both major actions in the play. Having seen Bianca once, the Duke must have her. Even Guardiano, the opportunist at court, expresses surprise: 'How strangely that one look has catched his heart' [II ii 21]. When Leantio returns to find Bianca fallen from innocence and corrupted by experience, the centre of her defence is, ironically, a philosophy that lovers' constancy is tantamount to blindness:

> I would not stand thus,
> And gaze upon you always. Troth, I could not, sir;
> As good be blind, and have no use of sight
> As look on one thing still. What's the eye's treasure,
> But change of objects? [III ii 60–4]

And at the famous banquet scene, when Leantio is humiliated as the eyewitness to his wife's adultery, he becomes conscious of the finality of his loss only when Bianca walks out of sight: 'As long as mine eye saw thee, / I half enjoy'd thee' [III iii 251–2]. Livia's lust, like De Flores's, is visual and sensual. She has not the 'power / To keep from sight' of Leantio [III iii 349–50], while Leantio, delirious with remorse and shame, dreams of what happiness might have been his had he never set eyes on Bianca.

But eventually he succumbs to Livia, and the Duke then prevails upon Hippolito to avenge himself against Leantio, who has become 'blinded with her [Livia's] appetite' and now boasts openly of his attachment [IV i 153]. What persuades Hippolito is the strange maxim that if sin one must, 'there's a blind time made for't', and so

Leantio, a 'daylight lecher', deserves to die [iv ii 5–10]. When, at the end of the play, the Duke offers repentance to his brother, the Cardinal is moved to say: 'Take up those lights; there was a thicker darkness, / When they came first' [iv i 264–5]. Now, too, Leantio speaks of Bianca as a 'glist'ring whore' who 'shines like a serpent' [iv ii 20]; the lesson he has learned is that his jewel 'cased up' in the dark seemed deceptively brighter than when exposed to the light of day.

Beyond these more obvious examples, there are, in both plays, subtler and richer instances of Middleton's handling of his metaphor. In several scenes, sight – or the lack of it – actually functions in developing the action of the plot, as Middleton employs the device of exhibiting to his victims certain 'sights' – a castle or a room lined with pictures – under false pretences. In each case the person persuaded to enter upon such a tour sees indeed more than he bargained for. Beatrice suggests to her father that Alsemero be shown the castle, her real motive being to ingratiate the stranger to the head of the house; it is a visit that Alsemero had been wiser to refuse. Later in the play De Flores tempts Alonzo (Beatrice's intended husband) with the secrets of the castle, which the latter is anxious to see. They enter a passage 'somewhat narrow'. Ironically, De Flores says to the admiring Alonzo, 'All this is nothing; you shall see anon / A place you little dream on' [iii ii 1–2]. He places his unsuspecting victim by a window and instructs him: 'Look, spend your eye awhile upon that object . . . keep your eye straight, my lord' [iii ii 8, 12]. And while Alonzo keeps his eye straight (yet how crooked it is) upon the wrong object, De Flores stabs him in the back.

Livia, in *Women Beware Women*, acting as pander to the Duke, instructs Guardiano to show Bianca the 'rooms and pictures', while her intention is, of course, to bring her to the waiting Duke. Bianca, like Alonzo, is impressed: 'Trust me, sir, / Mine eye ne'er met with fairer ornaments' [ii ii 310–11]. Whereupon Guardiano, echoing De Flores, answers facetiously:

> There's a better piece
> Yet than all these . . .
> You'll say so when you see't. Turn but your eye now,
> Y'are upon't.   [ii ii 314–17]

What she is upon is the lecherous Duke. While Bianca is being seduced, Middleton parallels this action in the chess game which Livia is using to distract the mother; the irony of this scene has often been commented upon, but the irony is verbal as well as situational:

LIV.   I have given thee blind mate. . . .

MOTH.   You may see, madam,
My eyes begin to fail.   [II ii 392–3]

Bianca returns presently to say, astonished, 'I have seen that I little thought to see' [II ii 456], and Guardiano, proud of his success, boasts that he had properly whetted Bianca's appetite by showing her 'naked pictures' on the way. In a later scene, Livia, now suddenly impassioned with Leantio, tries to attract his straying attention by again suggesting a tour: 'I pray let's walk, sir; / You never saw the beauty of my house yet' [III iii 357–8]. And so they walk and gaze, always in the wrong direction: Alsemero, Alonzo, Bianca, Leantio, each receiving, like Alonzo, the eventual stab in the back.

Even the comic action of *Women Beware Women* is sometimes managed by the motif of blindness. In a cruder play, *The Witch*, the foolish Almachildes, blindfolded, is persuaded by the Duchess to murder the Duke, enjoyment of her bed being his promised reward. Instead, both Almachildes and the Duchess are fooled by each other: he thinks he is seducing the Duchess, although a common harlot is hired for the occasion; she thinks the Duke is dead, but he is spared and appears to the startled woman at the end of the play.

But Middleton's ironic parallelism of comic and serious 'seeing' in *Women Beware Women* is far subtler. Early in the play Livia pleads with Isabella's father that, if there is to be a wedding, Isabella should be allowed at least 'one look' at the Ward. Sordido, the Ward's servant, also asks to 'Let me alone to see what she is: if I but look upon her', he boasts, he will be able to detect all her faults at a glance [II ii 96–8]. Later the Ward takes the responsibility of examining 'every part' of Isabella himself: 'I take delight to view you', he says, 'on both sides' [III iv 121]. He even feels convinced that seeing her naked before marriage would immeasurably enlighten him as to her character.

The irony is obvious: the foolish Ward who views Isabella 'on both sides' is as easily and as damagingly deceived as was the impulsive Alsemero who looked but once, or as the gullible Bianca who looked upon paintings one moment and upon the Duke the next. When the Ward discovers he has been cheated, he turns upon Sordido for not living up to his promises; but the servant quickly justifies himself: 'Alas, how would you have me see through a great farthingale, sir? I cannot peep through a millstone, or in the going, to see what's done i' th' bottom' [iv ii 116–18]. Even after such a labored and painstaking examination as he had given Isabella, the Ward's poor eyesight is to him a puzzle. It never occurs to him that his anatomical observation could reveal little else but anatomy. And Middleton, in pointing to this overly cautious, foolish lover, who is tricked as effectively as those who are rash, convinces us that mere looking is not the antidote to quicksightedness.

Middleton, it would seem, came by stages to his uncompromising view of human nature. It is revealing to look at an earlier play, *More Dissemblers Besides Women*. Potentially a play in which the actions of its characters invite disaster, it resolves happily – and somewhat unconvincingly – the very situations that bring *The Changeling* and *Women Beware Women* to tragic ends.[6] The main action ensues from an oath of chastity offered by the Duchess to her dying husband. Her uncle, the Lord Cardinal of Milan, as self-appointed guardian of this oath, nearly precipitates a tragic involvement for his niece. Although the Duchess has kept her vow for seven years, she is clearly successful only because the Cardinal, like Leantio in *Women Beware Women*, has kept her 'cased up' out of sight of suitors.

Moreover, it is evident that her seclusion is intended primarily not to keep sin away from her, but to keep her away from sin: the Cardinal fears that the very sight of men will awaken lust in the Duchess, he himself wearing 'so severe an eye . . . / It not endures the sight of womankind / About his lodgings' [i i 49–51]. But his moral zeal gets the better of his judgement, and he is persuaded by one of the lords to test the Duchess's will power. The acid test is to 'see and be seen, / And yet resist' [i ii 34–5]. The Cardinal himself elaborates the challenge, and the Duchess accepts: 'I'll come forth / And show myself to all . . . and shine clear' [i iii 56–9].

But the Duchess has more faith than power to carry this out; beholding a handsome general lately come to Milan, she succumbs at once (just as Beatrice and Bianca had): 'O hard spite, / To lose my seven years' victory at one sight!' [i iii 127–8]. The astounded Cardinal asks whether the lover (the Duchess has deceived him into thinking she loves his nephew) wears 'Such killing poison in his eye' [ii i 120] that he can captivate the Duchess at first sight. 'No basilisk', he vows, 'that strikes dead pure affection / With venomous eye, lives under my protection' [ii i 130–1]. At the end of the play, the Duchess says truly, but sententiously, 'The love of woman wears so thick a blindness, / It sees no fault' [v ii 54–5].

With this realisation, the Duchess escapes the consequences of her rash sight more, one feels, through machinations of plot than through any convincing insight on her part. In *The Changeling* and *Women Beware Women*, Middleton seems to have recognised the powerful effects of restraining the *deus ex machina* and permitting his blinded characters to plunge into the abyss which, in this earlier play, they merely approach.[7]

There is, of course, aimlessness in this Middletonian world, for in *The Changeling* and *Women Beware Women*, the single-mindedness of the inflexible characters (once they are committed to a goal) drives them with abandon and indifference toward an amorality which is monstrous. Leantio, in speaking of Bianca, describes this Middleton character tellingly:

> A monster with all forehead, and no eyes.
> Why do I talk to thee of sense or virtue,
> That art as dark as death? And as much madness
> To set light before thee, as to lead blind folks
> To see the monuments.   [iv i 93–7][8]

Being 'all forehead', the 'monster' is incapable of regeneration. As Una Ellis-Fermor has remarked, in Middleton's tragedies 'it is the promise of a fine flowering that is destroyed'; and with special irony he takes 'elements of great beauty' that he subsequently poisons with the 'spiritual evil set at work within them'.[9] In Middleton's tragic world there can be little resistance to deterioration, few spiritual struggles that question the moral order.

Denied the opportunity of seeing past the wilfully distorted views of their own worlds, these characters play out their roles in a confinement of spirit and body which invests at least the two major plays with a palpable sense of constriction. Both *The Changeling* and *Women Beware Women* are landlocked: the sea journey which Alsemero has planned before he sees Beatrice is never taken, and he is drawn into the castle where, behind the doors of his own closet, the final catastrophe is played out. Almost all of the action in the main plot of *The Changeling* is confined indoors; and De Flores's setting fire to the maid's room in a desperate effort to cover up his liaison with

Beatrice is characteristic of a play in which the atmosphere is close, thick, and impenetrable.

Nor is the air any clearer in *Women Beware Women*. Bianca, a virtual prisoner in Leantio's house, looks wistfully out of the window into the light of the street just as the Duke passes beneath it. Yet, in her efforts to liberate herself, she succeeds only in exchanging prisons. Leantio's apartment is replaced by the Duke's bedchamber, and eventually her sense of imprisonment becomes not only physical, but spiritual as well. Both Beatrice and Bianca discover themselves trapped by the superficiality of their visual perceptions; but neither is able to achieve redemption, for their insight is cynical, not humble.

Harsher even than Webster, Middleton opposes no real clarity of sight to blindness, no rational and ordered universe to offset the optical illusions of his blinded characters. Bianca laments the hard fate of such an uncompromising world:

> From a man that's blind
> To take a burning taper, 'tis no wrong,
> He never misses it; but to take light
> From one that sees, that's injury and spite.   [IV iii 61–4]

Deprived of light, Middleton's characters collapse rather than disintegrate, and with astonishing suddenness. And collapse precludes the possibility of arriving at that slow and painstaking awareness which we have come to expect from tragedy. Yet, while the absence of the larger tragic dimension is a limitation in both plays, the confined field of vision that the theme of human blindness necessarily dictates gives *The Changeling* and *Woman Beware Women* a convincing and terrifying focus.

Source: essay on 'Tragic Blindness in *The Changeling* and *Women Beware Women*', in *Modern Language Quarterly*, XXIII (1962), pp. 20–28.

NOTES

[Reorganised and renumbered from the original – Ed.]

1. [Ed.] See Eliot's essay, above, in this selection.
2. Samuel Schoenbaum, *Middleton's Tragedies* (New York, 1955), and R. H. Barker, *Thomas Middleton* (1958). Schoenbaum and Barker ascribe controversial plays to Middleton. Although they sometimes offer very convincing evidence, I have felt it wiser – in a paper of this kind – to restrict myself to Middleton's undisputed works.
3. I am aware, of course, that the eye, as image and metaphor, is common

throughout Elizabethan and Jacobean drama. But the insistence and frequency with which Middleton uses the eye to project a major theme in his plays is unique. There are, in the main plot of *The Changeling*, some fifty-odd references to the eye and its functions and disorders; nearly the same number of references occur in *Women Beware Women*. Although the eye as an agent of tragic blindness is alluded to in *A Fair Quarrel*, *The Old Law*, *The Witch* and *Hengist, King of Kent*, it never assumes a really functional stature in these plays.

4. Barker recognises that 'in Middleton's view sin *is* blindness' (*Thomas Middleton*, p. 125). Of course, Alonzo and Leantio, before revenge and lust possess him, are not 'evil' characters. But their innocence is blindness to evil, which counts against them as much as the evil man's blindness to good. Ultimately, blindness is the inability to see the world truly: it is ignorance.

5. The first scene of *The Changeling* is traditionally ascribed to Rowley, though E. H. C. Oliphant (ed.), *Shakespeare and His Fellow Dramatists*, 2 vols. (New York, 1929), II, p. 907, conjectured that 'some lines' are Middleton's. In any case, certain lines in the first scene do at least anticipate the theme of distorted vision. When Beatrice first encounters Alsemero's attentions, she chides this skilful man who 'can sing at first sight' [I i 67]. She even delivers a sententious speech which ironically points up her own flaw in the action to follow:

> Our eyes are sentinels unto our judgements,
> And should give certain judgement what they see;
> But they are rash sometimes, and tell us wonders
> Of common things, which when our judgements find,
> They then can check the eyes, and call them blind.   [I i 72–6]

Yet, only moments later, she reverses herself: 'Sure, mine eyes were mistaken; / This was the man was meant me' [I i 84–5]. The later theme is here clearly anticipated.

6. For an illuminating discussion of this play, see Samuel Schoenbaum, 'Middleton's Tragicomedies', *Modern Philology*, LIV (1956–7), pp. 7–19.

7. In plays like *The Witch* and *Hengist*, Middleton loses control of his material and employs such crude devices as the blindfold to project his theme of tragic blindness.

8. The irony of this becomes sharpened when one recalls that on the day Bianca succumbed to the Duke, Guardiano had first led her to see the monument, a sight Livia had particularly recommended as worth seeing.

9. [Ed.] See Ellis-Fermor's essay, above, in this selection.

Inga-Stina Ewbank Realism and Morality in
Women Beware Women (1969)

In this essay I wish to examine the unity of Thomas Middleton's *Women Beware Women*. The art of this play is a compound of realism and morality – a compound which has laid the play open to some fundamental criticisms. Middleton has been praised for the naturalism and psychological insight of the first three and a half acts, and reprimanded for (allegedly) betraying his own vision and art by concluding the play in terms of conventional Jacobean morality and theatrical sensationalism. Recent critics have, on the whole, abandoned T. S. Eliot's view of Middleton as a playwright who 'has no message; he is merely a great recorder'; and at the other extreme we have been given the 'highly moralistic artist who could skilfully pattern his actions in terms of a central theme'.[1] It seems to me that in *Women Beware Women* realism is not at war with morality; nor is one simply subservient to the other, like the two layers of an allegory. To understand their relationship one should, I think, look at the play through two (necessarily interrelated) questions: is there a unity of viewpoint? and, is there a dramatic unity?

I

'It isn't difficult to be a country gentleman's wife', Rebecca thought. 'I think I could be a good woman if I had five thousand a year . . .' And who knows but Rebecca was right in her speculations – and that it was only a question of money and fortune which made the difference between her and an honest woman? . . .

It may, perhaps, have struck her that to have been honest and humble, to have done her duty, and to have marched straightforward on her way, would have brought her as near happiness as that path by which she was striving to attain it. But . . . if ever Becky had these thoughts, she was accustomed to walk round them, and not look in . . .

We grieve at being found out, and at the idea of shame or punishment; but the mere sense of wrong makes very few people unhappy in Vanity Fair. [Thackeray, *Vanity Fair*, ch. XLI]

Middleton has often been seen as a seventeenth-century Ibsen, but it might be more helpful to suggest that, if we were to look for a nineteenth-century equivalent of *Women Beware Women*, we would find it in the social novel. The themes of the play are the favourite domestic and social ones of love, money and class – indeed, G. R. Hibbard has spoken of *Women Beware Women* as 'the most powerful criticism of the education of women and of the *mariage de convenance* in Elizabethan drama'.[2] The structure is formed not so much by plot and sub-plot as by interlinked groups of characters, so that the interest is spread over a cross-section of society rather than being centred on the development of a few characters. And, most important, Middleton's handling of the moral perspective is, in its combination of apparent objectivity, implicit evaluation and outright moralising, curiously like that of some nineteenth-century novelists.

The passage from *Vanity Fair* which I have quoted seems to me in many ways a paradigm of the viewpoint of *Women Beware Women*. Like *Vanity Fair*, *Women Beware Women* is a work without a hero (or heroine). Like Becky Sharp, all the characters in the play confound the relation between money and honesty. But it is the handling of the moral point-of-view which chiefly makes this passage a parallel in narrative form to the dramatic art of *Women Beware Women*. Thackeray has the novelist's advantage – which he uses particularly fully in this novel – of being able to illuminate his work 'by the author's own candles', but he does so in a variety of ways. First, Rebecca is given apparently free rein in the dialogue; then ('And who knows . . .') the author, with pretended objectivity, explains her in purely social-economic terms; then ('It may, perhaps, have struck her . . .') the omniscient observer becomes a moral judge of her actions; and finally his focus widens out to a universal moral statement, and to reveal the 'preacher in cap and bells'.

In much the same way Middleton deals with his characters in *Women Beware Women*. For most of the play, their own speeches are remarkably lacking in ethical insight into their own actions. There is a great deal of documentation provided, of a sociological rather than psychological nature, so that we may see how they have become what they are. Who knows but that Bianca and Leantio's marriage would have had a chance if they had been rich? Who knows but that Bianca, as she asks in her soliloquy in iv i, would have been less easily corrupted, had she had a less restrained upbringing? Who knows but that Isabella would have been saved from incest, adultery and ultimately murder, but for the loveless and mercenary attitude of her father which has thrown her and Hippolito 'whole nights

together in discourse' and leads to the miseries of enforced marriage
with the Ward? This is not to say that Middleton, while making us
ask these questions, remains the clinically detached observer, for
throughout the play there is an undertow of reminders of an
inexorable moral order. Many commentators have drawn attention
to the persistent imagery of love / money, and love / gluttony, which
interprets and judges the corruption of the play's world. But the
characters are kept away from comprehension of the moral order,
even while referring to it, just as Becky Sharp uses the word 'good'
without knowing what it means. Middleton manages this in several
different ways. In the opening scene, Leantio delivers a diatribe
against adultery:

> Methinks it should strike earthquakes in adulterers,
> When e'en the very sheets they commit sin in
> May prove, for ought they know, all their last garments:
>
> [I i 22–4]

which, on the face of it, has a Vindice-like vigour. But it is undercut
by his own blatant Pharisaism: 'Now when I go to church, I can
pray handsomely' – much as his speech, in III i, on 'a glorious
dangerous strumpet' is undercut by being in praise of this smug
youth's sexual self-control. It is undercut, too, by searing irony, for
when Leantio self-rightously proclaims

> I find no wish in me bent sinfully
> To this man's sister, or to that man's wife: [I i 28–9]

he is in fact unwittingly telling us exactly what is going to happen
to sisters, brothers, men and wives, in the rest of the play. Such
counterpointing (of the blindness of a character with generally valid
judgements) is, however, dramatically uneconomic – hence the
wordiness and drag of the opening scene. More successful is
Middleton's technique of making his characters themselves thwart
our ethical expectations. Hippolito, for example, first tells of his
incestuous desires in a speech which, from its tense beginning, we
might have expected to be one of inner struggle:

> I would 'twere fit to speak to her what I would; but
> 'Twas not a thing ordained, Heaven has forbid it.   [I ii 152–3]

But it peters out into a clichéd resolution to stay silent – which he
immediately proceeds to break. Finally, there is the technique of
making the mercenary imagery invade what should be moral

statements: so that in Livia's mock-sermon on incest even religion becomes a matter of economics:

> So he Heaven's bounty seems to scorn and mock
> That spares free means, and spends of his own stock.
> [II i 15–16]

'Spatially', then, the play judges its characters throughout; but in terms of the time-sequence of the plot the Cardinal, with his explicit judgements in IV i and IV iii, becomes a wondrous necessary man. He is necessary because all the other characters, like Becky Sharp, 'walk round' such thoughts of sin as occur to them. His appearance corresponds to the omniscient judge stance in the Thackerary passage ('It may perhaps have struck her') and represents, to the play audience, a closing-in on the characters of the moral scheme they have ignored. And so, finally, that scheme is made explicit in action, in the moral retributions of the masque.

In terms of viewpoint, the masque corresponds to the generalisation that concludes the Thackeray passage: as the characters are made to destroy themselves and each other with fiendish irony, the focus widens and the Cardinal becomes the preacher, left to point out what 'these ruins show too piteously'. The very deliberate contrivance of the ending, the patterning of the ironies:

> vengeance met vengeance
> Like a set match, as if the plagues of sin
> Had been agreed to meet here all together.   [v ii 157–9]

detach us and put us in the Cardinal's position. We see, too, that the moral view of the play is a question of the movement of the whole: rather than moral confusion, or inconsistency, there is a dynamism of viewpoint. This is where, ultimately, the dramatist scores over the novelist, for, because of the very nature of the form, his art is one of progression. In shaping his viewpoint, and so controlling our reactions, Middleton has used the art of drama to the full.

II

For, of course, *Women Beware Women* is supremely a work of the theatre. The strength of its dramatic poetry lies less in the obviously poetic speeches than in apparently unmemorable lines which are thrust into dramatic life through the context of character and action. Thus Isabella's words,

> In that small distance from yon man to me
> Lies sin enough to make a whole world perish,   [IV ii 134–5]

which articulate the perverse horror of her situation, combining kinship and theatrical fact (for 'that small distance' is in blood as well as stage area) into what is virtually a metaphysical conceit, are in the theatre a far more powerful evocation of the reality of sin than any of the speeches of the Cardinal. Middleton's poetry is, to use Francis Fergusson's distinction,[3] more *of* the theatre than *in* it. It lies in the texture and the structure of his play, in the way social context is established, in the handling of characters and their relationships, and in the movement of the play as a whole. It is to these aspects of the play that I should now like to turn my attention.

One of the remarkable features of *Women Beware Women* is the realistic density of its *milieu*. Like no playwright outside Shakespeare, Middleton is able to give a solid context to his play world. It is partly a matter of his almost documentary use of objects – like Bianca's list of the furnishings lacking in Leantio's home, or the *two* handkerchiefs which the Mother runs to fetch in order to 'pocket up some sweetmeats' from the banquet. Partly it is a matter of scattering pieces of apparently irrelevant information – like the history of the room 'at the end of the dark parlour' where Leantio wants to immure Bianca, or of the genesis of the masque: prepared for the Duke's first wedding and cancelled because of the death of Isabella's mother (a lady who, like Leantio's father and Bianca's parents, is more present in the play than the cast-list would suggest). These hints create a sense of continuous life. How many husbands Livia has had *matters*, and so does her story about the lady who, at the age of forty-nine, kept a young 'friend' – who, in his turn,

> kept a quean or two with her own money,
> That robbed her of her plate, and cut her throat.
> [II ii 165–6]

It is through carefully planted details like this little tragi-comedy, as well as through the action itself, that the quality of life in the play is rendered.

One of the main sources of the density of *Women Beware Women* is a type of metaphorical language which is common throughout the play and used by all the characters, from the Ward to the Cardinal. This is a simile, usually beginning 'as if' or 'as when' and going on to draw an analogy between the dramatic situation and another human situation. Thus, around an already large group of characters, there is formed a whole background cast, ranging, in the social spectrum, from the country-maid 'dressing her head / By a dish of water' to 'great gallants the next day / After revel'. Genre-paintings like the Ward's reaction to kissing Isabella – 'methinks it tasted as if a man had stepped into a comfit-maker's shop to let a cart go by' – are obviously an inheritance from Middleton's city comedies; but the technique as a whole is put to a specific use in the play. The analogies which the characters are made to make so elaborately tend, on the one hand, to play down and trivialise their emotions, so as to suggest that they are composing satires on their own experiences rather than coming to grips with them. Hippolito's view of himself in the banquet scene –

> Like the mad misery of necessitous man
> That parts from his good horse with many praises,
> And goes on foot himself,   [III ii 197–9]

– is an inept version of the emotions he should have, but is structurally apt as an anticipation of the following scene, in which Isabella is literally put through her paces before the Ward and Sordido. Leantio is constantly referring his experiences of love, for good or ill, to events in the life of 'some rich man', thus judging himself by the play's prevailing image-pattern of commercialised relationships. On the other hand, these analogies build up a dramatic metaphor of characters masquerading in other selves: selves which are parodies on human experience. This metaphor, which is a product of the play's realism as well as of its moral commentary, is also structural: it helps to prepare us for the masque which is the greatest masquerading, the climactic 'as if' image, of the play. No wonder, in a world where people so consistently relegate their experiences to some imaginary character, that Fabritio is confused about the identity of Livia's real and her masque self: 'I hope / *My sister Juno* has not served me so'.

Within the social context which Middleton so carefully establishes, the most outstanding 'figure in the carpet' is that of human relationships. For all T. S. Eliot's praise of Middleton's insight into the psychology of a few great individuals, the dramatic impact of *Women Beware Women* is made not so much through single characters – who are often static, or who, when like Bianca they change, are treated very much in dramatic shorthand – as through the dynamism of relationships. It is significant that Leantio, who has more and longer soliloquies than anyone else in the play, gives far less sense of an inner life than many of the other characters; and that he only really comes alive when he and Bianca, in IV i, are pitted against each other in their new corruption and new finery. From the opening lines, where the Mother (who has no other name than 'Mother', or 'Widow') expounds the most intimate of all ties:

> Welcome, with all the affection of a mother,
> That comfort can express from natural love

to Fabritio's outcry:

> Dead? My girl dead? I hope
> My sister Juno has not served me so,   [v ii 144–5]

the dramatic mechanism is a pattern of family relationships, confounded and criss-crossed by erotic links. The ordinary appellations of kinship are used with more than ordinary care and point – for example in Livia's scenes with her two brothers, or in the Mother's little ritual of the two kisses with which she moves from a 'gentlewoman' to a 'daughter' relationship with Bianca – and as relationships tangle so these words are fed with peculiar significance. There is pathos as well as irony in Isabella's appeals to her 'sweet uncle' when we know that his feeling for her is 'somewhat too unkindly' and that he loves her 'dearlier than an uncle can'; and Guardiano's shrewdness about other relationships makes his words to the Ward doubly ironic when he explains that

> he that weds her
> Marries her uncle's heart too.   [III iii 18–19]

The reverberations of the action can make simple lines extremely sinister, as in Guardiano's gloating, Pandar-like greeting:

> How now, ward and nephew,
> Gentlewoman and niece! Speak, is it so or not?
>   [III iv 136–7]

And in the end, the conjunction of kinship words can produce an effect like oxymoron, as when the Duke asks Hippolito: 'How does that lusty widow, thy kind sister?' [IV i 142].

The action of the play is a progressive perversion of natural relationships, one violation of a natural bond leading to another – as Leantio sees in a moralistic speech which anticipates the symmetry of retribution in the masque:

> Oh equal justice, thou hast met my sin
> With a full weight; I'm rightly now oppressed;
> All her [Bianca's] friends' heavy hearts lie in my breast.
>
> [III iii 94–6]

Livia, the king-pin of the *liaisons dangereuses* in the play, is, of course, the centre of these perversions. She forgets words of kinship when she sees people as touchstones against which to sharpen her wit (then both Fabritio and Hippolito become just 'man'); and she tramples on their meaning when it comes to a game of sexual intrigue:

> y'have few sisters
> That love their brothers' ease 'bove their own honesties.
>
> [II i 70–1]

In the scenes where she presides, complete havoc is played with family bonds; and well may she remind Isabella, after she has slandered 'your dead mother, my most loving sister' and set the niece on the way to an incestuous union: 'I pray forget not but to call me aunt still' [II i 167]. There is an ironic echo of this line in Isabella's recognition speech, perhaps the most sinister expression of what relationships have come to mean in the play:

> I'd fain bring
> Her name no nearer to my blood than woman,
> And 'tis too much of that.   [IV ii 131–3]

Under the impact of this pervading dramatic image, the masque at the end becomes an integral part of the figure in the carpet. It has been defended, when at all, as a moral ritual 'utterly without logic in terms of human probability'.[4] Certainly, in real life, no people would plot so heedlessly against each other, or be subject to such coincidences. But within the play's own world, 'human probability' has come to mean the utter perversion of blood relationships; and so it seems logical enough that in conclusion an aunt should kill her niece, a niece her aunt, a sister her brother – and, a fitting irony, that in her own masque Bianca should kill the wrong brother. The context of the play makes us accept it, much as we accept the spontaneous combustion in *Bleak House*: in terms not of realism in the ordinary sense but of the reality of the central image, which is one of self-destructiveness.

Destructiveness, of self and others, is also the ultimate effect of the wit which is such an outstanding feature of the social world of

the play – wit in language and in action. 'It's a witty age', Guardiano
gloats after he has assisted in the seduction of Bianca; and Livia is
forever priding herself on her wit, from the harmless 'I think I am
more than witty; how think you, sir?', to the more sinister:

> Sir, I could give as shrewd a lift to chastity
> As any she that wears a tongue in Florence:
> Sh'ad need be a good horsewoman, and sit fast,
> Whom my strong argument could not fling at last.   [ii i 36–9]

Wit in the play, as in this speech, means control of language as well
as situation – that is, of other people. Leantio is bought by Livia,
and Livia, who, when she first set eyes on Leantio, declared herself
'dumb to any language now / But love's', finds exactly the right
love's language for Leantio. Her analysis of marriage-for-love puts
in clear and persuasive terms what was an undertone in Leantio's
speeches in Act i:

> It brings on want, and want's the key of whoredom.
> I think y'had small means with her.   [iii iii 285–6]

And her direct offer to Leantio picks up his favourite term of
reference, the 'rich man':

> I have enough, sir,
> To make my friend a rich man in my life,
> A great man at my death.   [iii iii 360–2]

The way in which people's wit in the play is directed towards *using*
each other is epitomised in the clinching of their bargain:

> LIV.   Do but you love enough, I'll give enough.
> LEAN. Troth then, I'll love enough, and take enough.
> LIV.   Then we are both pleased enough.   [iii iii 374–6]

The chess scene is obviously the best example of wit in action
and language: double action and double talk. It shows, too, how, as
previously innocent characters are drawn into the whirlpool of the
play's sex-game, they join, as it were, the group language and the
group action. We learn how corruption has affected Bianca through
her single speech of outrage – 'Now bless me from a blasting!' –
but, more sustainedly, through her new use of words. In almost
exactly the same terms as she spoke of Guardiano at the outset of
the scene, she now, with ironical doubleness, refers to him as 'this
kind, honest, courteous gentleman'; she makes bawdy, albeit feeble,
jokes in the banquet-scene and in the scenes [iv i] with the court

ladies (this functions as an image of court-wit) and with Leantio. And, of course, the ultimate product of her wit is the masque she devises, fatal to the Duke and herself.

It has been well said that, throughout the play, Livia uses other people like pawns in a game of chess;[5] but this is true for all the other characters as well, even if they are not as clever at the game as Livia. Guardiano plays on Fabritio, for Isabella; Fabritio uses Isabella as a pawn in the monetary game; Isabella and Hippolito use the Ward as 'the only veil wit can devise / To keep our acts hid from sin-piercing eyes'; the Duke uses Hippolito to rid himself and Bianca of Leantio. By the time death is involved as an element in the game, only one outcome is possible; and, again, there is a particular rightness about the masque, with its doubleness of language and action, as the climactic and fatal game of this society.

This is where, finally, the 'realism' of the masque scene lies. In itself – even if there were not a long tradition of masques in plays to support it – the masque is as natural a form of social occasion in the world of the play as is the ball in *The Cherry Orchard* or the coffee-party in *Pillars of Society*. It is justified, too, by expectancies within the play itself, such as Leantio's image of how the idle rich live: 'Grow fat with ease, banquet and toy and play.' It is set within a realistic framework of preparation, supplied by the scene between Guardiano and the Ward [v i] and by Fabritio's bustling around with 'the model / Of what's presented'. All this, together with Middleton's careful attention to the reaction of the masque audience, makes it a fully realised social occasion – as against the very schematic masques of, say, *The Revenger's Tragedy* and *Antonio's Revenge*.

But the 'realism' of the masque is also a matter of the structure of *Women Beware Women* as a whole. Middleton has a unique power of constructing group scenes, in which a very large number of people – virtually the whole cast – interact, take cues from each other, clash and score off each other. The three such scenes (if we may include the chess-scene, which in fact gradually involves nearly all the characters) form nodal points in the structure of the play. They form, too, a progression up the social scale. In the chess scene, Livia presides, and the Duke is hidden 'above'; in the banquet, the Duke presides, but the scene takes place in Livia's house; in the masque scene, the Duke presides, and the location is the Court. The structural irony of the masque is the ultimate involvement of all the characters in the masque. Bianca acts, in her aside, as a Presenter of her own private 'antimasque':

> But I have made surer work; ...
> Cardinal, you die this night, the plot's laid surely –
> In time of sports death may steal in securely.   [v ii 17–22]

Soon she also has to act as an Epilogue:

> Pride, greatness, honours, beauty, youth, ambition,
> You must all down together, there's no help for't.
> Yet this my gladness is, that I remove,
> Tasting the same death in a cup of love.   [v ii 218–21]

The supposed audience become real masquers, just as in Livia's masque real death hits the masquers proper. The masque scene demonstrates in a stage image how the very ethos of their society has overtaken the characters. And, within this image we are prepared to accept that people speak their last words not as (psychological) characters but as masquers in the masque of retribution:

> HIP.   Lust and forgetfulness has been amongst us,
>   And we are brought to nothing.

Critics have spoken of the coolness and detachment of this play which would seem to preclude a tragic vision. It is true that there is an extraordinary precision about the 'puppet show' at the end; but in the theatre, I think, our reaction is not all detachment. The masque scene shows Middleton's peculiar power of combining the ordinary with the horrible. As, in the chess scene, the ordinary surface of the game between Livia and the Mother is counterpointed with the horror of the act 'above', so, in the masque scene, the horror of the surface is placed in relation to the ordinary reactions of bystanders like Fabritio. The greatest emotional moments in the play are when a character gives voice to the tension between these two levels: Bianca's outcry at the evil she has seen 'above', or Fabritio's 'Dead? My girl dead? I hope / My sister Juno has not served me so'. Within Middleton's vision, as crystallised in these moments, there was room for a tragedy which not only dealt in conventional terms of retribution and damnation, but also saw the horror of life precisely in what men will do to men (or women to women). Therein, I think, lies Middleton's particular morality, as well as his realism; and as a theatrical image for this vision *Women Beware Women* has a unity of its own.

SOURCE: essay on 'Realism and Morality in *Women Beware Women*', in *Essays and Studies*, XXII (1969), pp. 57–70.

NOTES

1. Irving Ribner, *Jacobean Tragedy: The Quest for Moral Order* (1962), p. 152.

2. G. R. Hibbard, 'The Tragedies of Thomas Middleton and the Decadence of the Drama', *Renaissance and Modern Studies*, I (1957), p. 44.

3. See Francis Fergusson's essay, '*Don Pimperlin*: Lorca's Theater-Poetry', *Kenyon Review*, XVII (1955), reprinted in *The Human Image in Dramatic Literature* (New York, 1957).

4. Ribner, op. cit., p. 151.

5. Hibbard, op. cit., p. 50.

J. B. Batchelor   The Pattern of *Women Beware Women*   (1972)

The critical endeavour in modern studies of *Women Beware Women* tends to follow, to some extent, the lines of Eliot's essay and of M. C. Bradbrook's remarks in *Themes and Conventions of Elizabethan Tragedy* (1935). It is true that all the imagery of the play creates a pattern which reduces love to lust, and lust to a saleable article in a corrupt society, and it is also true that the tone of the play changes abruptly with the entrance of the Cardinal in IV i. This is where, in this traditional view of the play, the division comes between the realistic and the didactic parts, and this is where Miss Bradbrook does for *Women Beware Women* what Leavis did for *Daniel Deronda* by separating the bad part from the good part. The traditional view of the play is expressed with great clarity by G. R. Hibbard when he remarks that 'What begins . . . as seventeenth-century Ibsen, ends as a kind of mongrel'.[1] Christopher Ricks [see his 1961 essay on the play, above] tends to put aside this aspect of the criticism of the play by suggesting that the line of argument has been overdone: the play is 'very obviously a play about the corruption of life and love by money'. My own feeling is that the discussion is not yet concluded.

The sources for the Bianca plot, sources that are translated and set out at length by J. R. Mulryne,[2] contribute to an understanding of the supposed conflict of realism and morality in *Women Beware Women*. In the source for the Isabella plot it is clear that the episode is thought of as an example of monstrous duplicity, but the sources for the Bianca plot tend to be much more sympathetic to Bianca than is Middleton.

The story of Bianca Capello had been transmitted by a number of authorities, but in Dr Mulryne's view the only printed source that could have been available to Middleton in 1620 is in the *Ducento Novelle*, by Malespini, published in Venice in 1609. The fact that it was published in Venice is interesting, as the story is a Florentine one: the Medici seem to have been at some pains to erase the memory of Bianca in Florence, and one can see Malespini's account as a gleeful, irreverent exposure of a Florentine scandal seen from a Venetian point of view. Bianca herself was a Venetian, and Malespini's narrative is full of sympathy for Bianca and the Duke, and suggests that both of them were, possibly, murdered by Cardinal Ferdinand who was to succeed as Duke after his brother's death.

Malespini's narrative can be summarised as follows: Bianca Capello, the daughter of a wealthy Venetian, elopes to Florence with one Pietro Buonaventura, and lives in poverty with him in his parents' home until she has the 'good fortune' to catch the eye of the young Francesco di Medici. Francesco's tutor, Mondragone, and his wife, arrange a meeting with Pietro's mother, and thereby with Bianca herself (clearly the function of the Mondragones has been taken over, in the play, by Livia and Guardiano). Bianca becomes the Duke's mistress, and she and Pietro enjoy for some years a life of great luxury, until Pietro unwisely involves himself in a liaison with a widow who is a member of a powerful Florentine family, and is assassinated (with Francesco's connivance) by the widow's relations.

Malespini hints that Bianca and the Duke are murdered by the Cardinal, and this is contradicted by Fynes Moryson's *Itinerary*, Part IV, where the provenance of the poison (as in the play) is Bianca herself. Bianca sends a piece of 'marchpane' (marzipan) to the Cardinal, which the Cardinal refuses. The Duke, however, breaks off a piece and eats it; Bianca, realising that her plan has miscarried, eats some herself, and both she and the Duke die within the hour. There is an obvious difficulty over this source, as Dr Mulryne points out, in that this part of the *Itinerary* was unpublished until 1903 (when it appeared in *Shakespeare's Europe*, edited by Charles Hughes), yet the resemblance between the misadventure of the marchpane and the confusion over the poisoned goblet in Middleton's play is remarkable.[3] Like the conflicting versions of the American Civil War, the Bianca–Francesco story has two perspectives, depending on where the commentator lives: the Venetians would presumably regard Cardinal Ferdinand as the villain of this story, while the Florentines would regard Bianca as the most culpable and the Duke as weak and misguided.

In order to achieve a streamlining of this material for dramatic purposes a number of changes, all obvious and all in one direction, have to be made in the Bianca story. In Malespini Bianca loves her husband, but she also, and simultaneously, loves the Duke; Middleton has Bianca fall out of love with Leantio, and she has to be forced into her relationship with the Duke. Point is added to this by making the Duke in the play into an old lecher, whereas historically Francesco was twenty-three in 1564, the year in which time Bianca became his mistress. (There is also a great deal of compression in the time scale; Francesco was married, and historically he and Bianca had to wait twelve years before she could become his Duchess. But this compression is as much Malespini's as Middleton's.)

Middleton reorganises the structure of events so that they accord, to some extent, with the Cardinal's morality, and I hope to show that it is only with the Cardinal's intervention that the story is brought into focus. Until that point the play acts upon the observer, enticing and then betraying him through a series of carefully patterned dramatic devices. For some of the play Middleton seems to be writing with much of Malespini's comfortable complaisance and worldliness, allowing an audience to feel that the orthodoxy of the outraged husband is a nagging, prejudiced provincialism obstructing the tolerant elegance of a sophisticated society. This pragmatism, this comfortable ability to let things slide without worrying too much, is brought to a halt by the Cardinal. With his intervention in Act IV a searchlight is turned on the action of the play, and the persons presented are forced to see themselves judged by an objective morality. If one can discard concepts of 'realism' and 'morality' in conflict and see the play as a diptych, a double perspective in which a Venetian and then a Florentine present contrasting versions of the same picture, one brings the play almost within reach.

To appreciate not only this large binary form but also the subtleties of detail in this play, one would like to see it run backwards and forwards simultaneously. This would be to see Leantio's bitter soliloquies (Act III) in the light both of his parochial innocence in the first scene, and of his wrist-flicking cynicism in IV i, where he and Bianca encounter each other in their new-found finery; or, again, to see Livia's unreflecting commitment to pleasure in the light of the Cardinal's reminder that life can offer more than the gratification of lust. Livia's code, such as it is, is crucial, since she dominates the first three acts and provides in them the only enduring standpoint among the shifting sands of eroded personality and collapsing standards; yet her eminence is only gradually achieved.

The opening scene, presenting as it does an anonymous lower-class family (none of the characters are named) can seem dull in the theatre. The elements of exposition in it are compressed:

> From Venice her consent and I have brought her,
> From parents great in wealth, more now in rage.
> But let storms spend their furies; now we have got
> A shelter o'er our quiet innocent loves,
> We are contented. Little money sh'as brought me;
> View but her face, you may see all her dowry.   [I i 49–54]

The only names voiced in this scene are the two place names, Venice and Florence, and in these lines is contained the essential information about Leantio's marriage; he has committed hypergamy, bringing the girl out of her class into pauperdom. Yet the dialogue with the mother with which Middleton fills out his scene is not without purpose; the argument over the unbalanced marriage and the tensions that it may bring operates significantly on two levels. The first is immediately apparent; the mother's affectionate anxiety establishes the attractive qualities of warm, closely-held family relationships in a tight-knit unit. These qualities are thrown into strong relief by the following scene in which Livia establishes, with equal certainty, an atmosphere of comfortable and expedient worldliness proper to a class with better prospects and broader horizons. To return from this scene to the first is to be nudged by Leantio's primitive notions of a husband's authority, by his dangerous failure to see his wife as a woman rather than as a possession, and by the restrictive action of his self-righteousness:

> As often as I look upon that treasure,
> And know it to be mine – there lies the blessing –
> It joys me that I ever was ordained
> To have a being, and to live 'mongst men.   [I i 14–17]

It is clear that Bianca will not be content to be locked up by the mother for long.

Leantio's fragile happiness is left in the balance, and his limited philosophy of marriage is contrasted with Livia's philosophy of love. The first part of I ii is seen to be in a symmetrical relationship with the opening episode. In the mother's house the mother, nominally the authoritative figure, is the least effective, and Middleton has sharpened this situation by removing the father, who is an important figure in Malespini's narrative. In Livia's house Livia emerges, and ascends, by a series of related epithets from 'experienced' to 'wise' to 'more than witty', and she is the manipulating figure among the three characters; Guardiano and her brother Fabritio are mere agents. This triangle inverts the mother's situation; but as the scene develops with the entrance of the second brother, Hippolito, and of Isabella, who is forced to witness the exhibition of the revolting Ward, it looks forward to the shape of I iii, in which Bianca witnesses the Duke resplendent in his procession.

One may observe, before leaving I ii, that at this point the title of the play would seem to have been conceived in a spirit of parody. Isabella and Bianca have no cause to beware women, but great cause to resent, and fear, men. Bianca has been ensnared into a wholly unsuitable marriage by the contrary pressures of repressive parents and an ardent but foolish lover, and Isabella's case is far worse: Fabritio's greedy stupidity, Guardiano's complaisant unscrupulousness, and Hippolito's perverted sensuality threaten her on all sides, and in this predicament Aunt Livia must seem to preside over her disreputable brothers like a saint surrounded by demons. And while civilised man is misguided, corrupt and mercenary, natural man in the person of the Ward, the husband intended for her, is a horrifying blend of childish futility and mature lust. After the removal of the Ward, Livia's intervention must come to Isabella, who remains speechless, as the voice of sanity in a mad world:

> FAB. How do you like him, girl? This is your husband.
> Like him or like him not, wench, you shall have him,
> And you shall love him.

> LIV. Oh soft there, brother! Though you be a justice,
> Your warrant cannot be served out of your liberty;
> You may compel out of the power of father
> Things merely harsh to a maid's flesh and blood;
> But when you come to love, there the soil alters,
> Y'are in another country.   [I ii 128–36]

Livia's nature is discovered to us by a progression; from Fabritio's 'you're an experienced widow, lady sister', to Livia's 'I am blown, man! / I should be wise by this time', our sense of these words, of 'experienced', 'wise' and 'witty', undergoes a continuous modification until it comes to rest on an infinite and all-embracing worldliness.

Livia's understanding of 'love' undergoes a comparable moral descent, from the speech quoted, in which it seems to refer to something pure and idealised, to the dialogue with Hippolito culminating in 'thou art all a feast, / And she that has thee a most happy guest' [I ii 149–50]. Middleton does not deceive us to the extent of allowing us to suppose that Livia is virtuous, but in theatrical terms she is the most attractive figure that has yet appeared, and the most responsive of the group with whom Isabella must contend.

The definition of love takes another turn in the scene which mirrors this one, where the mother unwittingly brings Bianca face to face with her future lover, the Duke. The idealism of Leantio as he leaves for work parallels that of Isabella: for him love means responsibility, just as for her it meant purity:

> then man loves best
> When his care's most: that shows his zeal to love.
> Fondness is but the idiot to affection,
> That plays at hot-cockles with rich merchants' wives –
> Good to make sport withal when the chest's full,
> And the long warehouse cracks. 'Tis time of day
> For us to be more wise, 'tis early with us;
> And if they lose the morning of their affairs
> They commonly lose the best part of the day.   [I iii 22–30]

Unfortunately the more Leantio explains himself the more he disappoints. His aspirations, the long warehouse and the full chest, are the product of an impoverished imagination and do not measure up to the nobility of the opening sentiment. In the dialogue with Bianca this fatal explicitness reduces his predicament to a coarse equation; time spent getting money is balanced against time spent in sexual intercourse:

> If I stay any longer I shall turn
> An everlasting spendthrift. As you love
> To be maintained well do not call me again,
> For then I shall not care which end goes forward.   [I iii 53–6]

The application of the title becomes apparent as soon as Livia is seen to enjoy her power. 'This I can do' [II i 32]; in this chilling little line, where she promises to prostitute her niece to her brother, one sees why she is deadly to other women. She has the moral outlook of a man, and of a sensual man at that:

> I take a course to pity him so much now
> That I have none left for modesty and myself.
> This 'tis to grow so liberal – y'have few sisters
> That love their brothers' ease 'bove their own honesties.
>
> [II i 68–71]

She has forgotten what innocence is like; the total inadequacy of 'loss of modesty' to the monstrous action that she is preparing to perform is a mark of this. Yet with her effortless control and her air of genial self-knowledge she remains the most attractive person on stage.

The corruption of both Isabella and Bianca is presented emblematically in II ii; Isabella's off-stage surrender to Hippolito is understood, since she has accepted the Ward as a husband, allowing Fabritio a triumph which is rich with dramatic irony. In the Bianca plot, Middleton has allowed himself an economy over the relationship between Livia and the mother. In Malespini Signora Mondragone has to seek out the mother's acquaintance, but Middleton simplifies this by making them already acquainted; it is an unlikely friendship, and one learns with surprise that the factor's mother is a Sunday-dinner and Thursday-supper woman in the Livia household. With the tale of the friend who 'had a friend at nine-and-forty' Livia practises some erosion of moral standards on the mother before going to work on the daughter-in-law. This establishes the mother's helplessness; moving into a higher social class by her entry to Livia's house, she surrenders her own fragile standards to Livia's robust worldliness. Bianca, on the contrary, is moving into the class to which she naturally belongs, and in theatrical terms the transformation in Bianca after the rape is a transformation for the better; she has far more life, in her rage, then she did as the sweet wife of the first scene.

Another significant adaptation of the source is Guardiano's function; in Malespini it is the wife who leads Bianca to the Duke, but here Guardiano is the sordid instrument while Livia remains the aloof, controlling agent. Guardiano's malice ('How prettily the poor fool was beguiled') also sets Livia in a relatively flattering contrast with him.

In III i the play returns to the lowest social grouping, that of the Leantio household, to witness the effects of corruption: Bianca is bored, the mother indignant, Leantio first incredulous and then enraged. The effect of Bianca's exchange with the mother is to discredit the mother as a moral focus, since it is seen that her scale of values differs only in degree from that of Bianca herself:

> She'd be served all in silver by her good will,
> By night and day; she hates the name of pewterer
> More than sick men the noise, or diseased bones
> That quake at fall o'th' hammer.   [III i 76–9]

Leantio is equally discredited as a moral focus. On his first return, eager after his 'five days' fast' to enjoy the fruits of marriage, he may command some allegiance, but the more he talks the more he forfeits one's sympathy; the final explosive conflict with Bianca is seen not just as collision of husband and wife, but as a collision of class habits:

> LEAN. Thou hast been seen, Bianca, by some stranger,
>   Never excuse it.
> BIAN.   I'll not seek the way, sir.
>   Do you think y'have married me to mew me up
>   Not to be seen?   [III ii 136–9]

With the invitation to the feast, Middleton removes the last props and leaves his audience floundering in a welter of shifting moral attitudes and class perspectives. The mother surrenders to the delight of being invited to a feast, Bianca seem vulgarly ambitious, Leantio hysterical; and yet, after all, why should they not accept Livia's invitation? Particularly (and here Middleton's adaptation of Malespini serves his purpose) if Livia is an old friend of the mother?

III iii, the banquet at Livia's house, is the third of the five spectacles that punctuate the play and contribute to its form. Each act has a piece of pageantry, and with each pageant we move up the social scale; if the code of social success were the only code operating in the play, the progress of its settings would suggest a triumphant comedy. In the first act the ducal procession, in which the Duke sees Bianca, passes under the mother's house and therefore operates at the mother's social level. The game of chess in Act II takes place at the level of Livia in her domestic rather than her public role; one assumes that Livia and the mother are in a private parlour, and not in the grand reception rooms of the palazzo – Bianca is taken off by Guardiano to see these rooms, 'the monument and all', and there finds the Duke. The banquet scene operates at the level of fashionable society; a level at which Livia can successfully play the hostess, and the Duke can appear as a gracious and condescending guest. In Act IV and Act V the pageants operate at the Duke's level, and are indeed royal occasions – the wedding procession in IV iii, and the masque (part of the wedding celebrations) in Act V.

In the Act III pageant, the banquet, one can feel the social horizons broadening for Bianca, for Leantio, and for the mother. If Act II erodes all moral codes, Act III establishes the code of success, which is adopted, to some degree, by all the protagonists.

Leantio, seduced by the contrast between the glitter of this scene and the squalor of his mother's house, accepts first the captainship ('This is some good yet, / And more than e'er I looked for; a fine bit / To stay a cuckold's stomach!' [III iii 45–7]), and then Livia as a mistress, and one can sense that his intensely held notions about marriage dissolve in the sunlight of a cultivated society; with Livia he turns his back on idealism, and accepts in its stead a deadly adequacy:

> LEAN. Troth then, I'll love enough, and take enough.
> LIV.   Then we are both pleased enough.   [III iii 375–6]

Bianca, at the dinner-table of fashionable society, is back where she belongs; she falls naturally into the diction of that society:

> He talks as if his daughter had given suck
> Before she were married, as her betters have;
> The next he praises sure will be her nipples.   [III iii 158–60]

Isabella, forced to sing to the company and display herself for its benefit, is prepared to act the plaything of this society since she has beaten it at its own game by her intrigue with Hippolito. Her compromise is complete; she will submit to any indignity offered her, including the dance with the Ward, and the succeeding 'market' scene in which she undergoes inspection by him, because her own secret is assured.

So far the play has been a series of formal scenes, mirroring each other, in which the two girls are seen as duplicate victims of society who come to terms with their predicament in contrasting ways, the one secretly and the other openly. In Act IV the action becomes at once more rapid and more stylised, but before the catastrophes are set in motion one has a brief and necessary glimpse of Bianca's upbringing:

> How strangely woman's fortune comes about.
> This was the farthest way to come to me,
> All would have judged, that knew me born in Venice
> And there with many jealous eyes brought up,
> That never thought they had me sure enough
> But when they were upon me. Yet my hap
> To meet it here, so far off from my birth-place,
> My friends or kindred; 'tis not good, in sadness,
> To keep a maid so strict in her young days;
> Restraint breeds wand'ring thoughts, as many fasting days
> A great desire to see flesh stirring again.
> I'll ne'er use any girl of mine so strictly.   [IV i 23–34]

This is to equal up the balance with Isabella; Isabella is obviously a victim, and her greedy father and diabolical relations are there in the play to remind us of the repressive forces that have shaped her. Bianca's parents are never seen, but here Bianca puts, at its strongest, the Venetian view of her story: the loving girl who runs away from repressive parents and becomes the helpless victim of monsters. Since one is about to hear the Florentine view of the tale put by the Cardinal, it is important that one has the Venetian view restated thus plainly at this stage of the play.

There follows the lively exchange with Leantio which sets in motion the catastrophes of the play. Both figures are at their most energetic in this scene, and in theatrical terms success has done them no harm; but Bianca reports Leantio's threats to the Duke, the Duke resolves to murder Leantio by Hippolito's agency, and the downward turn of the wheel is commenced.

It is alleged that Hippolito's motivation is obscure, at this point; but the code of success is still operating, and it is perfectly appropriate, within the terms of that code, that Hippolito should wish to avenge Livia's supposed honour. If the Duke were in fact planning a match for Livia with Vincentio, then the family fortunes of Livia and her brothers have indeed been dashed by Leantio's impertinence.

The play is transformed by the entrance of the Cardinal, who opposes Christian orthodoxy to the loosely held code of success and expediency which has so far operated. The Cardinal enters with lights, and his imagery, full of light and fire, is designed to force the Duke to see his own sin glaring 'like a fire upon a mountain'. The Duke responds to this in precisely the wrong way; his reaction to the spectacle of his own sin is to conceal rather than to repent. The same state of mind is echoed in Hippolito; sin can flourish in the darkness, but as soon as light is turned upon it it becomes a source of humiliation and must be hidden. The strongest motivation for the murder of Leantio is that he has dared to sin openly:

> Art, silence, closeness, subtlety, and darkness
> Are fit for such a business; but there's no pity
> To be bestowed on an apparent sinner,
> An impudent daylight lecher.   [IV ii 7–10]

The figures in the play have gone too far for the Cardinal to save them.

Theatrically, Livia has remained inviolate to this point, but with the murder of Leantio she loses her balance and forfeits the allegiance of the audience. With a misplaced instinct for revenge she reveals Hippolito's incestuous relationship with Isabella to Isabella herself, to Guardiano, and the Ward. The collapse of Livia precipitates the collapse of the world she has dominated, and she, Guardiano, Isabella, and Hippolito set up their symmetrical plots to murder each other in the masque.

With the withdrawal of Livia as the focus of control, Isabella and Bianca reveal themselves as apt students of her methods. Bianca is capable of an elegant, relaxed, and disdainful justification of her actions while her intention to murder the Cardinal is, presumably, already formed [IV iii 47–69]. She neatly inverts the Cardinal's characteristic light and vision imagery to serve her own purpose:

> From a man that's blind
> To take a burning taper, 'tis no wrong,
> He never misses it; but to take light
> From one that sees, that's injury and spite.   [IV iii 61-4]

'Light', here, is to be not a means of showing Bianca to herself and to the world, but an implement, or resource, for Bianca's own convenience. Bianca is completely convincing here because she has become manipulative and totally self-centred; the world is seen only in terms of her own requirements and the Cardinal's external scale of values is inconceivable to her. For her, 'seeing' is now synonymous not with moral perception, but with ability to control. Thus, on the Cardinal's offer of friendship in v ii, she continues the image in this form:

> But I have made surer work; this shall not blind me;
> He that begins so early to reprove,
> Quickly rid him or look for little love.
> Beware a brother's envy; he's next heir too.   [v ii 17–20]

The snakepit has been exposed to the light; the reaction is found in the masque itself, where Livia, as Juno Pronuba, appears as a diabolical parody of the Cardinal, bringing light to the involved lusts of the two shepherds and the nymph:

> Though you and your affections
> Seem all as dark to our illustrious brightness
> As night's inheritance hell, we pity you.   [v ii 104–6]

The light and fire images carry through to the death of Isabella, the precise nature of which is uncertain. The stage direction for Livia, '*Throws flaming gold upon Isabella, who falls dead*' is found only in an annotation to the Yale copy of the 1657 edition, and has been adopted by the modern editors. One assumes that the writer of the annotation was recording a performance that he had seen.

> LIV. Now for a sign of wealth and golden days,
>   Bright-eyed prosperity which all couples love,
>   Ay, and makes love, take that. – Our brother Jove
>   Never denies us of his burning treasure,
>   T'express bounty.
> DUKE   She falls down upon't,
>   What's the conceit of that?
> FAB.   As over-joyed, belike.
>   Too much prosperity overjoys us all,
>   And she has her lapful it seems, my lord.   [v ii 115–22]

Whatever the exact nature of Isabella's death, it is clear that gold, lust and the fire of hell are identified in the image of the burning treasure. The image applies to all the lovers in the play, but has a special application for Isabella; to die from a lapful of love from Livia's brother (therefore from Hippolito himself) has a fiendish appropriateness comparable with that of the death of Edward II.

Until the end of Act III the play moves experimentally through a range of social and moral attitudes without reaching any conclusion, and it moves on only one level; the physical, the immediate, the here and the now. Against this monism is set the dualism of the Cardinal's orthodoxy, with its uncompromising stand on final values, and on a medieval cosmology polarised by an unchanging heaven and an unchanging hell. After this intervention the action accelerates and the rapid deaths in the masque can be seen as consistent with this increasing rate of acceleration; each death is a moral emblem, a carefully worked model of appropriate retribution seen from the perspective of orthodox Christian dualism. Livia dies from incense because she has sought homage; Guardiano is impaled on his own caltrop for his pride in his ingenuity; and Hippolito's sin is passion for one too close to himself, for which he is punished first by the torture of the Cupid's poisoned arrows, then by self-slaughter on a guard's halbert. As Bianca dies, her face is corroded by the Duke's poisoned lips as a punishment for her fatal beauty: 'A blemished face best fits a leprous soul.' She pleads with the audience for their human sympathy, and the Cardinal, in counterpoint, iterates the point of view of the Florentine citizen:

> The greatest sorrow and astonishment
> That ever struck the general peace of Florence
> Dwells in this hour.   [v ii 198–200]

Bianca once more emphasises her Venetian origins:

> What make I here? These are all strangers to me,
> Not known but by their malice, now th'art gone,
> Nor do I seek their pities.   [v ii 206–8]

We are reminded that it is not just the masquers who are on stage; there should be an entire court of solid Florentine citizens, only too pleased to see the age of misrule pass away. The Cardinal's epilogue puts the falling of the Duke's sinful court into political terms:

> Two kings on one throne cannot sit together,
> But one must needs down, for his title's wrong;
> So where lust reigns, that prince cannot reign long.

Two scales of values – Venetian and Florentine, humanist and Christian, dualist and monist, or however else one seeks to express the contrast – cannot be held simultaneously in a single society; an explosion is inevitable.

If plot is conflict, then this play has a great deal of plot. Bianca, Isabella, Leantio, and Hippolito are each engaged in a struggle with their respective predicaments: poverty, ill-treatment, a hasty marriage and an incestuous passion. Each of these predicaments except the last can be seen as a product of the pressures exerted by social change, and while the playwright engages in open-ended speculation about the moral problems of persons subjected to such change in the first three acts, in the last two the problems are, in a sense, solved; all these persons are submitted to the judgement of a stern orthodox code from which there is no appeal.

In the images with which I have tried to describe this process – the mirror, the diptych, the beam of light in the snakepit – I have been anxious to emphasise the formal properties of the play. With its five pageants, of which the central one is the most elaborate and the final one is the most spectacular; with its series of mirrored scenes in which the divergent stories of Isabella and Bianca are set out in careful comparison with one another; and with the closely organised sequences of imagery and word-play which have attracted the attention of every critic who has looked at this play, the sophistication and the artifice with which the playwright has presented his moral argument cannot be overstated. That the characterisation of Isabella and Bianca could lead critics to regard Middleton as a seventeenth-century Ibsen may be a tribute to the success with which Middleton conceals his craft, but to proceed from such a judgement to lament the artificiality of the latter part of the play is to miss the point with a thoroughness that the playwright himself would have relished. His purpose is to act upon the unwary auditor in precisely that way; to seduce him, to bring him to extreme moral perplexity, and then to betray him.

Source: essay on 'The Pattern of *Women Beware Women*', in *Yearbook of English Studies*, II (1972), pp. 78–88.

NOTES

[Reorganised and renumbered from the original – Ed.]

1. G. R. Hibbard, 'The Tragedies of Thomas Middleton and the Decadence of the Drama', *Renaissance and Modern Studies*, I (1957), pp. 35–64 (p. 54).

2. J. R. Mulryne (ed.), *Women Beware Women*, Revels Plays (1975), pp. 168–84.

3. [Ed.] Middleton's Bianca mentions marchpane at III ii 189.

David L. Frost 'Notes on *Women Beware Women* and *The Changeling*' (1978)

Predeterminism and Subconscious Knowledge in *Women Beware Women*

Beyond the degree of social and economic determinism suggested by the action of the play is a deeper determinism conveyed through persistent dramatic irony. Characters seem to have a subconscious knowledge of the pattern of events, past, present and future, yet they are unable to raise this knowledge to a level at which they might benefit from it. Before the seduction of Bianca, the Mother whose office is to guard the girl comments on the role of the *rook*, otherwise the 'duke', in a chess game which has already become disturbingly proleptic: 'when you spoke there came a paltry rook / Full in my way, and chokes up all my game' [II ii 292]. When Bianca has fallen, the Mother observes of the rook/duke whose moves have ironically paralleled those of the stage action: 'H'as done me all the mischief in this game' [II ii 416]. Yet in the next scene she has no conscious apprehension that anything has taken place. Similarly, the Ward appears to have subconscious knowledge of his actual situation when he expects Isabella 'to send me a gilded bull from her own trencher, / A ram, a goat, or somewhat to be nibbling' [III iii 73–4]: these animals are not only emblematic of lechery, but they are all horned – and the Ward is cuckolded even before he is married. His 'knowledge' seems to condition his unwillingness to dance with Isabella and his insistence that her uncle lead off with the Ward's betrothed: 'Look, there's her uncle, a fine-timber'd reveller; / Perhaps he knows the manner of her dancing too; / I'll have him do't before me' [III iii 182–4; also 212–13].

Leantio has perhaps an intimation of the two 'riders' – himself and the Duke – which his wife will bear, an intimation which occasions the irony at I iii 51–2: 'I have such luck to flesh / I never bought a horse but he bore double'. Leantio, deserted by Bianca, gives vent to sentiments which ironically anticipate his own elimination as a block to Bianca's 'redeeming' marriage with the Duke: 'Methinks by right, I should not now be living, / And then 'twere all well' [III iii 322–3]. Yet more disturbing is the language of Leantio's reproach to Bianca in the confrontation scene: 'as much madness / To set light before thee, as to lead blind folks / To see the monuments, which they may smell as soon / As they behold – marry, oft-times their heads, / For want of light, may feel the hardness of 'em' [IV i 95–9]. Bianca was seduced by being led 'blind' to see the 'monument' – she felt his 'hardness' and smelt the 'infectious mists and mildews [which] hang at's eyes'. But Leantio does not know consciously the circumstances of Bianca's seduction, so it seems that some supra-rational recollection of them is here influencing the terms of his denunciation.

The total effect of these ironies is to extend the metaphor of the chess game to the whole action, where characters play according to a predetermined pattern and may on occasions have an intimation of their role in it, without being able to influence the progress of the game.

The Title of *The Changeling*

Though the Dramatis Personae relates this title only to the supposed idiot Antonio, the speeches at v iii 196–219 clearly indicate that the dramatists intended it to have a wider application. A 'changeling' was an ugly or mentally deficient child substituted by the fairies for a normal child which they had stolen, and the term was also applied to the stolen child. By extension the word comes to mean 'half-wit' or 'idiot', and is thus used of Antonio. But 'changeling' had further meanings: a woman who was inconstant in her affections, an untrustworthy or wavering person, an inferior substitute, someone who has undergone transformations. One or other of these meanings is appropriate to most of the characters in the play.

Beatrice-Joanna is the most obvious 'changeling': her affection, as De Flores reminds her, ''Twas chang'd from thy first love, and that's a kind / Of whoredom in thy heart' [III iv 143–4], and later her love will be transferred from Alsemero to De Flores, a change indicative of her moral decline and of the alteration in her spiritual and social standing [III iv 133–40]. Moreover, her amorality – though she is a daughter of the upright Vermandero – makes her a spiritual 'changeling', a cuckoo in the nest.

Beatrice's change conditions other changes: the unfortunate Alonzo is 'chang'd' from life to death [III iv 144]; Diaphanta must change from virtue to whoredom and become a 'changeling', an inferior substitute in Alsemero's bed, and then suffer the same change as Alonzo; Alsemero unwittingly 'chang'd embraces / With wantonness' [v iii 200–1]. At the close, the revenger Tomazo is changed 'from an ignorant wrath / To knowing friendship' [v iii 202–3]. The lovers of the sub-plot are made idiots, 'changelings', by love's madness, but the husband Alibius will 'change now / Into a better husband' [v iii 213–14]. Finally, the whole cast, 'circumscribed' by Hell, are descendants of the original changelings, Adam and Eve, who lost their 'first condition' and were turned out of Paradise.

The Changeling and the Myth of the Fall

The ostensibly naturalistic plot of the play is by persistent allusion related to the Biblical story of the Fall of man in Genesis iii. Alsemero interprets his encounters with Beatrice-Joanna in the temple as indicating that he will by marriage re-establish a prelapsarian state: 'that, methinks, admits comparison / With man's first creation, the place blest, / And is his right home back, if he achieve it' [I i 7–9]. But Beatrice is another Eve, 'that broken rib of mankind' [v iii 146] – alluding to Genesis ii: 21–3, Eve's creation from Adam's rib – and she is haunted by a 'fallen' gentleman, De Flores, whose lust and physical repulsiveness [II i 58, 82–5 *et passim*] associate him with the Devil in stage moralities. De Flores is persistently linked with the Satanic Snake, being called 'serpent' [I i 225, v iii 66] and 'viper' [III iv 166], and, more explicitly, 'lust's devil' [v iii 53]. He swears by the pleasures of Hell, linked with those of sexuality – 'by all the sweets that ever darkness tasted' [III iv 146] – and he interprets Beatrice's complicity in his murder of Alonzo as a second Fall, initiating another Expulsion from Eden: 'You lost your first condition, and I challenge you, / As peace and innocency has turn'd you out' [III iv 138–9]. Beatrice herself accepts her sexual corruption as eternal damnation: 'This fellow has undone me endlessly' [IV i 1].

Submission takes her out of moral conflict to the 'peace' of permanent commitment to one side: 'Thy peace is wrought for ever in this yielding' the Devil-figure assures her [III iv 169]. Finally, Alsemero invites De Flores to prepare to re-enact his seduction of Beatrice for the amusement of the devils in Hell, who relish the torments of the damned: 'rehearse again / Your scene of lust, that you may be perfect / When you shall come to act it to the black audience / Where howls and gnashings shall be music to you' [v iii 114–17], alluding to the 'weeping and gnashing of teeth' of those cast into 'outer darkness' and 'the furnace of fire' [Matthew viii:12; xiii:42, 50; xxii:13; xxiv:51; xxv:30].

Calvinist Predestination in *The Changeling*

According to Calvin's teaching, the Fall of Adam and Eve not only predestined all their descendants to depravity but was itself predestined. Beatrice / Eve has some understanding of the inevitability of her fate – 'Was my creation in the womb so curs'd, / It must engender with a viper first?' [III iv 155–6] – and she finally acknowledges De Flores as her destiny: 'Beneath the stars, upon yon meteor / Ever hung my fate, 'mongst things corruptible; / I ne'er could pluck it from him: my loathing / Was prophet to the rest, but ne'er believ'd' [v iii 154–7]. Similarly, Alsemero / Adam, already uneasy in the first scene, turns in Act v to explicit questions about predestination: 'Did my fate wait for this unhappy stroke / At my first sight of woman?' [v iii 12–13].

In the days of her naivety, Beatrice is made to express the position of the execrated Arminians on the question of divine Grace: 'Requests that holy prayers ascend heaven for, / And brings 'em down to furnish our defects, / Come not more sweet to our necessities' [II ii 9–11]. In effect, Beatrice is shown as regarding prayer as 'turning on the tap' of God's grace, which will then repair the 'defects' of human nature: she is in complete opposition to the Calvinist view that no human action can initiate the gift of Grace, which is bestowed by God on his elect, irrespective of human merit – merit which is anyway an illusion, since mankind does not merely have 'defects' but is totally depraved.

Beatrice learns in the course of the play to accept the Calvinist position as an accurate analysis of the human situation; and in this she is representative of the other characters. The Gnostic strain of Calvinism is apparent in the symbolism of the game of barley-brake, played by the fools and madmen of the sub-plot [III iii 165] and made an image of sexual congress by De Flores at the close; the initial couple draw all the other couples into the central circle, until all are enclosed by 'hell' – 'I coupled with your mate / At barley-brake; now we are left in hell' [v iii 162–3]. Vermandero grimly assents to the Calvinist doctrine of hereditary damnation, transmitted by copulation: 'We are all there, it circumscribes here' [v iii 164].

Biblical Allusions in *The Changeling*

II i 103–4 – 'The day will steal upon thee suddenly . . . I will be sure to keep the night': An abstruse but disturbing use of Biblical allusion. Vermandero's injunction to 'prepare' associates the marriage with Judgement Day itself: 'For ye yourselves know perfectly, that the day of the Lord shall come, even as a thief in the night . . . But ye, brethren, are not in darkness, that that day should come on you, as it were a thief' [1 Thessalonians v:2–4 (in the Geneva version, 1560)]. Revelation iii:3 takes up the theme: 'If therefore thou wilt not watch, I will come on thee as a thief, and thou shalt not know what hour I will come upon thee'; and in the context of Beatrice-Joanna's intention to 'keep the night', Revelation xvi:15 is grimly appropriate: 'Behold, I come as a thief. Blessed is he that watcheth and keepeth his garments, lest he walk naked, and men see his filthiness.'

III iv 14 – 'And if that eye be darkened that offends me': A savagely ironic echo of Scripture. Beatrice-Joanna, contemplating murder, recalls Zechariah [xi:17] prophesying against the worthless shepherd of Israel – 'his right eye shall be utterly darkened' – and the Psalmist [lxix:23–8] cursing the ungodly: 'Let their eyes be darkened, that they see not . . . Let them be blotted out of the book of life.' There is further recall of Matthew xviii:9: 'And if thine eye offend thee, pluck it out and cast it from thee' (in the Authorised version, 1611). The nexus of allusions is completed by one more appropriate to Beatrice's own darkened eye: 'But if thine eye be evil, thy whole body shall be full of darkness. If therefore the light that is in thee be darkness, how great is that darkness?' [Matthew vi: 23].

v i 25, 59 – 'The day-star, by this hand! See Phosphorus plain yonder': The importance of this stage appearance will be clearer when it is realised that Phosphorus is in Latin *Lucifer*, the morning star, identified in Isaiah xiv:12–15 with Satan: 'How art thou fallen from heaven, O day star, son of the morning! . . . And thou saidst in thine heart, I will ascend into heaven, I will exalt my throne above the stars of God . . . I will be like the Most High. Yet thou shalt be brought down to hell, to the uttermost parts of the pit.' Under this star the Devil-figure De Flores conceives his plan for murder amidst a last-act conflagration; but when the shadow of Alonzo's ghost [line 58] interposes between the Vice character and the Satanic *light* under which he acts, De Flores endures a temporary 'mist of conscience'. Probably pyrotechnics were used to represent the star emblematically in the Jacobean theatre, and modern productions should attempt something similar.

SOURCE: extracts from editorial commentary in *The Selected Plays of Thomas Middleton* (1978), pp. 411–15.

John Stachniewski   Calvinist Psychology in Middleton's Tragedies   (1989)

Since Nicholas Tyacke's article, 'Puritanism, Arminianism and Counter-Revolution' (1975),[1] the recognition that Calvinism was the orthodoxy of the Church of England from the latter part of the sixteenth century till the accession of Charles I and the rise of the Arminian party has itself become the orthodoxy of students of history. With few exceptions, literary critics have not caught up with this fact. The reasons are not far to seek. It was convenient for those who believe in literature's embodiment of transcendental verities to bundle together Calvinists and Puritans, whose supposed hostility to literature added testimony both to their perversion of the human spirit and to art's spiritual grandeur in resisting this. Drama especially remained uncontaminated since it was the butt of such moralists as William Prynne, Philip Stubbes and William Perkins. Reassessment is, however, now required, both of religiously-minded interpretations of texts, which, following T. S. Eliot, tend to assume that literature registers the influence of Anglo-Catholic or 'moderate Anglican' Church teaching, and of secular readings which discreetly ignore theology in the plays, regarding it as epiphenomenal cultural jetsam, immaterial to the universal values art proclaims.

If Saussure and the parti-coloured offspring he is supposed to have spawned have taught us anything of scarcely disputable importance, it is that meaning does not inhere in particular words but is generated by the differentiation of synchronic terms. This being so, the neglect of aspects of the language of a text disfigures the meanings even of those aspects which are examined. Instead of looking for permanent truths about human nature (and ending up with a handful of banalities) literary critics should, in my view, see themselves more as anthropologists who are lucky enough to have literature as their primary subject matter, since it gives the most direct access to the codes of a culture at their highest level of sophistication. Whatever our view of this or that religio-cultural formation – and we ought in the end, in justice to ourselves, to come clean about our own moral evaluation – we should attempt a criticism which gives attention to the religious language of that culture commensurate with its density in the text.

It would be otiose, in the space available here, to pursue any further the specific question of Calvinist hegemony or the general question of how alien discourse should be approached. The minimum has been said for the purpose of this essay, which is to consider the tragedies of Thomas Middleton, especially *The Changeling*, in the light of the contemporary authority and currency of Calvinist discourse and to gauge the effect of the interdefining terms in the plays' lexicon. There are two critics who may look as though they have been here before me: Irving Ribner and Margot Heinemann.[2] Ribner sees the importance of Calvinist predestination and reprobation in *The Changeling*, especially as it is symbolised by De Flores, but he offers no close examination of the play's language. Heinemann, who dislikes Ribner's stress on predestination, argues that Middleton had close links of a personal and political kind with city Puritans, who were not generally hostile to plays. This is useful in as much as it helps to break down the barrier protecting literature from Calvinism (along with Puritanism as she understands it). But in her enthusiasm to see Puritans as forming a coherent political opposition at this early date (highly dubious in itself), she cannibalises the plays for social documentation, largely ignores their language and structure, and overlooks their culture-locked Calvinist psychology.

My term, Calvinist psychology, may seem odd, an anachronism inconsistent with the anthropological model just proposed. But the Reformation, especially Calvinism, seems to me to be the main cultural origin of what eventuated in Freudian depth-psychology. The term 'psychology' was coined by Luther's disciple Melanchthon in 1575 (see *OED*). And Freud himself realised that he was the legatee of a Protestant tradition when, in *The Question of Lay Analysis*, he dubbed analysts 'secular *Seelsorger*' (soul-searchers).[3] William Haller entitled the first chapter of *The Rise of Puritanism* (1938) 'Physicians of the Soul' because this was commonly the appellation of divines who were thought able to delve beneath apparent character and discover the underlying spiritual state. Haller describes the leading English expositor of Calvin's teachings, William Perkins, as 'a sixteenth-century William James' [p. 92]. Interest in the logic of an inner, unknown self was mobilised by the Calvinist determination to read polarised endings, in heaven or hell, back through entire lives which might not always exhibit extreme differences. What we find in the drama pervaded by Calvinism is a conception of character as strung between conscious purposes and unconscious identity. The discovery of the hidden logic of character is the unifying purpose linking the play's disparate episodes and propelling its action.

Middleton was fascinated by the secrecy of the operation of divine truth. His understanding of human affairs is keyed to the Calvinist idea that truths have been established long before they are revealed. The little tract *The Marriage of the Old and New Testament* (1609) evidences his interest, expressed here by biblical prefiguration, in the truth of things not yet manifest. 'In reading the Prophets', Middleton says in the preface, 'you shall finde that they speake of things to come as if they were already past; But note that they do this of purpose to shew the certainty of all their prophesies, which they know could not chuse but happen, because God himselfe was the revealer of those secrets to them' [p. 7]. John Reynolds, author of *The Changeling*'s source story, was interested too, in a cruder way, in the gradual disclosure of divine attitudes: 'But God', he says, 'is as just as secret in his decrees.' Reynolds's Alsemero is acquitted for the punitive killing of Beatrice-Joanna (whom he was 'ordained of old to chastize') and of De Flores, and then erroneously convicted of Alonzo de Piracquo's murder. Reynolds applauds the divine justice of this: God, he says, 'seeth not only our heart but our thoughts, not only our actions but our intents', and God engineers Alsemero's execution because he knew 'how ready and willing Alsemero was to ingage himselfe to Beatrice-Joana to kill Piracquo'.[4] This attests, crude morality though it is (especially since Alsemero had only intended a duel), the interest the Puritan Reynolds shares with Middleton in mentalised, inward evil. Attention is directed in *The Changeling* towards a mysterious tendency of character, a spiritual essence.

The title of *The Changeling* gives the first clue to this mode of character and play construction. We note in *OED*, among definitions of 'changeling': sb. 2 – 'A person or thing (surreptitiously) put in exchange for another'; and sb. 3 – 'A child secretly substituted for another in infancy'. Both definitions point to the importance of a hidden unknown identity – unknown alike to its possessor and its supposed kin – which has supplanted ostensible identity. If these senses are applied to Beatrice-Joanna she does not, as influential critics such as Muriel Bradbrook and Helen Gardner have maintained,[5] gradually change into a different moral creature; she is, from the start, a different person from the one she is taken (from the external badges of birth and beauty) to be. Richard Levin notes the relevance of sense 3 but does not apply it in the aptest way. De Flores, he says, 'is the agent of Beatrice's transformation, the evil fairy who makes the exchange'.[6] He clings to the idea of transformation which *OED* supports less well than that of mistaken identity, omitting to quote the definition which indicates a substitution 'in infancy'. Her reprobate character, though unperceived, inheres in her from the start.

The opening of the play cleverly launches the theme of the spiritual changeling by exploiting the convention of the comic heroine. A stock situation shapes up. Master and servant pair up with mistress and maid; a wedding is in the offing; obstacles in the form of a rival suitor and a father's choice present themselves to be surmounted; a faithful retainer offers his services as an intriguer. Sucked in by the conventional configuration, we share Beatrice-Joanna's sense of herself as a comic heroine, a virtuous (because beautiful) darling of the gods to whose needs events will finally bend. Consequently we are as rudely disabused as she of her apparent elect identity. J. B. Batchelor concludes of *Women Beware Women* that Middleton's 'purpose is to act upon the unwary auditor . . . to seduce him, to

bring him to extreme moral perplexity, and then to betray him'.[7]
No reason is assigned, however, for this sadistic proceeding. The
play's heuristic Calvinist function can make sense of it: auditors are
alerted to the interior operation of spiritual principles. That the
predestinarian message tends to invalidate moral purpose is an
objection to which all Calvinist teaching was vulnerable. Middleton
was, as an artist, probably more interested in the psychological
mechanisms he was exhibiting than their moral upshot. Nevertheless,
the plays gravitate towards the self-recognition of the characters
and, like morality plays, invite audience participation.

The 'bitterest blasphemy against God', thought Luther, was the
unconscious despair of those who evaded conviction for sin.[8] From
The Changeling's first scene Beatrice-Joanna's unconscious despair
is represented by De Flores. He confronts her with something
ineradicable in herself which her conscious violence is directed to
repress: that is, her own reprobate character. Middleton prepares
us to realise this by withholding external explanation for her hostility.
De Flores tells us she has 'no cause for it', and she herself calls it
her 'infirmity' [ɪ i 107–9]. For her, characteristically, the word
suggests no moral awareness. Puritan divines regularly spoke of
spiritual states in medical language, as Haller's 'Physicians of the
Soul' indicates. Middleton elsewhere favours the metaphor. In The
Marriage of the Old and New Testament, he adds such glosses to his
selected biblical texts as 'a Physition was comming' [p. 2], referring
to Christ, and 'God was mindfull of our saving health' [p. 2]. In
The Second Maiden's Tragedy, the guilt-stricken Helvetius takes up
Govianus's Puritan surgical injunction to introspective retrospection
('search thy conscience for thy sins of youth') with the words:
'Such a wound as mine / Did need a pitiless surgeon. Smart on,
soul; / Thou't feel the less hereafter!'[9] Gratiana in The Revenger's
Tragedy begs the heavens to 'Take this infectious spot out of my soul'
[ɪv iv 51] and then speaks of herself as 'recover'd of that foul disease'
[121]. The Puritan divine Richard Greenham contrasted the diligent
precautions people took to avoid 'corrupt humors, which in time
may breede (though presently they doe not bring foorth) some
dangerous sicknes' with their negligence (exemplified by Beatrice-
Joanna's casual apology for her foible) towards comparably latent
'diseases of the soule' [Works (1599), p. 230].

Such medical analogies no doubt seemed the best way of making
sense of Calvin's idea that men are totally depraved (since the

observable evidence for it was wanting). That appearances told against the doctrine led him to emphasise a psychological evil not necessarily recognised in oneself, still less in others. 'In dede I graunt', said Calvin, 'not that all these faultes do appeare in every man: yet it cannot be denied that this *hidra* lurketh in the heartes of all men. For as the body while it already fostreth enclosed within it, the cause and matter of disease, although the paine be not yet vehement, can not be called healthy: no more can the soule be reckened sound, while it swarmeth full of such diseases of vices.'[10]

By the end of the play despair of salvation has irrupted into consciousness:

> Beneath the stars upon yon meteor
> Ever hung my fate, 'mongst things corruptible;
> I ne'er could pluck it from him; my loathing
> Was prophet to the rest, but ne'er believed.   [v iii 154–7]

This avowal shows very clearly how the Calvinist doctrine of reprobation introduced an idea of the unconscious. Beatrice-Joanna had a destiny from which she consciously recoiled, but the strength of her revulsion measured her need to repress what her unconscious intimated to her. In saying she 'ne'er believed' it, she admits to having had, early on, to struggle against its admission to consciousness. She now sees the continuity, the psycho-logic, between her original loathing and final exposure. Her unconscious despair has gradually been raised to consciousness.

This belated self-recognition might seem to relieve Beatrice-Joanna of some of her guilt. Was she not, as T. S. Eliot and others suggest, merely amoral, morally ignorant, unself-aware?[11] This again is where the Calvinist viewpoint sets up reverberations between the conscious mind and a lower region which is at the same time available and not available to inspection. The term 'self-ignorance' was a Puritan coinage which carried a strong moral charge.[12] Robert Bolton speaks of those whose 'ignorance hath betraied them to the Divell'.[13] It has, though, been a wilful ignorance: Calvin strongly dissents from Plato's view that sins are committed only through genuine ignorance [*Inst.*, 2.2.22] and proceeds to point out the difference between an abstract knowledge of evil and the self-delusion people practise in individual cases. One might recall Beatrice-Joanna's eloquent homily on how the eyes should be sentinels to the judgement. Calvin's example might have been Middleton's brief for the portrayal of his heroine: 'Every man if it be generally asked, will affirme that manslaughter is evell: but he that conspireth to kill his enemies, deliberateth upon it, as on a good thing' [*Inst.*, 2.2.23]. Beatrice-Joanna, we shall see, even seeks to sanctify her conspiracy with biblical allusions. While the understanding was, in Calvin's view, 'seldome deceived', a kind of 'blindnesse' entered in 'when he cometh downe to the special case'. To 'pretend ignorance' on this basis was no extenuation [*Inst.*, 2.2.24]. A firm note in Middleton's *Marriage* concurs that 'None shal bee blinded with ignorance' [p. 44].

The idea of a deliberate resistance to confrontation of one's spiritual destiny is suggested by Govianus in *The Second Maiden's Tragedy*:

> O, who dares play with destiny but he
> That wears security so thick upon him,
> The thought of death and hell cannot pierce through!
> [v ii 57–9]

Such a person could, in William Perkins's words, take 'the numnesse and securitie of a defiled conscience, for the true peace of conscience'.[14] The security is an assumed protection against knowledge he prefers not to face.[15] In *Women Beware Women* the combination of fleshly desire and suppression of spiritual awareness is highlighted at the end by Hippolito:

> Lust and forgetfulness has been amongst us,
> And we are brought to nothing.   [v ii 146–7]

Leantio connects the idea of ignorance with the inner disease which is destined to recrudesce when he leaves Bianca with the thought that she will discover something more sinister than illegitimate offspring:

> So to an ignorance darker than thy womb
> I leave thy perjured soul: a plague will come.   [iv i 103–4]

Like Beatrice-Joanna's self-ignorance, the forgetfulness is always pregnant with what has been forgotten. When the idiot Ward exclaims absurdly, 'I'm damned, I'm damned!' [iv ii 79], on discovering that he has been cuckolded, he voices the despairing knowledge of being 'a plain reprobate' from which the others shrink. In *The Revenger's Tragedy* Vindice, a self-deceiver, thinks 'man's happiest when he forgets himself' [iv iv 84]. And Beatrice-Joanna shares the repressive facility of characters in *Women Beware Women*: 'y'are grown much forgetful', De Flores tells her [III iv 96].

In Calvin's view, self-ignorance had been facilitated by scholastic and Catholic writers who put misleading emphasis on wicked actions and therefore distracted people from the mentalised evil indispensable to the total depravity thesis: 'For a naturall man', said Calvin, 'suffreth not himself to be brought to this, to acknowledge the diseases of his desires. The light of nature is choked up before that it come to the first entry of their bottomlesse depth. For when the Philosophers note immoderate motions of minde for faultes, they meane those motions that appeare and shew foorth themselves by grosse tokens, but they make no accompt of those evell desires that do gently tickle the minde' [*Inst.*, 2.2.24]. Beatrice-Joanna is just such a natural (meaning unregenerate) individual who senses the 'danger' (a recurrent word in the play) of the abyss and shrinks from such self-understanding, distancing herself from actual crimes. De Flores says she recoils from him 'As if danger . . . hung in my looks' [II i 36]. And Beatrice's rapport with her spiritual doppelgänger is suggested in her words a few lines later: 'I never see this fellow, but I think / Of some harm towards me, danger's in my mind still' [II i 89–90]. Danger signs are dismissed until what was dangerous in herself has spilt out onto the external world. When she worries about the danger of De Flores's fire, he is amazed by her slowness to understand her predicament: 'You talk of danger when your fame's on fire?' [v i 34]. Sin will, wrote a Puritan, 'set the whole soule on fire, which for a time the sinner may shift, he cannot eschew.'[16] Events have caught up with the spiritual danger she has failed to confront; it is matched by the danger of an actual fire (a fire Alsemero describes as 'not so dangerous' [v i 85]), which in turn anticipates the hell fire she is bound for. It is at this moment, when De Flores lights the fire, that his demonic identity is fully disclosed in his allusion to the influence of Phosphorus (synonym for Lucifer). She now embraces the destiny she cannot elude, extolling De Flores and replying to Vermandero's 'That fellow's good on all occasions': 'A wondrous necessary man, my lord' [v i 90–1]. The redundant seconding is a cue for ulterior meaning: the stress on 'necessary' indicates her newly gained deterministic awareness. There has been a movement from unconscious (when Beatrice-Joanna shrank from her danger as something alien) to conscious (she sees the necessity of the dangerous fire and of De Flores) and to its fitting counterpart, the actual fire, and then that of hell to which she is resigned. Her (wilful) ignorance has betrayed her to the Devil.

For the Calvinist, who believed in the total depravity of the unregenerate, particular sins were merely symptomatic of a diseased consciousness. Even the vulgar Puritan John Reynolds who trades in scandalous crime appears to see things in this light. In his preface to *The Triumphs of God's Revenge* he says of his punished subjects: 'they builded not their faith on God ... and this, and only this, was both the Prologue to their destruction, and their destruction it selfe', and in the dedication for volume II he describes murder as 'frequently *coincident* to unregenerate Christians'. Murder is coincident to Beatrice-Joanna in this sense: not a one-off crime important for itself but a natural spin-off from the values regulating her life. Although real crimes are committed in the play, stress is thrown, Calvinistically, onto interior experience. It may be significant that we never see Beatrice-Joanna committing physical crimes; Middleton conveys his spiritual meaning with sufficient skill for us to realise their symptomatic status.

There is in Middleton's vision a stark dualism of flesh and spirit, derived from the Pauline theology revived by the Reformation, which lies at the root of his psychological treatment of evil. Predestination to damnation unfolds through the constraint 'the flesh' places on men to sin. The term is often substituted in Middleton by 'blood'. At Junior's trial in *The Revenger's Tragedy*, the Second Judge asks of his rape 'What mov'd you to't?' To which he replies: 'Why, flesh and blood, my lord' [I ii 47]. A few lines later he adds: 'Her beauty was ordain'd to be my scaffold'. The straightforwardly reprobate Husband of *A Yorkshire Tragedy* protests against the unfairness of such inevitable self-destruction:

That Heaven should say we must not sin and yet made women; gives our senses way to find pleasure which being found confounds us! Why should we know things so much misuse us?

''Tis our blood', he concludes, 'to love what we are forbidden.'[17] This is echoed by Lussurioso in *The Revenger's Tragedy*: 'It is our blood to err though hell gap'd loud' [I iii 72].[18] The Tyrant in *The Second Maiden's Tragedy* confesses that 'In vain my spirit wrestles with my blood' [v ii 1], while Helvetius refuses to be 'bawd to mine own flesh' and uses the contemptuous compound noun 'flesh-brokers' to impart the pejorative Pauline sense to the word in addition to that of 'kin' [II iii 39–46]. In the more complex *Women Beware Women*, social and economic duress compounds the theological determinism of fleshly desire; Guardiano finds

> no spider's web
> Made of a daintier thread, than are now practised
> To catch love's flesh-fly by the silver wing.   [II ii 398–400]

Economic deprivation assures the success of the Duke's well-baited seduction. Livia later explains the law ('want's the key of whoredom' [III iii 285]) that doomed Leantio's love-match. More condensed, too, is Livia's punning reaction to Hippolito's declaration of his incestuous love for Isabella: 'Yet does love turn thy point to thine own blood?' [II i 7]. *Blood* is used here, as in *The Changeling*, to refer both to kin and life-blood. Hippolito's sexual interest in his niece is tantamount to spiritual (and actual) suicide, as events reveal. Asked a moment before how he came by such an affection, Hippolito had replied: 'E'en as easily / As man comes by destruction, which oft-times / He wears in his own bosom' – echoing his earlier reference to Calvinist teleology: 'Ev'ry man has something / To bring him to his end' [I ii 188–9]. The mechanism by which predestination to damnation appears to operate, then, in Middleton's plays is the enslavement of characters to the Pauline 'flesh'. The lure of riches can be subsumed to this: Vindice comments on 'gold and women' with the familiar predestinarian phrasing:

> But 'twas decreed before the world began,
> That they should be the hooks to catch at man.   [II i 260–1]

For the preponderant reprobates in Middleton's tragedies (reflecting Calvinist statistical expectation), the effectiveness of the hooks is assured by the fact that, denied God's spirit, men are entirely actuated by fleshly desire. 'Flesh', as Middleton himself glosses it in *The Marriage*, is 'a figure . . . for the whole man' [p. 27], but the whole man unregenerated by the Holy Spirit and consequently totally depraved, capable only of willing evil.

If we return to *The Changeling* we can see how important the idea of flesh and blood, as opposed to spirit, is to the understanding of the play's psychology. Christopher Ricks points out in his 1960 essay (reproduced above) how the word *blood* is used to show that one kind of blood (meaning lust) entails another (murder) which in turn, assuming a moral order, entails a third (retribution). The use

of the same word insists on their inseparability.[19] This insistence
derives from the biblical concept of the flesh for which *blood* can
stand as a synonym. Paul says, for instance, in 1 Corinthians xv:50:
'Now this I say, brethren, that flesh and blood cannot inherit the
kingdom of God; neither doth corruption inherit incorruption.' *Blood*
in the play can clearly mean, in addition to the meanings Ricks
assigns, kinship or pedigree. In the crucial interview with De Flores
in III iv, Beatrice-Joanna loftily reminds him of 'the distance that
creation / Set 'twixt thy blood and mine' [130–1].

Middleton handles the shift to partial realisation in this scene
with characteristic play on alternative meanings – meanings guided,
simply enough, by the essential Protestant dualism as to the orders
of nature and grace. When later in the scene Beatrice-Joanna asks
with dawning awareness, 'Was my creation in the womb so curs'd
. . . ?' [165], her understanding of the word 'creation' has been
revised. Formerly in addressing De Flores she thought only of her
congenital social standing; now she sees that God (no respecter of
persons) assigns a spiritual identity in a creation prior to birth.[20] In
The Revenger's Tragedy the Duchess describes Spurio as, like Beatrice,
'The curse o' the womb . . . Half-damn'd in the conception, by the
justice / Of that unbribed everlasting law' [I ii 161–4]. There is a
spiritual as well as a physical (natural) creation, and spiritual birth
is 'not of blood' [John i:13]. In her conscience (the umpire, for
Puritans, which pronounced on spiritual identity) Beatrice-Joanna
will, De Flores assures her, 'find me . . . your equal' [III iv 133]. De
Flores is her conscience, a mirror confronting her with her moral
image, but her wilful self-ignorance has prevented the inspection
of conscience Puritans enjoined. Beatrice-Joanna has accordingly
disregarded all values except those tied to 'the flesh' by way of
birth, physical beauty and social institutions with which she has
automatically equated spiritual privileges. She suffers from what
Calvinist divines called 'spirituall blindnesse'.[21]

Middleton conveys this blindness allusively at times, in the irony
of Beatrice's biblical reference – for instance, when she thinks of
disposing of Alonzo: 'And if that eye be darkened that offends
me / (I wait but that eclipse) . . .' [III iv 14–15]. David L. Frost
(see the excerpt reproduced above) lists a number of scriptural
references for this, but in the context the most significant is Matthew
v:29: 'And if thy right eye offend thee, pluck it out, and cast it from
thee: for it is profitable for thee that one of thy members should

perish, and not that thy whole body be cast into hell.' She thus unconsciously anticipates her fate by misconstruing the scripture and taking the offending object to be Alonzo rather than her own eye. In *The Marriage* [p. 37], Middleton quotes the accompanying text about cutting off an offending right hand. The eye is frequently a metonym for fleshly perception. 'I have', Beatrice says 'within mine eye all my desires' [II ii 8]. The incommensurability of spiritual and fleshly values was suggested in the first scene when Vermandero boasted of 'our citadels . . . plac'd conspicuous to outward view', but added: 'within are secrets' [I i 164–6]. Physical fortifications should not be confused with interior moral ones any more than physical beauty should be equated with spiritual. Middleton draws attention to the citadel again in the last scene to point up the contrast between the external defences (which might have been involved in the play's action) and the moral-psychological plane on which the action has in fact occurred: 'An host of enemies enter'd my citadel / Could not amaze like this' [v iii 147–8]. X-ray perception of the inner spiritual secrets was no easy matter. 'Who can perceive this', asks Vindice in *The Revenger's Tragedy*, 'save that eternal eye / That sees through flesh and all?' [I iii 65–6].

The polarisation of humanity based on the Pauline distinction between flesh and spirit cut across social divisions, and no doubt it was with some relish that Middleton, a tradesman's son, undermined the traditional equation between social and moral worth (reflected for centuries in words like *gentle, noble, villein* and *churl*). That Middleton rejects the presumption that the high-born will be more virtuous than the low-born is confirmed when we learn from De Flores [II i 49] that he, too, is a gentleman born; his criminal nature is also independent of his 'blood' in the sense of pedigree. The relish is conveyed in the scene [III iv] in which Beatrice-Joanna is disabused. *Blood*, then, encompasses, in addition to the meanings Ricks identifies, the natural man's mistaken equation of privileges of birth with divine election. The mistake indicates an orientation to flesh which implies the lust, murder and punishment which 'blood' also evoked. The last use of 'blood' in the play is Beatrice-Joanna's, who plays on the ambiguity of kinship and sinful dependence on the flesh (both meanings ignored by Ricks) and connects it with the medical-spiritual analogy: she describes herself as 'that of your blood was taken from you / For your better health' [v iii 150–1].

The word *flesh* is moreover used in the play in significant allusion to the Bible. De Flores says of the ringed finger he presents to Beatrice-Joanna: 'He was as loath to part with't, for it stuck / As if the flesh and it were both one substance' [III iv 37–8]. This evidently alludes to Christ's saying: 'For this cause shall a man leave father and mother, and shall cleave to his wife: and they twain shall be one flesh' [Matthew xix:5]. Although Beatrice-Joanna is not yet Alonzo's wife, it is clear from this that Middleton wishes us to think of them as symbolically married – married in intent. The sexual meaning of the ring and finger is explicit in the sub-plot[22] and here we are meant to be shocked not just by the physical violation of the severed finger (noting another instance of Beatrice-Joanna recoiling from herself) but by the attempt to put asunder (in the phrase of the marriage service) what God has joined together.

De Flores is the character in the play most conscious of biblical teaching though, as befits his demonic function, he perverts and parodies it for his own purposes. He it is who tells Beatrice-Joanna she has committed 'whoredom in thy heart' and that she is a 'whore in thy affection' [III iv 142–4], taking his cue from Christ's pronouncement [Matthew v:28] that looking on a woman to lust after her amounted to adultery in the heart. The words immediately precede, as it happens, Christ's advice in the Sermon on the Mount to pluck out an offending eye. De Flores also suggests, however, that the murder of Alonzo has united her to him in a macabre marriage: it has 'made you one with me' [140]. He directly parodies the marriage service, indeed, when he intones, 'Nor is it fit we two, engag'd so jointly, / Should part and live asunder' [88–9]. Although this is a clear case of the devil quoting scripture for his own purpose, De Flores does have a kind of biblical authority for what he is suggesting. Paul alludes to Christ's dictum that husband and wife are one flesh (literally, in the sexual act, as the ring and finger betoken) when he exclaims to the wayward Corinthians: 'What? know ye not that he which is joined to an harlot is one body? for two, saith he, shall be one flesh. But he that is joined to the Lord is one spirit' [1 Corinthians vi:16]. In this text Paul diverges from his master. Christ implied, of course, no disparagement of marriage in his use of the word *flesh*, but Paul adds to Christ's words the associations he has given to it, and as usual places it in a pejorative antithesis to *spirit*. (Calvin also stresses this antithesis because it reinforced the polarisation of the totally depraved reprobate and the elect whose virtue was totally attibutable to divine grace.) Paul's words enable Middleton to unite the characters of Beatrice-Joanna and De Flores sexually to symbolise their spiritual identity: they are one flesh in their enslavement to the flesh (or blood) and she therefore cannot (though it takes her most of the play to see it) inherit incorruption. That Middleton thought of sexual congress as not only symbolising but mystically effecting marriage and divorce is confirmed by *The Second Maiden's Tragedy* when the Lady says to her husband, Govianus, that the Tyrant's 'lust may part me from thee, but death, never' [III i 144].

Fortifying the sinister effect is the lurking idea, belonging to popular theology and folklore, of reprobate women and witches copulating with the Devil.[23] In the first scene De Flores was referred to as 'serpent' [225], and the demonic suggestion is reinforced by his adept infernal casuistry in III iv. He later exposes himself as being under Lucifer's influence. Both he and Beatrice-Joanna are called 'devils' at the end, and De Flores exhibits a gloating satisfaction as if claiming his own when he announces, 'now we are left in hell'. Alsemero seems in no doubt as to his demonic identity when he says 'Take your prey to you'. The plays closes with an explicit realignment of family ties, on spiritual not fleshly lines. Beatrice-Joanna's kinship with her father is abrogated, while Alsemero — whose desire for Beatrice-Joanna has always been subordinate to his devotion to God (it is 'to the holy purpose' and he keeps 'the same church, same devotion' [I i 6, 35]) — allies himself to Vermandero as his spiritual son [v iii 216–17]. There is a surprising air of general acceptance, as though misunderstandings had been cleared up rather than that tragic events had occurred. Innocence can 'joy again' [186–7].

The chilling detachment which led one critic to describe Alsemero, without any encouragement from the text, as 'a grotesque moraliser'[24] is a product of the Calvinist habit of rigidly polarising humanity. The Duchess Renata of Ferrara, a disciple of Calvin, wrote in 1563:

> If I knew that the king my father, and the queen my mother, and my late husband and all my children were rejected by God, then I would hate them with a deadly hate and would wish them to be consigned to hell and would wholly order myself in accordance with the will of God.[25]

Doubtless the Duchess's faith was exceptionally ardent. But the Calvinist doctrines inevitably had something of this twisting effect on social and human attitudes even in the most intimate relationships. Alsemero and Vermandero quickly perceive that their beloved Beatrice is really a piece of human refuse and take comfort in their spiritual brotherhood.

Certain key words draw attention to themselves and alert one to the play's conceptual scheme. There are somewhat abstract leitmotifs doing the work of patterns of imagery in directing us to Middleton's psychological-theological concerns. The terms *will*, *appetite* and *judgement*, picked out by M. C. Bradbrook, are abstract and refer to discussions of their interrelations by humanists and divines. Even Ricks's discussion of *blood* (as compounding lust, murder and retribution) abstracts swiftly from the physical an inexorable moral law. All this is I think justified by Middleton's own concentration on mysterious inner and spiritual processes. There are other words as well as those already mentioned – *blood, flesh, creation, necessary, danger* – which are charged with Calvinist meaning and deployed to sensitise us to the Calvinist worldview.

The use of the word 'will', for instance can be further illuminated if its relations with 'reason' and 'passion' are perceived. Because for Calvin the post-lapsarian will was capable only of willing evil, the reason was powerless to influence virtuous conduct.[26] Calvin excepted 'civile or outward doinges' which 'belong not to the kingdome of God' [*Inst.*, 2.2.5], in which will and reason remained as serviceable, distinctively human attributes. When, therefore, Beatrice-Joanna's will is referred to, we should think of it as concurrently her faculty for manipulating her world to secure pragmatic ends and for directing herself unerringly towards evil. 'Will' is consistently given pejorative force in this play – for instance when De Flores announces ominously at the close of the first scene: 'Though I get nothing else, I'll have my will' [i i 237]. This connects him with Beatrice-Joanna who has just pitted her will (in an aside) against her father's legitimate authority [219–20]. Repetitions of the word 'reason' suggest its inefficacy and domination by the dark driving force of will. Livia has a powerful line in *Women Beware Women* when Hippolito seeks to propose his 'reason' for killing Leantio: 'The reason! That's a jest Hell falls a-laughing at' [iv ii 63]. The devils are amused by the self-duping propensity of humans to suppose their conduct to be directed by reason. Leantio's early confidence that it is 'Not the licentious swinge of her own will' [i i 92] that governs Bianca's behaviour is shown to be naive.

Guardiano observes in an aside that fools are not foolish 'at all hours' when Fabritio asks rhetorically: 'Why, do you think that women love with reason?' [I ii 16–17]. When Beatrice-Joanna seeks to justify her violence to De Flores in the first scene, she admits, 'Nor can I other reason render you'; De Flores has just ascribed it to her 'peevish will' [I i 107–10]. De Flores similarly admits to the inefficacy of his own reason when he remarks on his dogging Beatrice-Joanna: 'and I have small reason for't' [II i 31]. He comforts himself a few lines later with the thought of 'daily precedents of bad faces / Belov'd beyond all reason' [II i 83–4]. Reassurance is had from the evidence that reason in many does not govern conduct. Beatrice-Joanna does indeed turn out to be one of them; her eventual surrender to him has as little to do with reason as her original loathing. Vermandero, on the other hand, thinks, not knowing Beatrice-Joanna's motives for requesting postponement of the wedding, that 'the request / Is not far out of reason' [II i 115–16]. Reason is his criterion of evaluation. The term most commonly opposed to reason was 'passion', closely allied to blood. Thus Alsemero, too, gives a sign of his own election when he insists: 'And prithee do not weigh me by my passions' [IV ii 109]. Beatrice-Joanna, contrastively, implies that she is ruled by passion when she admits: 'This ominous ill-fac'd fellow more disturbs me / Than all my other passions' [II i 53–4]. For non-Calvinists the will remained, after the Fall, capable of recognising and choosing the good. Middleton makes the very word seem sinister. Will is a pre-Schopenhauerean force energising the characters of De Flores and Beatrice-Joanna, and reason (as for Donne) 'proves weak or untrue'. (It is because Aristotle and his scholastic followers believed 'that reason and the rational part are by nature rulers over the sensory part'[27] that his psychology could not accommodate the idea of unconscious drives.)

So we see that Middleton juggles with terms belonging to the same semantic field (*will, reason, passion, blood* etc.) to envelop the characters of De Flores and Beatrice-Joanna in a Calvinist miasma. He is adept at injecting words with special, usually sinister, sense. Even the innocent monosyllable 'still' acquires a metaphysical resonance. 'I'll haunt her still', says De Flores [I i 236], and, in the next scene, 'It seems 'tis my luck / To be i' th' way still' [II i 75–6] is instantly followed by 'I must see her still!'. Close on the heels of this repetition is Beatrice-Joanna's echo, 'danger's in my mind still' [90]. 'Still' is used to express De Flores's persistence and Beatrice-

Joanna's impatience. The two uses oppose one another, but at another level of the word's meaning they are united – if, that is, the available meaning 'always' is entertained. Beatrice-Joanna's 'danger's in my mind still' expresses her conscious surprise and expectation of release; unconsciously she is alluding to her permanent spiritual condition. The two characters use the same word to anticipate the way their identities fold into one another. That Beatrice-Joanna uses it suggests economically that awareness of her plight is buried in her own unconscious: it is an instance of parapraxis.

Beatrice-Joanna is a hypocrite. When in the exposure scene she offers to 'strain a tear to fill the vault', Alsemero retorts that this would be 'hypocrisy of a sadder colour' [v iii 26–8]. Like other Calvinists (Bunyan for instance), Middleton presents hypocrisy less as conscious pretence than as an inability to distinguish between the outward (flesh) and the inward (spirit): 'They are condemned for hypocrisie', he glosses in *The Marriage of the Old and New Testament*, 'because they made the Kingdom of God to stand in outward things' [p. 25]. 'Within', as Vermandero says, 'are secrets'. Beatrice's conscious (sadder) hypocrisy, expressed by her literal acting in the scene of the virginity test, is in a continuum with her earlier unself-conscious pretensions. 'The Hypocrite', wrote John Abernathy, a Calvinist divine, 'may *cover* or *colour* his flesh and affections, but he cannot crucifie them. But none do *crucifie* them, but they that are *Christs*.' She does not change but has been, again in the terms of Abernathy, 'long ignorant of [her]selfe'. Eventually, as to other reprobates, 'Gods secret judgement is cast open to [her]self'.[28] What we have heard rumbling in her unconscious makes its way to the surface.

That a subterranean spiritual identity unrolls itself relentlessly along the axis of an individual career while its owner is distracted by other ideas is consistently an ironic focus for Middleton in his tragedies. The sub-plot of *The Changeling* itself is clearly designed to mirror it. What Antonio actually does in the play is to behave as a madman, and his assumption of aloofness to the instrument of his purposes is as ignorant as Beatrice's to hers. He is unable to divest himself of his identity as madman when he wishes to disclose 'within / A gentleman that loves you' [iii iii 139–40]. Although he avers 'I know this shape / Becomes me not' [187–8], the danger is precisely that the role will become him, both in the sense of 'suit' and 'turn into', revealing itself, by Calvinist gradualism, to be his real self, 'a great fool as I am' [v iii 205]. The play presents a paradoxically determinist existentialism: you are the sum of your choices ('the deed's creature') whether or not you believe those choices to express an essential self.

When Vindice assumes his disguise in *The Revenger's Tragedy*, he quips to Hippolito: 'What, brother? am I far enough from myself?' [I iii 1]. He has a firm sense of his essential identity. He and his brother, he says, are 'innocent villains' [170]. But the oxymoron draws attention to the moral contamination the role entails. He will, he says, 'apply myself / Unto the self-same form, forget my nature' [181–2]. As with Beatrice, however, his choices do constitute him and his confidence that he is with the angels turns out to be misplaced. When Lussurioso conveniently asks Hippolito for his brother's services, Hippolito is relieved: 'Brother, disguise must off; / In thine own shape now I'll prefer thee to him' [IV i 58–9], adding, in the following scene, 'So, so, all's as it should be, y'are yourself' [IV ii 1]. Unfortunately, however, all is not as it should be since the self Vindice now is, is indistinguishable from the disguise (vindictively treacherous servant) which he has abandoned. His cry 'O, I'm in doubt whether I'm myself, or no' [IV iv 24] resounds beyond its context.

The occult continuity of human character is dramatically presented again in *The Revenger's Tragedy* when Castiza disowns or disrecognises her mother whose behaviour has invalidated the spiritual identity on which the filial relationship has been based: 'I cry you mercy, lady, I mistook you; / Pray, did you see my mother? Which way went she?' [II i 161–2]. When Gratiana promised the disguised Vindice, 'If she be still chaste, I'll ne'er call her mine', he had muttered: 'Spoke truer than you meant it' [II i 135–6]. As with Beatrice, Middleton uses the characters' unconscious equivocation, not as crude dramatic irony, but to dramatise a latent spiritual awareness (which Gratiana later brings profitably to consciousness). Livia in *Women Beware Women* may also speak truer than she means when she lyingly convinces Isabella that she is not related to Hippolito: 'I told you I should start your blood. / You are no more allied to any of us' [II i 134–5]. In the order of grace rather than nature she may be right (although Isabella's own blood is effectively started – stimulated as well as shocked – as the play degenerates, sacrificing characterisation in its moral holocaust). As in *The*

Changeling there are, in *The Revenger's Tragedy*, two orders of experience: the ostensible order of the flesh and the inner life of the spirit.
When Castiza exclaims 'Mother, come from that poisonous woman
there!', Gratiana swivels round with understandable alarm, demanding 'Where?' Castiza rejoins, 'Do you not see her? she's too inward,
then' [II i 239–41]. Castiza shares Calvinist habits of thinking of
identity as inward and spiritual, while the unself-aware Gratiana is
baffled. In the end Gratiana's original grace is restored, and she
confirms the underlying meaning of her name ('gratia' means grace)
with the words: 'to myself I'll prove more true' [IV iv 37].

Middleton's reprobates are not exposed; they expose themselves
when God's secrets are ripe for disclosure. Vindice's realisation
comes later, or at least more suddenly, than Beatrice's. Yet her
dying words, ''Tis time to die, when 'tis a shame to live' [v iii 179]
echo Vindice's, ''Tis time to die, when we are ourselves our foes'
[v iii 110]. The revelation to both of what they in fact are clashes
irreconcilably with the image they entertained. Exposure and self-
exposure are simultaneous. Vindice is foe to himself both in the
sense that he has given himself up and in the sense that the
instrumental identity he assumed to be alien to him has acquired
autonomy. It is because of Vindice's failure to recognise the self that
has possessed him that he is given the name 'Piato', which means
'hidden' or 'secret'. Just as Tomazo said that De Flores will 'bring
it out in time' [IV ii 58], referring at once (grammatically) to De
Flores's 'heart' and (consciously) to detection of the murder, Vindice
similarly says of Piato: 'time will make the murderer bring forth
himself' [v iii 116]. Time is midwife to reprobation. Vindice gives
himself away (rather than up) because he has become so habituated
to the values of Piato that they are normative for him. Beatrice-
Joanna likewise assumes that Alsemero will find her murder for love
acceptable. This yielding up of essential identity is the *telos* informing
both *The Revenger's Tragedy* and *The Changeling*.

Belief in predestination mobilises Middleton's interest in psychological consistency. The contingent is eliminated. No action or
choice, Beatrice-Joanna learns, can be excluded from the trajectory
of a life: she must 'settle . . . / In what the act has made' her
[III iv 134–5]. For the reprobate protagonist the play's essential
movement is from unconscious to conscious despair of salvation:
psychology, character determinism, and predestination unite as the
intellectual dynamic of this theatrical movement. Formally, for the

Calvinist Middleton, as for Aristotle, 'the end is more important than anything else', and, as Aristotle prescribed, he concentrates on the two essential ingredients of tragedy, irony and disclosure, prepared for by 'a chain of probability (or necessity)'. 'A Disclosure, as the term indicates', said Aristotle, 'is a change from ignorance to knowledge.' It 'produces its finest effect when it is connected with Irony, as the disclosure of *Oedipus* is'. Ironic disclosure could be of the identity of things or of persons: 'Assuming then that it is a disclosure of persons, it may be of one person only, to the other, when the former knows who the latter is; or sometimes both have to be disclosed.' Middleton, with the aid of Calvinism, is able to strengthen the potency of ironic disclosure, bringing incident and character into more intimate relationship, since the chain of necessity has a purely internal operation and disclosure is of the person to him or herself. For Aristotle 'it is their characters that give men their quality, but their doings that make them happy or the opposite'.[29] Middleton brings the two into alignment, still enabling ironic disclosure by dramatising the Calvinist idea of the unconscious and its eventual irruption into consciousness.

SOURCE: first published in this Casebook.

NOTES

1. Nicholas Tyacke, in Conrad Russell (ed.), *The Origins of the English Civil War*, (London and Basingstoke, 1975), pp. 119–43.

2. Irving Ribner, *Jacobean Tragedy: The Quest for Moral Order* (London, 1962); Margot Heinemann, *Puritanism and Theatre: Thomas Middleton and the Opposition Drama under the Early Stuarts* (Cambridge, 1980).

3. *The Complete Psychological Works of Sigmund Freud*, trans. James Strachey and Anna Freud, 24 vols. (London, 1953–74), xx, p. 255.

4. John Reynolds, *The Triumphs of God's Revenge*, 3 vols. (1621–4), i, pp. 132, 139–40.

5. M. C. Bradbrook, *Themes and Conventions of Elizabethan Tragedy* (Cambridge, 1935), pp. 213–24; Helen Gardner, 'The Tragedy of Damnation', in R. J. Kaufmann (ed.), *Elizabethan Drama: Modern Essays in Criticism* (Oxford, 1961), pp. 320–41. Gardner speaks of 'the absolute contrast at the beginning and the identity at the close of Beatrice-Joanna and De Flores' (p. 329).

6. Richard Levin, *The Multiple Plot in English Renaissance Drama* (Chicago, 1971), p. 45n.

7. J. B. Batchelor, 'The Pattern of *Women Beware Women*' (1972), reproduced, above, in this selection.

8. Luther, quoted by S. S. Snyder, 'The Left Hand of God: Despair in

Medieval and Renaissance Tradition', *Studies in the Renaissance*, XII (1965), p. 48.

9. *The Second Maiden's Tragedy*, ed. Anne Lancashire, Revels Plays (Manchester, 1978): II i 148, 155–7.

10. Calvin, *The Institution of Christian Religion*, trans. Thomas Norton (1562): 2.3.2. Further references to this translation will be embodied in the text.

11. Eliot speaks of 'the not naturally bad but irresponsible and undeveloped nature, caught in the consequences of its own actions' (see Eliot's essay reproduced, above, in this selection). The idea of being 'not naturally bad' is, of course, in direct conflict with Calvin's view of human nature and, I argue, with Middleton's.

12. M. van Beek, *An Enquiry into Puritan Vocabulary* (Groningen, 1969), p. 119.

13. Robert Bolton, *Instructions for a Right Comforting Afflicted Consciences* (1631), p. 211.

14. William Perkins, *The Works* (1605), p. 439.

15. Anne Lancashire's gloss on *security* in *The Second Maiden's Tragedy*, as '(1) confidence; (2) carelessness', fails to observe the Calvinist sense of wilful imperviousness to anxiety about salvation. It is interesting to note that the only use of *security* in this sense in Shakespeare's work is in one of Hecate's speeches in *Macbeth*, which comes from the pen of Middleton [*Macbeth*, III v 32].

16. John Abernathy, *Physic for the Soul* (1615), p. 236.

17. *A Yorkshire Tragedy*, IV 55–62, in *Three Elizabethan Domestic Tragedies*, ed. Keith Sturgess (Harmondsworth, 1969).

18. I am indebted to R. V. Holdsworth who pointed out this parallel to me.

19. This compounding of the meaning of *blood* is not peculiar to Middleton. Vittoria in *The White Devil* dies with the confession, 'O my greatest sin lay in my blood. / Now my blood pays for it' [v vi 240–1].

20. Calvin was aware that his doctrine of election could elicit the objection that God was 'an accepter of persons', but replied that God's choosing 'one man, refusing an other . . . cometh not of respecte of man, but of his mercy alone, which ought to have libertie to shew forth and utter it selfe where and when it pleaseth him'. He went out of his way to insist that those attributes of a person which 'being seen with eyes in man are prone to procure eyther favor, grace, and dignitie, or hatred, contempt, and shame: as richesse, wealth, power, nobilitie, office, contrye, excellency of beauty and such other: on the other syde poverty, nede, basenesse, vilenesse, contempt and such other' had no bearing on God's election and reprobation [*Inst.*, 3.23.10].

21. Bolton, *Instructions*, p. 211; also Calvin, *Inst.*, 2.2.24, quoted above.

22. Alibius, worried about being cuckolded by his young wife, tells Lollio: 'I would wear my ring on my own finger'. Lollio replies: 'You must keep it on still then; if it but lie by, one or other will be thrusting into't' [I ii 27–31].

23. Compare Bellarius's retort to Anselmus's description of the Wife in

The Second Maiden's Tragedy as 'A constant lady!': 'To the devil, as could be!' [v i 126–7].

24. David M. Holmes, *The Art of Thomas Middleton* (Oxford, 1970), p. 184.
25. Quoted by Oscar Pfister, *Christianity and Fear*, trans. W. H. Johnston (New York, 1948), p. 400.
26. For Calvin's view of the will's depravity, see *Inst.*, 2.2 and 2.3. Elsewhere he criticises philosophers who, he says, 'always . . . imagine reason to be that in man, whereby man may rightly govern himself' [1.15.6].
27. Franz Brentano, *The Psychology of Aristotle* (1977), p. 103.
28. John Abernathy, *The Dignity and Duty of a Christian* (1620), p. 126.
29. L. J. Potts (ed.), *Aristotle on the Art of Fiction* (Cambridge, 1968), pp. 25, 28, 31.

R. V. Holdsworth   *Women Beware Women* and *The Changeling* on the Stage   (1989)

Women Beware Women

It is impossible to be certain when, where, or by whom *Women Beware Women* was first performed. Links with *The Changeling* (1622) and *A Game at Chess* (1624) have been taken to indicate composition at about the same time. Both *Women Beware Women* and *The Changeling* chart the decline of a female protagonist into adultery and actual or attempted murder, via a sexual liaison which is first enforced and later enjoyed; both have a subplot heroine named Isabella; and both begin with a situation in which 'hopes of amorous bliss initiate disaster'.[1] A symbolic chess-game, as in *Women Beware Women*, ii ii, is the governing device of *A Game at Chess*, and all three plays closely echo one another in passages which compare their sexually beleaguered heroines to a 'panting turtle' [*Women Beware Women*, ii ii 320–3; *The Changeling*, iii iv 169–71; *A Game at Chess*, iii iii 4–7].

Middleton's habit of self-repetition, however, which often operates across wide distances, jeopardises such arguments. A case for an earlier date for the play could be based, for example, on the ironic presence of the Cupids in the closing masque, which resembles the equally ironic appearance of Cupid in the masques in *The Nice Valour* (1615–16) and Middleton's share of *Timon of Athens* (1605–8), and may have resembled the action of his lost *Masque of Cupid* (1614). There are also parallels of imagery in Middleton's pageant of 1613,

The Triumphs of Truth, which have led one critic to claim that *Women Beware Women* must have been written in or near that year.[2] Nor can one place much weight on the fact that the plot motif of a sexually threatened female (Bianca), flanked by two men (Leantio, the Duke) who represent her choice between virtue and corruption, is matched in *The Changeling* by Beatrice-Joanna's relationship with Alsemero and De Flores, and in *A Game at Chess* by the dilemma of the White Queen's Pawn, who hesitates between the white and black houses. This is, in fact, Middleton's favourite dramatic situation from his earliest plays onwards. Notable instances include Fidelio, Castiza and Proditor in *The Phoenix* (1603–4), Vindice, Castiza and Lussurioso in *The Revenger's Tragedy* (1606), Govianus, the Lady and the Tyrant in *The Second Maiden's Tragedy* (1611), Touchwood Junior, Moll and Sir Walter Whorehound in *A Chaste Maid in Cheapside* (1613), and Fitzallen, Jane and the Physician in *A Fair Quarrel* (1615–16).

Allusions in the text are sometimes cited, unconvincingly, as dating evidence. At ɪ iii 91–3, the Mother gives the Duke's age as 'About some fifty-five', and Bianca comments that a man is 'then at best / For wisdom, and for judgement'. Since this is Middleton's invention (the historical Duke was twenty-three when he met Bianca), critics have detected a compliment to James I, who was fifty-five in June 1621. It is hard, though, to see how the King could feel flattered by comparison with a rapist, and anyway Middleton had an odd fancy for the number fifty-five.[3] The real point of the passage is that whereas in general 'Wisdom in men grows up as years increase' [*A Fair Quarrel*, ɪ i 129], the Duke will prove a shocking exception to this proverbial rule. At ɪɪɪ ii 71–2, Bianca taunts the newly returned Leantio by seemingly deviating into gossip when he demands a welcoming kiss: 'Let's talk of other business . . . What news now of the pirates, any stirring?'. The Revels editor spots a reference to some pirates who were active in 1620–1, but this again is to miss an internal point: as the sexual puns on *business* and *stirring*, harped on elsewhere, make clear, Bianca is dwelling on her own bitter knowledge of what has happened to her in her husband's absence, for she has herself become a pirate's prize ('news' Leantio will get wind of a few lines later). Similarly misguided is the search for an actual pageant to which the Ward apparently alludes at v i 7–9, when, pointing to the trap-door down which Hippolito is to drop, he remarks, 'here rose up a devil with one eye,

I remember, with a company of fireworks at 's tail'. Middleton's aim is partly to suggest the lurking proximity of hell, waiting to receive all the main characters at the end, but also to give the Ward another chance to vent his obsessive coarseness: the whole reference is a phallic joke.

There are, however, stronger pointers to a late date. The Italian and French literary sources of *Women Beware Women* indicate composition after 1614, when Middleton began to make regular use of such material, and the play's borrowings from *The Duchess of Malfi* again imply a link with *The Changeling*, which also echoes Webster's tragedy.[4] Middleton wrote a dedicatory poem for the publication of *The Duchess* in 1623, the year after *The Changeling* was licensed for performance. Finally there is the question of *More Dissemblers Besides Women*. This Middleton tragicomedy, which can be firmly dated 1619–20, also deals with female chastity and sexual betrayal in an Italian setting, and features a moralising Cardinal and yet another Cupid ironically employed in a masque. It was published with *Women Beware Women* in 1657 in a single volume, where it is placed first. If this coupling of the two plays is the result of an earlier one, in the form of performance in successive seasons by the same company, there would have been special point in Middleton giving them similar titles, in order to call attention to the thematic continuities between them. This is guess-work, but it is supported by the fact that *Women Beware Women* seems to glance not only at its own title [at v ii 211–12], but at that of *More Dissemblers Besides Women*: 'dissemble . . . Be but a woman so far' Guardiano urges Livia, and Isabella takes this up with 'I had a mother, / I can dissemble too' [iv ii 156–7, 183–4]. The balance of probabilities thus favours performance about 1621, and by the King's Men, the leading company of the time, who staged both *More Dissemblers Besides Women* and *Anything for a Quiet Life*, a Middleton comedy of the same date.

A further reason to suppose that Middleton was counting on the expertise of London's best company is that *Women Beware Women* is by far his most theatrically ambitious and demanding play. This is not merely a question of the large number of major roles it contains, including four sharply differentiated women (itself a challenge to a Jacobean all-male acting troupe). *Women Beware Women* is also unusually long, nearly a third as long again as the Middleton average, and a fast pace needs to be maintained if substantial cutting is to be avoided.[5] At the same time variations of pace need to be registered, for the action switches between private, often tense exchanges between pairs or small groups of characters and busy *ensemble* scenes, such as the banquet in III iii and the nuptial entertainments in v ii. There is yet another challenge in the sheer size of the company required: if, for example, the Boys and Citizens remain with the Mother and Bianca to watch the ducal procession, some twenty-five actors, plus musicians, are needed to stage the end of Act I.

Middleton is constantly alert to the symbolic possibilities of action and spectacle. A simple but vivid instance is in III iii, where the Ward refuses to dance with his wife-to-be and she is partnered by Hippolito. Since Hippolito and Isabella are engaged in a furtive and incestuous affair, the resulting stage-image shockingly violates the ideas of harmony and decorum of which the dance was conventionally an emblem, but it has a measure of fitness too, for to *dance* was Jacobean slang for copulation. The Ward's idle but all-too-relevant quip, 'Perhaps he knows the manner of her dancing', brings this meaning into focus, though even without it the sexual connotations of the spectacle are clear (as they are, for example, in Pinter's *The Homecoming*, when Lenny dances with Ruth while her husband looks on).

A more complex case of action assuming symbolic status is kissing. A sequence of at least twelve kisses extends through the play, sharpening its themes of estrangement and betrayal, and bringing widely-separated turning-points in the plot into poignant alignment. In the first scene Bianca is kissed twice by the Mother, who will instigate her ruin (it is 'Your fortune to mar all' Leantio prophetically jokes); Bianca then kisses and is kissed by Leantio, whom she will cuckold and whose death she will precipitate. Returning from his trip Leantio anticipates more kisses, only to have them denied [III ii 23–7, 56–69], and in the next scene he is obliged to watch while Bianca is kissed by her new partner [III iii 33, 235]. This prompts a bitter memory of the kisses he once enjoyed and propels him into his affair with Livia, which is sealed by a kiss [III iii 262–6, 366]. The Duke kisses Bianca again when she rebuts the Cardinal's strictures [IV iii 70], and just before the masque Bianca is kissed forgivingly by the Cardinal, whom she intends to murder [v ii 16]. All these kisses are in a sense poisoned, and this is literally true of the play's last kiss, planted by Bianca on the poisoned lips of the

Duke, by which she secures her own death [v ii 193–6]. The subplot supplies an abridged version of the same sequence: Isabella kisses Hippolito as she agrees to their illicit liaison [II i 203], and in the finale Hippolito, himself poisoned by the Cupid's arrows, kisses Isabella's corpse [v ii 134].

Locations as well as gestures are subject to ironic patterning. Both Bianca and Leantio fall into adultery in the same place, Livia's house, a link which is signalled verbally and which on the stage the reappearance of scenery should reinforce. Taken on a tour of Livia's 'rooms and pictures' Bianca is delivered to the Duke, who suggests 'We'll walk together' [II ii 386]. Livia takes Leantio on the same tour: 'let's walk, sir; / You never saw the beauty of my house yet' [III iii 357–8]. A more concerted harping on location involves the image of Bianca in an upper window. This is where she stands as Leantio takes his early-morning leave: 'See and she be not got on purpose now / Into the window to look after me' [I iii 13–14]. One of the play's cruellest manoeuvres follows, for it is this affectionate action which exposes Bianca to the Duke's view. Leantio departs, Bianca remains where she is, and the man who will supplant him supplants him now on the stage, entering to catch sight of her. It is a moment to which the play keeps returning: 'a gentlewoman . . . spied from the widow's window!', Livia muses as she plans her trap [II i 1–2], and the Mother realises that it was when Leantio 'left us both at window' and the Duke 'looked up twice to th' window' that Bianca was spotted [III ii 148–52].

Middleton fixes on this image because it evokes contradictory associations of romantic fidelity and prostitution, and this is apt because it is in the instant that the Duke spies Bianca that she is doomed to be transformed from chaste wife to whore. On the one hand there is the Petrarchan tradition of the earth-bound lover and his elevated mistress, and more specifically the balcony and aubade scenes in *Romeo and Juliet*, which Leantio's parting from Bianca inevitably recalls;[6] on the other there is the suggestion of the whore offering herself at the window, an idea at least as old as the Bible. Compare Jezebel's attempt to seduce King Jehu: 'And when Jehu was come to Jezreel, Jezebel heard of it, and she painted her face, and tired her head, and looked out at a window . . . And he lifted up his face to the window' [2 Kings ix: 30–2]. Bianca herself taunts her husband with this association – harking back privately to the moment of her own undoing – when she demands a better lodging:

''Tis a sweet recreation for a gentlewoman / To stand in a bay-window, and see gallants' [III ii 49–50].[7] Nor does this exhaust Middleton's use of the image. By a brilliant stroke he links it to an earlier betrayal, when Bianca deserted her family and, Leantio recalls, 'my love . . . received thee from thy father's window / Into these arms at midnight' [III iii 258–9]. Later, when Bianca has got her new lodging and bay-window, Leantio relives the event a second time: 'I took her out / Of no such window, I remember, first: / That was a great deal lower, and less carved' [IV i 43–5]. Though the stage-directions of the text suggest otherwise, it is hard not to treat this as a cue for Bianca to appear again at the window, for the bleak exchange of insults with her husband which follows.

The kissing and the dancing evoke ideas of human concord which the characters of *Women Beware Women* fail to match up to, while Bianca and Leantio's separate betrayals of their marriage bond in the alien territory of Livia's house, and Bianca's removal to the upper stage, enforce the sense of human isolation which is the play's dominating concern. Both language and stagecraft work to detach the audience from the characters, and the characters from one another. 'Strange' and 'stranger' are key words. They occur some twenty-five times, and with especial frequency in the two adjacent scenes [II i and II ii] which juxtapose the play's two central acts of betrayal. In the former, Livia convinces Isabella that she is not Livia and Hippolito's niece but 'the merest stranger' [138], so that Isabella feels able to urge her uncle into a different intimacy: she implores him to 'make your love no stranger' [226]. The family ties of aunt, uncle and niece thus give way to a set of relationships based on sexual exploitation, something which semantically has been latent all along, for 'aunt', 'uncle' and 'niece' were common Jacobean slang for 'bawd', 'whoremaster' and 'whore'. Livia's request, 'I pray forget not but to call me aunt still' [167], shows she appreciates the pun.[8]

In the following scene Livia engineers Bianca's ruin by insisting that Bianca, too, is a 'stranger' [II ii 219, 222, 272, 283, 430] to whom such friendly courtesies as a tour of the house are due. The result of both betrayals is that the victims become strangers indeed, both to themselves and in their relations with those around them. Isabella's 'alteration' [II ii 44] dumbfounds her father, and Bianca likewise is 'strangely altered' and undergoes the 'strangest alteration' [III i 7, 63]. Returning to her marital home she finds it 'the strangest house', full of 'defects' [III i 16–17]: perplexed by her new self-image, she is projecting it onto her surroundings. This experience of strangeness is shared by other characters: by Hippolito who, along with his niece, is compared to a sleep-walker;[9] by Leantio, who rebounds abruptly from Bianca to Livia; and by Livia herself, who in her sudden passion for Leantio ironically suffers the same violent access of feeling to which she has exposed her victims. Bianca's dying cry expresses a dislocation which is not hers alone: 'What make I here? These are all strangers to me' [v ii 206].

Various features of the acted play enhance this sense of alienation, imposing it also on the audience, whose response becomes one of dispassionate judgement rather than of sympathy. An important distancing device is namelessness. We naturally treat the discovery of names as fundamental to the formation of relationships and to the knowledge of who a person is, and dramatists are normally anxious to get this information across as early as possible. In *Women Beware Women* it is persistently withheld. A reader as much as a spectator will be struck by the fact that several characters, the Mother, the Duke, the Ward, the Cardinal, never acquire personal names; but as regards the rest, the reader's immediate encountering of their names in the *dramatis personae* list, in stage-directions, and in speech-prefixes will create a sense of contact and familiarity which is at odds with Middleton's intention. If one attends to the spoken text, and thus to the audience's experience of the play in the theatre, quite contrary impressions of anonymity and remoteness are conveyed.

Remarkably, although all the major characters are introduced in Act I, not a single personal name is divulged: Leantio omits to tell his mother his new wife's name, making do with 'her' and twice with 'it' [I i 15, 43], and the courtiers who replace them in I ii identify one another only in terms of family connections ('lady sister', 'brother', 'uncle', etc.). It is not until II i 58 that a character's name, Isabella's, is disclosed, and then it is by a servant and it is never mentioned again: of her two lovers, one continues to call her 'niece' and the other 'gentlewoman'. Livia's name is not released until III ii 106 and Hippolito's not until III iii 203, and even at IV i 128 its owner needs to be identified ('Hippolito, / Brother to Lady Livia'). Bianca is the play's most frequently named character, but use of her name is confined entirely to the two consecutive scenes, III ii and III iii, in which she passes from Leantio's possession to the Duke's. Her name parallels this transference. We do not learn it until III ii 34, after her marriage with Leantio has broken down, when he observes 'y'are not well, Bianca'. He then uses it repeatedly for the rest of the scene, and it is taken up by the Duke with the same frequency in the scene which follows. Disclosure of Leantio's name is even more delayed. It is not mentioned until IV i 162, when Hippolito needs to know whom he must kill, and it is not used by Bianca until her dying speech: 'Leantio, now I feel the breach of marriage / At my heart-breaking' [v ii 210–11]. Nor is she here harking back nostalgically to her marriage with him: she means that now, beholding her dead second husband, she feels an agony of marital separation like that which she had inflicted on her first. One other character's name, Guardiano's, is discoverable only by a reader; it is never mentioned in the play's dialogue. All this reticence is the more striking because of the play's openness about place: Venice, Florence, Bologna and St Mark's are referred to in Act I, Naples and Rome in Act II. We know where the characters are, but who they are, in terms of our having names to attach to them, is deliberately held back.

The action, too, transmits impressions of distance and division. Asides are extraordinarily frequent, pulling characters away from one another even (and especially) at moments of apparently intimate contact, and Middleton continually ensures that characters remain on stage for long periods without speaking, or converse in separate groups isolated from others who are also present. The first two scenes set the trend. In I i, Leantio's response to his mother's welcome is an avoidance of contact, an aside, after which the two discuss Bianca who has entered with her husband but says nothing until line 125. In I ii, Hippolito and Isabella enter at line 69 but are virtually silent for another hundred lines, and the Ward and Sordido enter at line 87, supposedly to inspect the mute and masked Isabella, take over the dialogue for forty lines but ignore her and speak only to each other, and then exit. Every subsequent scene involves similar failures to interact. A recent study of *Women Beware Women* labels such tactics 'the stagecraft of apartness': 'stagecraft' is well chosen, for in a film or television version of the play the use of close-ups would blot out the fragmented stage-picture these techniques aim to create.[10]

Repeated employment of the upper stage, more sustained and elaborate than in any other play of the period, makes the apartness physical as well as mental. Crucial action takes place on the upper level on three occasions: each presents Bianca at a key moment in her journey from chaste wife to court whore to would-be murderess, and each involves simultaneous lower-stage action which comments obliquely on what we see above. At I iii 73ff. Bianca and the Mother linger on their balcony while below a citizen awaits the passing-by of the Duke and his train. The Duke, a boy tells him, is 'hard at hand', whereupon he instructs his apprentice to 'get a standing for your mistress, / The best in all the city', and the apprentice assures him ''Tis ready at her pleasure'. 'Fetch her to't then', the citizen replies. More than time-filling chat is occurring here, nor are the sexual puns built into each of these phrases merely a means of providing a few belly-laughs for the groundlings. The dialogue predicts Bianca's fate, giving it an air of being predestined. The Duke will be aroused ('hard at hand' and 'standing') when he spies Bianca, she will be fetched to him, and she will enjoy both his social and his sexual 'standing' – 'The best in all the city' – as a result. 'Did not I say my duke would fetch you over?' Livia will ask the Mother over their chess-game [II ii 388], and Bianca will receive 'the best content / That Florence can afford' [III ii 40–1].

The predictions in this little episode are fulfilled in II ii, when Bianca reappears on the upper stage to be delivered to the Duke. Again lower-stage business intervenes. We watch Bianca's entrapment over the heads of Livia and the Mother as they play chess, and their game spells out what is about to happen above, reinforcing its predestined quality and fostering an attitude of analytical detachment. Nor does this symbolic chess-game seem abruptly stuck in, for game-playing images proliferate in the spoken text, as well as receiving further visual embodiment in the form of the Ward's cat-stick and battledores. As early as I i 57 the Mother asks Leantio 'If your obedience will give way to a check', and this is quickly followed by Guardiano's demand for 'fair play' in the betrothal of the Ward and Isabella, Livia's advice to 'mark how the game goes', the Ward's declaration 'I think of nobody when I am in play', and Leantio's reluctant abandonment of 'game / In a new-married couple' [I ii 2, 37, 102; I iii 9]. Such images recur up to the final massacre, itself compared to 'a set match' [v ii 157]. Their function is twofold. Most obviously, they point to a besetting frivolousness of mind in those who habitually reduce life's serious issues to a matter of playing games; and more subtly, they imply that the

characters are themselves like the pieces in a game where freedom
of manoeuvre is limited in advance. Constrained by their weak and
corrupt natures, their careers can only unfold along fixed lines, so
that at the end each character will, like Livia's black duke, have
merely 'showed himself in 's kind' [II ii 417].

It is tempting to try and work out the correspondences between
the chess-game and Bianca's fall in exact detail,[11] but some of the
parallels are left deliberately ambiguous. Livia's 'duke', for example,
the piece now known only as the rook or castle, is primarily
Guardiano, but its name invites simultaneous identification with the
Duke (who is at the same time the 'black king' of II ii 299). Similarly,
Bianca, whose name means 'white', is the Mother's pawn at line
302, but thanks to the queen/quean pun she can also be seen as
the piece Livia terms 'my queen' two lines before. The confusion is
apt, as a transformation of a white pawn into a black queen (and
quean) is what is taking place above. Nor should one restrict the
chess-game's symbolism to the play's main action. Isabella's as well
as Bianca's habituation to sin is summed up in Livia's telling remark
that 'Your pawn cannot come back to relieve itself' [302], and
Livia's dupings of both women into the adulterous acquisition of a
second partner are comprehended in her prediction that she will
win the game by ensuring that 'simplicity receives two for one'
[309]. Leantio has already joked about owning a horse which 'bore
double' [I iii 52], and Isabella will boast that she has 'catched two
in my lap at one game' [III iv 91]. The final masque will enforce
this parallelism by portraying 'a nymph . . . In love with two at
once' [V ii 33–4], a part taken by Isabella and watched by Bianca.

The masque is the last of these two-level spectacles. Bianca, the
Duke, the Cardinal and their train '*Enter above*' to see it performed
on the lower stage, facing out towards the audience as they watch.
What we and they see is officially intended as a celebration of the
Duke and Bianca's union, with the larger purpose, conventional to
court masques, of celebrating the order and concord made possible
by the Duke's rule. At the end the harmonies enacted in the masque
ought to reach out to include the courtly audience, as masquers and
spectators join in a dance. But just as the Duke and Bianca's union
has begun in adultery and been sustained by murder, and 'lust and
forgetfulness' have prevailed at the Duke's court, so the masque
provides a true 'celebration' of this by collapsing into anarchy and
killing; and the royal spectators do indeed become incorporated in

the final spectacle, as the poisonings spread to include Bianca and the Duke.

Many specific ironies strengthen the masque's appositeness. Not only does its plot re-enact the stories of Isabella and Bianca, those who act it perform versions of themselves. The masque is one which had been cancelled when 'death . . . turned the glory of it all to black' [IV ii 206–7] – a transmutation about to be repeated. Livia had been due to play Juno, the marriage goddess, who decides between two suitors competing for the same girl, and now she will take her 'old part still' and play 'good aunt Juno' to Isabella's nymph [IV ii 215, v ii 101]. This is indeed Livia's old part, for she has played the aunt (in the sense of bawd) to both Isabella and Bianca, directing their choices between the Ward and Hippolito, and Leantio and the Duke. Similarly, Hippolito, as one of the nymph's suitors, is struck by Cupid's arrows, an event 'Fitting his part' [v i 34] in fact as well as in fiction, especially since the arrows – like his love for Isabella – are poisoned. His death has the same emblematic fitness. When he confessed his incestuous passion to Livia, she promised to 'minister all cordials' to him [II i 48]. The first of these cordials, the delivery of Isabella, amounted to moral and spiritual poison; now Livia completes her ministrations by conniving in his physical poisoning as well. Livia had also exclaimed, 'does love turn thy point to thine own blood?' [II i 7], the triple pun on 'point' (compass-needle, penis, and sword) deftly suggesting that Hippolito's attraction to his niece is at once irresistible and a form of suicide. This comment, too, receives physical fulfilment when Hippolito in his death agony impales himself 'upon a weapon's point' [v ii 169].[12]

The original staging of this last, hectic scene is hard to establish from the octavo text, where directions are scanty, but recent analysis has solved most of the problems. In the antemasque, how did Hebe and Ganymede reach up from the lower to the upper stage to offer their 'cups of nectar' to the Duke and Cardinal, a distance of some twelve feet? Leslie Thomson plausibly suggests that they clambered onto 'Juno's altar', a structure mentioned in the stage direction at v ii 50 for use in the masque proper which follows.[13] Though such an action would hardly look decorous, it would aptly symbolise the desecration of marriage, providing a visual echo of the Cardinal's earlier complaint that 'lust's offerings are / On wedlock's sacred altar' [IV iii 23–4]. It is less easy to guess how Middleton expected the confusion of cups to be managed, whereby Hebe, who has the poisoned one intended for the Cardinal, gives it to the Duke. There is irony, of course, in the fact that she is charged to 'give that to innocence', and gives the cup instead to the guilty brother, not the innocent one, but is Ganymede's learned joke about Hebe's 'stumbling' [v ii 59], which in classical myth created the Milky Way, prompted by an actual stumble which causes the mistake? If so, the joke is an ad-libbed remark which fails to alert Bianca to the fact that something has gone wrong.

Some of the deaths also cause problems. Why does the Ward drop Guardiano rather than Hippolito down through the trap? G. B. Shand[14] has the right answer: Guardiano's 'All's fast' [v ii 123] implies that he is standing on the trap as he checks it, and just at this moment Hippolito discovers that Isabella is dead ('Oh treachery, cruelly made away!') and accompanies this discovery with a stamp, a traditional stage-gesture to mark grief or anger. The Ward, under the stage, takes this to be the stamp Guardiano was to give to signal that Hippolito is in position, and promptly opens the trap, spiking Guardiano on the caltrop below.

A further difficulty concerns the deaths of the Duke and Bianca. Dying on the balconied upper stage, as in the octavo text they seem to do, they would sink down out of sight of the audience. Leslie Thomson[15] ingeniously supposes a prior series of descents to the lower level: Fabritio comes down at line 145, on learning that his daughter is dead; the Duke at line 167, having heard Hippolito's dying speech (a lord is able to hand him Guardiano's confession at line 176); and then Bianca at line 186, as the Duke falls and she rushes to join him, telling the attendants who crowd round his body to 'give me way'. These descents, along with Guardiano's more spectacular one, would symbolise the moral debasement that has been occurring throughout the play, as well as permitting the five corpses (not counting Guardiano's) which strew the stage to be shown as levelled in death. Isabella, one recalls, has imagined 'a whole household down together' [I ii 184], and a descent which was moral as well as physical has already occurred in the chess scene, when Bianca returns to the lower stage ('there's somebody coming down' Guardiano observes). Repeated reference in the finale to downward movement – the word 'down' itself appears nine times in the last 120 lines, receiving heavy emphasis in the closing speeches – also supports the staging which Thomson proposes. She may be wrong, however, to suggest that the Cardinal comes down too, leaving the upper stage, and thus the play's moral high ground, 'symbolically empty'. Keeping him above would add weight and didactic authority to his austere closing lines, reaffirming Bianca's initial view of him, which she and everyone else will fatally ignore, that 'He's worthy to be marked' [I iii 96].

The theatrical complexities of *Women Beware Women* may account for its relative neglect on the stage. A census of Middleton productions up to 1985 lists twenty-six revivals, beginning with a radio version in 1955, as against forty-one of *The Revenger's Tragedy* and seventy-three of *The Changeling*.[16] There have been two major professional productions, both by the RSC. The first of these, directed by Anthony Page at the London Arts Theatre in 1962, suffered from a cramped, single-level set, prosaic delivery of the verse, and Bernard Bresslaw's over-exuberant Ward, but it was carefully attentive to divisions of class. Nicol Williamson as Leantio, challenged by Hippolito, attempted unaristocratically to run away, but Hippolito forced him to fight. Kenneth Tynan (*Observer*, 8 July 1962) describes what followed: 'you know from the panicky way in which [Leantio] fumbles and flinches that this is the first time he has ever wielded the expensive sword that hangs at his waist; he grips the hilt with both hands, and looks stupid as he is spitted, dying not comically or tragically, but in a state of bewildered unbelief'.

The second RSC production, by Terry Hands at Stratford in 1969, was played on a stage of black-and-white tiles resembling a chess-board, part of which rose up as a platform for the masque, the masque's courtly spectators sitting around it at ground level. A large statue of a naked Venus, ceremonial processions and gorgeous red velvet costuming stressed the decadence and power of the ducal state, and Richard Pasco's Leantio with his factor's bag and homely brown suit looked helpless before it. Pasco played Leantio as a pathetic victim, romantically naive and eager rather than vulgar or mercenary. As Bianca, Judi Dench was also vulnerably innocent, up to (and including) her encounter with the Duke. Grabbed by him from behind, both stared out towards the audience, Brewster Mason's Duke calm, firm and matter-of-fact, Bianca stunned and appalled. As he hustled her off after his last long speech, to which she makes no reply, there was no hint of compliance in her behaviour, though a steadily hardening cynicism began to assert itself as soon as she reappeared. Both RSC productions fought shy of the play's constant asides, omitting many of them and tinkering with others to make them part of the dialogue. One of Middleton's chief techniques for indicating the mutual isolation of his characters was thereby thwarted.[17]

The Changeling

As she dies, Bianca in *Women Beware Women* ponders the disjunction between her outward beauty and inward ugliness: 'my deformity in spirit's more foul – / A blemished face best fits a leprous soul' [v ii 204–5]. Middleton was fond of this contrast. 'The clearest skin may have the foulest soul', he notes in his earliest work, *The Wisdom of Solomon Paraphrased* [III vi 3], a perception repeated by the Father in *Michaelmas Term* when he finds his daughter decked out as a courtesan: 'Thou fair and wicked creature, steept in art! / Beauteous and fresh, the soul the foulest part' [III i 292–3]. In *The Changeling* both plots are a focus for the same preoccupation. Alsemero takes Beatrice-Joanna's beauty as proof of her virtue, protesting that 'modesty's shrine is set in yonder forehead' [IV ii 125]; later he recognises that though 'fair-fac'd' she is also 'all deform'd', and Beatrice herself acknowledges that whoredom 'blasts a beauty to deformity' [v iii 32, 77, 109]. In the subplot Antonio supposes that he need only discard his madman's disguise to become worthy of Isabella: 'in your eyes / I shall behold mine own deformity, / And dress myself up fairer' [III iii 185–7]. She, however, applies a more searching criterion, summed up in her response to Franciscus's letter: 'Compare his inside with his out' [IV iii 6]. Calvinism, which taught that the accidents of appearance and character merely camouflaged man's essential spiritual ugliness, no doubt fostered this habit of thought in Middleton, and perhaps also its verbal expression. Calvin preached, for example, that with the Fall the image of God in which we were created 'was so deeply corrupted that all that remains of it is a horrible deformity' [*Institutes*, 1 15 4].

The Changeling is Middleton's most powerful theatrical treatment of this theme. In his earlier plays it remains primarily a matter of verbal assertion, but here it is embodied in a recurrent stage image: the visual contrast between Beatrice-Joanna and De Flores. The point is that the contrast is merely visual, for the fair lady and the foul-visaged servant turn out to be alike under the skin, and 'twins of mischief' [v iii 142]. At the same time Middleton utilises the very neo-Platonism he is bent on rejecting, for, as with Dorian's picture in *The Picture of Dorian Gray*, De Flores's hideousness is the physical equivalent of Beatrice's inner evil, the mirror in which she sees her true self. In recoiling from him in the first scene she is, as she finally realises ('my loathing / Was prophet to the rest'), recoiling from an image of her own deformed nature; and in reconciling herself to his ugliness with the words 'When w'are us'd / To a hard face, 'tis not so unpleasing' [II ii 87–8], she is simultaneously describing her own habituation to sin. The De Flores of the source, John Reynolds's *The Triumphs of God's Revenge*, is merely 'a gallant young gentleman' whom Beatrice finds 'a fit instrument to execute her will'. Adapting the story for the stage, Middleton contrives a deeper fitness, which the new medium can vividly exploit.

De Flores's symbolic status is further emphasised by the timing of his entrances. They are almost always solitary, and are subject to an ironic cueing which signals his baleful function. He appears first at I i 92, just as Jasperino declares his intention to 'board' Diaphanta as a 'prize', a piece of piracy De Flores will imitate by seizing the 'prize' of Beatrice's honour [v iii 167]. His ostensible purpose, to announce Vermandero's arrival, is, Beatrice points out, superfluous: 'you must stall / A good presence with unnecessary blabbing' [I i 97–8]. This, too, is prophetic, for it will be De Flores's threat to blab, to 'confess all' [III iv 149], which will cheat her of Alsemero and complete her entrapment. After a brief aside describing his compulsion to be near the bride-to-be, De Flores then says nothing for 120 lines, but it would be quite wrong to remove him from the stage in the interim. Like the bad fairy at the feast, the custodian of the bride's dark future, he remains to menace by his very presence the scene of dalliance which follows.

His later entrances display the same ominous responsiveness. At II i 26 Beatrice contemplates the 'new comforts' of Alsemero's devotion; at II ii 56 Alsemero declares 'My love's as firm as love e'er built upon'; at III iv 17 Beatrice luxuriates in 'the refulgent virtue of my love; and in IV i bride and groom head the wedding procession '*in great state*'. On each of these exalted moments Middleton's staging makes the same grim comment, by means of a sardonic juxtaposition: '*Enter* DE FLORES', and 'DE FLORES *after all, smiling at the accident*'. As events turn against him, De Flores becomes the target of his own ironic cueing. Having been magnetised by Beatrice, he is so now by

Tomazo, entering at IV ii 35 while Tomazo is seeking an object for his revenge, and at v ii 8 just as Tomazo announces that 'the next I meet' will be the murderer. His timing is equally bad, from his point of view, at v iii 88, when Alsemero decides that De Flores's entrance has 'put me in' (given me my cue) in his effort to understand the tale of murder he has just heard. His final entrance at v iii 142 completes this pattern of declining dramatic authority. For the first and only time he enters at another's bidding, when Alsemero like a stage-presenter calls out 'Come forth, you twins of mischief!', and De Flores complies, bearing the dying Beatrice in his arms. The devil has claimed his own, but is himself now subject to a virtuous master of ceremonies.

This use of De Flores is part of a larger strategy of symbolic staging which embraces all of the play's visual effects. A simple instance is the tell-tale splash of blood on De Flores's collar [v iii 95]. Beatrice has been described as 'dipp'd in blood' [III iv 126]; true to his job of giving her guilt physical form, he now makes the metaphor actual. A more complex case is the episode in Act IV in which Beatrice finds the testing-kit for pregnancy and virginity in Alsemero's cabinet, administers the virginity-potion to Diaphanta in order to study the symptoms indicating a positive result, and then feigns them when Alsemero tries the test on her. Despite a recent effort to prove the contrary, it is unlikely that a London audience watching this in 1622 found it any more credible, on a literal level, than we do now.[18] The power of the episode lies not in its verisimilitude, but in its effectiveness as a theatrical device which enforces the distinction between Beatrice's false and true selves. Simulating the symptoms to deceive Alsemero, Beatrice acts out the part of an innocent virgin, but this is merely a more obviously fraudulent version of what she has been doing, in the complacent belief that it constituted her true self, all along; and the symptoms themselves, gaping and sneezing, a fit of laughter then of melancholy, turn her momentarily into one of the lunatics of the subplot, whose antics have already been used to spell out the more insidious madness of the main-plot protagonists.

Further visual details assist the episode's didactic point. Since Beatrice tries the test on Diaphanta and herself straight after the wedding procession, she must still be attired accordingly, in a white dress and with her hair down, as was the custom, to signify her virginity; yet it is the virgin bride whom the test demonstrates to be no virgin. The first potion Beatrice comes upon is a test for pregnancy, involving 'two spoonfuls of the white water in glass C', a glass she is tempted to 'break' [IV i 31–7]. But in holding up this glass Beatrice is exhibiting an emblem of her own deflowered (and possibly pregnant) condition, for in Jacobean bawdy 'water' meant semen, 'glass' the hymen, and the letter C represented the commonest slang term for a woman's genitals, puns – here embodied in a stage property – of which Middleton was fond.[19] In *No Wit, No Help* Twilight wishes to marry off his secretly-married daughter, 'for fear the glass should crack / That is already broken' [I i 108–9]. Beatrice's glass, too, is already broken, and as a result of her having undergone a universal form of the test she describes. Deaf to the word-play, she resolves that 'None of that water comes into my belly'. Middleton meant the line to be spoken with the emphasis on 'that', for De Flores's water has already done precisely this.

The play's most striking use of dramatic symbolism, however, involves a linked sequence. It begins at the end of the first scene when Beatrice drops her glove, De Flores tenders it back to her, and she spurns him by throwing the other one down as well. The director has a choice here: does he make Beatrice drop the glove accidentally or deliberately, and if the latter does she do it hoping that De Flores will pick it up, so that she can revile him, or intending that Alsemero should do so, as a sign of her love for him?[20] This last interpretation seems best. De Flores's unforeseen intervention then transforms this little scene, which is not in the source, into an enactment of what is to follow, when Beatrice plots to bestow on Alsemero the favour of her love, but De Flores appropriates it. The sexual implications are made coarsely clear by De Flores: 'She had rather wear my pelt tann'd in a pair / Of dancing pumps, than I should thrust my fingers / Into her sockets here' – lines which invite the actor to pull on the glove in a brutal defloratory gesture.

The subplot takes up the image in the next scene, as a means of encouraging a comparison between Beatrice and Isabella, who will stay true to her vows. Brooding on cuckoldry, Alibius observes, 'I would wear my ring on my own finger', and Lollio advises him, 'You must keep it on still then; if it but lie by, one or other will be thrusting into't' [I ii 27–31]. Lollio will try but fail to achieve this phallic thrusting, but with Beatrice De Flores will succeed, actually and emblematically. In III ii he cuts off the dead Alonzo's finger, bearing the ring which Beatrice sent him as the 'first token' of her faith. Horrified when he shows it her, Beatrice urges De Flores to be its 'keeper' [III iv 39]; a grimly prophetic instruction, for the finger in the ring symbolises both sexual and spiritual union. When he fell in love with Beatrice, Alsemero had hoped that the church would 'join us into one' [I i 11], and Beatrice's ring has 'stuck' to Alonzo's finger 'as if the flesh and it were both one substance' [III iv 38]. Now, holding the severed finger with its ring, De Flores tells Beatrice that her guilt has 'made you one with me'; it is they who must 'stick together' [III iv, 84, 140].

This visual motif recurs poignantly in the wedding procession, when the ghost of Alonzo, the dispossessed bridegroom, accosts De Flores, *'showing him the hand whose finger he had cut off'*. It may be present, too, in Beatrice and De Flores's death scene, when he urges her to 'Make haste . . . by that token to thee' [v iii 175]. The readiest interpretation of 'token' seems to be the wound De Flores has just inflicted on himself, as a pledge of his devotion; but since Alonzo's ring is three times called a token in III iv, perhaps the same ring is being drawn attention to here, but now it is on De Flores's finger. If this is so, an appropriate moment for De Flores to wrench the ring from Alonzo's severed digit and slide it on his own is at III iv 140, when he tells Beatrice she is made one with him – effectively the moment of their marriage. But whatever the truth of this, the finger-ring sequence is a remarkable demonstration of Middleton's use of stage imagery to add conceptual depth and theatrical vitality to his source. In Reynolds, Beatrice denies that 'she had the least shadow or finger' in Alonzo's disappearance, so that she and Alsemero can be 'united, and by the bond of marriage of two persons made one'. Middleton found in the first of these statements the hint for an image which could be embodied in the action and provide an ironic and macabre commentary upon the second.[21]

Locations receive similar emblematic enhancement. Reynolds switches events pointlessly between Alicante, where Vermandero is 'the captain of the castle', Valencia, and Briamata. In *The Changeling*, after the prelude outside the church ('Your devotion's ended?', Vermandero ambiguously asks his daughter), Middleton and Rowley site the main plot continuously inside the castle and the subplot in Alibius's madhouse nearby. The aim is not only to imply an equivalence between the two, but to exploit an allegorical tradition concerning castles, as metaphors for the human soul fortified by virtue and beseiged or usurped by vice, which went back to the Middle Ages. Castles of Virginity, of Truth, of Mansoul (the soul as resident in the body) and of Hell are commonplaces of medieval and early Renaissance literature and drama, and a homily by the fourteenth-century theologian John Bromyard shows the kind of elaboration the idea typically received:

The janitor is the Will, because, whatever may knock at the gate of Sight or Hearing or the other senses, the Will is immediately on the spot to let in or shut out, that is, what should be shunned or avoided. If a good thing comes up and the Will desires it, the gate is opened to God; if evil, and the Will desires that, the Devil is let in. . . . When Pleasures or Delights or things Angry or Vengeful present themselves to the Will, whether at the gate of the Senses, or the postern of the Heart, the Will ought not to open immediately, in seeking that thing or showing agreement with it or desire for it. . . . When the other external senses and actions are in suspense, good thoughts or evil enter the Castle of the Soul secretly, by way of the Heart. Whence sometimes the Soul is defended and fortified, sometimes lost. That castle God created so strong, and placed officers in it so well, that neither Hell, nor the World, nor demons, nor men can capture or conquer it, unless it is betrayed from inside.[22]

Middleton liked to imagine people as buildings (note, for example, the joke about the Duke as 'the Monument' in *Women Beware Women*), and such castle-metaphors are used frequently by his characters. Castiza, the representative in *The Revenger's Tragedy* of Chastity Beseiged, chimes with Bromyard in declaring 'A virgin honour is a crystal tower, / Which, being weak, is guarded with good spirits; / Unless she basely yields, no ill inherits' [IV iv 152–4]. In *The Second Maiden's Tragedy* Anselmus says of his wife, who is being tempted into adultery, 'The castle is but upon yielding yet; / 'Tis not delivered up' [v i 35–6]. These examples, from early plays, are confined to dialogue, but Middleton took up pageant-writing shortly afterwards, and the emblem-tradition on which the form drew encouraged him to realise his later castles physically. There is a property Castle of Fame and Honour in his pageant *The Triumphs of Honour and Industry* (1617), and a Tower of Virtue in *The Sun in Aries* (1621). Symbolic castle-settings begin to figure in Middleton's plays around this date. The chaste Duchess of *More Dissemblers Besides Women* is said to have 'kept the fort most valiantly' [I i 11], and the metaphor is made actual in the subplot where the wayward Aurelia is loved by the Governor of the Fort (also called 'the castle') and is shut up in it by her father. In *Hengist, King of Kent* a Hell's Castle, recalling Macbeth's Dunsinane, appears. In it the three villains (including the lustful Roxena, who, like Diaphanta, is burned alive) are destroyed at the end in a conflagration which presents, in the words of a recent critic, 'an image of the sinful, irreligious world doomed to apocalyptic burning'.[23]

The Changeling contains Middleton's most elaborate development of the castle-emblem, to the point where the house of Vermandero, the asylum of Alibius, and indeed the stage of the acted play may be viewed as representing Beatrice herself. Beatrice early hints at the analogy by calling her eyes 'sentinels' which may let down what they are guarding by proving 'rash' and 'blind' [I i 72–6], a truth she will proceed to ignore. The identification is confirmed when she tells her father that Alsemero is 'much desirous / To see your castle', and he agrees that the visitor 'must see my castle, / And her best entertainment' [I i 159–60, 201–2]. Since Alsemero has expressed no such wish, it is clear that Beatrice is using 'castle' as a code-word for herself (a knowing look at Alsemero should accompany the line) and Vermandero's choice of the feminine pronoun maintains the allusion. At first Vermandero hesitates, because 'we use not to give survey / Of our chief strengths to strangers; our citadels / Are plac'd conspicuous to outward view . . . but within are secrets' [I i 163–6]. This, too, has an obvious application to Beatrice. She will give survey of herself to a stranger (De Flores), and her secret evil self concealed within the innocent outward one will thereby be exposed. Once this has occurred, Vermandero may well exclaim, 'An host of enemies enter'd in my citadel / Could not amaze like this!' [v iii 147–8]. In the terms of Bromyard's exposition, the castle of his daughter's soul has been 'betrayed from inside'.

Thus launched in the opening scene, the castle-symbolism extends throughout the play. Alonzo, the defeated suitor, finds the castle 'impregnable', and a desire to be acquainted with its 'full strength' causes his death [II ii 158, III i 4]. De Flores and Beatrice, however, have keys which admit them to its secret recesses. De Flores's allows him to descend to the castle's centre, while Beatrice's unlocks a closet in which she finds a book called 'Secrets of Nature' [IV i 25], a book which will confirm the fraudulence of her exterior self. As this false self begins to dissolve, she cries 'I'm in a labyrinth!' [III iv 71]. The reference is doubly apt: Beatrice is being forced to explore her own dark interior, and the classical labyrinth harboured a monster which fed on maidens' flesh. Isabella, too, is hunted by sexual predators in 'the lower labyrinth' of Alibius's madhouse [IV iii 107], but no hidden evil in herself is thereby disclosed. Severed completely from her old self in the final scene, Beatrice declares that she is 'ruin'd' and beyond repair. Alsemero takes up the metaphor: 'I'll all demolish, and seek out truth within you' [v iii 34–6].

The truth is that Beatrice's infected will, activated in the first scene [I i 220] and fulfilled through De Flores, has turned the Castle of Virginity into the Castle of Hell. 'We are left in hell', De Flores finally perceives [v iii 163]. As in *Hengist*, Judgement Day portents matching those foretold in the Book of Revelation usher in this discovery. Darkness shrouds the action in v i (at lines 11–12 Beatrice and De Flores have difficulty finding one another), the dead rise in the form of Alonzo's ghost, a star appears [lines 25, 59], and fire and thunder follow as De Flores sets light to Diaphanta's chamber and shoots his musket. Time itself accelerates as judgement draws near. At IV i 52 it is 'seven hours to bedtime', but in v i a clock strikes the hours of one, two and three in the space of seventy lines. Language and staging then combine in a deliberate allusion to Revelation. De Flores is called a 'serpent' who will 'sink to fathoms bottomless' [v iii 66, 120], and Alsemero, no doubt using his key, locks Beatrice and later De Flores into his closet – the same closet in which Beatrice found the book of secrets – briefly releasing them before consigning them to hell. Compare Revelation xx, the climactic chapter describing Doomsday:

I saw an angel come down from heaven, having the key of the bottomless pit . . . And he laid hold on the dragon, that old serpent, which is the Devil, and Satan . . . And cast him into the bottomless pit, and shut him up . . . and after that he must be loosed a little season . . . And whosoever was not found written in the book of life was cast into the lake of fire.[24]

The play has begun [I i 7–9, 225] by associating Alsemero with Adam in Paradise and De Flores with the serpent who corrupted Eve (and, according to one tradition, copulated with her). Beatrice as Eve loses 'her first condition' [III iv 138] on contact with the serpent, betrays her husband in 'the garden', and becomes 'that broken rib of mankind' [v iii 2, 146]. The staging of Act v completes this biblical framework, so that the play, for all its localised, domestic setting, encompasses the entire spiritual history of mankind, from the Creation to the Last Judgement.

Stage business serves also to cement the links between main plot and subplot. Sometimes the verbal echoes are so pointed – as when

De Flores, anticipating a sexual share in Beatrice, says 'I'll put in for one' [II ii 60], and Lollio, hoping for the same from Isabella, decides 'I put in for my thirds' [IV iii 36]; or when Isabella proclaims her innocence by crying 'Come not near me' [IV iii 133], and Beatrice affirms her guilt with exactly these words [v iii 149] – that they seem an open invitation to the actors to signal the connection by means of similar gestures. Elsewhere gestures alone are used. At II ii 117 De Flores kneels to Beatrice as he begs for 'service', and at III iv 156 the stage-image, like the balance of power in their relationship, is reversed: Beatrice kneels to him. In between these moments we see Franciscus, one of the subplot's would-be seducers, kneel before Isabella and Lollio [III iii 56]. Kissing consolidates the parallel. In III iii both Antonio and Lollio try to kiss Isabella; she spurns them, and remains chaste. In the next scene De Flores tries to kiss Beatrice; she spurns him, but soon feels compelled to yield.

The Jacobean theatre's upper and inner stages, its balcony and discovery space at the rear of the main stage, provide further occasions for parallelism. At III iii 177 Lollio enters *above* to observe Antonio's sexual attempt on Isabella. If, despite the text's lack of directions, we place De Flores here in II ii to spy on Alsemero's courtship of Beatrice (he must observe them from somewhere, as he enters saying 'I have watch'd this meeting'), the two stage-pictures exactly mirror each other, pointing up the contrasting outcomes. Such a placing would also be a visual fulfilment of Beatrice's awareness that 'there's one above me' [I i 83]. She means her father, but her words are applicable both to God and to God's demonic agent who will bring her destiny home to her, De Flores.

About similar use of the inner stage we can be more definite. This is the closet of IV i–ii which Beatrice and Jasperino enter, each time using a key, to find the book of secrets. In the next scene the same place becomes Lollio's wardrobe which Isabella enters, with a key, to emerge dressed as a madwoman (though in her case the role is false). In v iii it becomes the closet once more, where Beatrice and De Flores are imprisoned, and her demented cries are heard *within*. This again associates Beatrice with the subplot's lunatics, whose cries *within*, no doubt issuing from the same alcove, have been continually heard [I ii 195, III iii 109, 165]. 'Enter my closet, / I'll be your keeper yet', Alsemero tells Beatrice [v iii 87]. By 'keeper' he means 'jailor', with a bitter pun on 'pimp' (keeper of prostitutes, and of the brothel-door). We can, however, understand a third sense, 'keeper of lunatics', for the word is used thus of Lollio in earlier scenes [ɪ ii 131, ɪɪɪ iii 87].[25]

Underpinning all these cross-references which make castle and madhouse merge is the Jacobean theatre's absence of scenery. With no visual instructions to suppose otherwise, the play's first audience was continuously primed to view the two settings as, fictionally as well as literally, the same place. The dramatists abet the confusion by having both sets of characters constantly refer to their whereabouts as 'the house'. In the main plot, for example, Jasperino tells of overhearing Beatrice and De Flores 'in a back part of the house', and Beatrice fears that fire 'may endanger the whole house' [ɪv ii 91, v i 33]. In the subplot, Lollio is sure that Isabella 'takes some pleasure in the house, she would abroad else' [ɪv iii 72]. Glimpsing Alonzo's ghost, Beatrice cries 'Some ill thing haunts the house' [v i 62], typically failing to register that her words more accurately describe both De Flores and herself. The subplot is afflicted by a less baleful visitation: Antonio is 'but a fool that haunts the house' [ɪv iii 198].

'House' could, at the date of the play, signify the playhouse and its audience, a sense still current today ('Is there a doctor in the house?') and one to which all the above examples slyly allude. The pun is not casual. It breaks down the play's fictional wall and incorporates the audience in the world-as-madhouse analogy which connects the two plots. An early joke points up the ambiguity, alerting us to later references. Lollio notes, 'We have but two sorts of people in the house . . . that's fools and madmen' [ɪ ii 44–5]. A knowing glance outwards should accompany the line, to indicate that it covers more than the two houses of the play itself. Lollio repeats the quip at ɪɪɪ iii 12–14 ('in the house . . . here's none but fools and madmen'), and Isabella offers a variation of it by mentioning 'your scholars in the upper room' [ɪɪɪ iii 110], 'room' being the Jacobean term for the modern theatre 'box'. The play's final version of this tactic is its most telling. The dying De Flores observes, 'We are left in hell', and Vermandero adds, 'We are all there, it circumscribes here' [v iii 163–4]. More than Vermandero's house, or the Jacobean theatre's projecting stage, or even the audience surrounding it, is embraced by 'circumscribes'. Playhouses at this date were themselves circular buildings.

Acted in 1622, *The Changeling* was not printed until 1653, in a text deriving from a promptbook. Despite the tinkering and recopying the manuscript may have undergone in the interim, the main plot presents few obscurities of staging. In iii iv, when Beatrice seeks to pay off De Flores, editors supply no direction, but since she shows him 'three thousand golden florins' she presumably throws open a chest (normally the male seducer's prerogative in his assault on innocent virginity, as in *Volpone* and *The Revenger's Tragedy*). In iii ii how does De Flores kill Alonzo? Editors, followed by directors, have him stab his victim with the sword he has hidden, but the dialogue implies something more elaborate. The episode begins with De Flores showing Alonzo the keys to the castle: 'here are all the keys . . . this for the sconce'. 'Sconce' (small fort) carries a sadistic pun on the sense 'head', covertly signalling De Flores's intention to club Alonzo with the same heavy key he is inviting him to inspect. He duly does this at lines 13–15 ('Take special note of that sconce before you . . . I am upon't . . . And so am I'), running to retrieve the sword while Alonzo is staggering from the blow.

The subplot is a different matter. Though its parodying of the themes and action of the main plot remains clear, it seems to have been heavily abridged, making the surviving version hard to follow on the stage. (A reader, aided by speech-prefixes, stage-directions, and the *dramatis personae* list, is apt to overlook the severity of the problems.) To begin with, the introduction of the fake lunatics into the madhouse is very abrupt. There is no hint that they are gentlemen from Vermandero's castle (a narrative element clearly meant to endorse the parallelism of the two plots) until iv ii 5, when they are about to be arrested. Antonio is at least given his name in the dialogue of i ii, but his escort Pedro, who is never seen or heard of again, remains nameless to the audience, and the fact that Antonio is shamming is not disclosed until iii iii 16, when he propositions Isabella. One could defend this last feature on the ground that the play's governing concern with the deceptiveness of appearance is thereby brought directly home to the audience, but the treatment of Franciscus is even more cryptic. No episode dramatises his arrival at the madhouse, and throughout his first appearance in iii iii there is nothing to indicate that he is not a genuine lunatic. Moreover, he is not named in this scene, so that when 'Antonio and Franciscus' are declared the suspected murderers of Alonzo in iv ii, and Isabella reads out the letter signed 'Franciscus' in iv iii, the audience has no means of identifying this person as the madman of iii iii. It is not until he next appears at iv iii 158, still mad and still unnamed, and

Lollio explains 'This is th'other counterfeit' that, for the audience, light begins to dawn, and even then the connection with the disappeared gentlemen of the castle can easily be missed. What seems to be lacking is a preliminary scene in which Antonio and Franciscus's identities and motives are firmly established.

A scene in Act v may also have gone. Plans are laid as early as III iii 251ff. to draw the two plots together with a wedding-masque at Beatrice's nuptials, danced by lunatics supplied by Alibius. Anticipation of its performance is boosted in IV iii when Lollio schemes first with Antonio, then with Franciscus, both of whom will participate, for each to kill the other at the masque's end. None of this comes to anything. The masque is not presented before the main-plot newly-weds, the fake madmen do not confront each other, nor is their public exposure dramatised, and Beatrice and De Flores never learn that other people have been arrested for their crime. If a missing scene is to blame its loss is serious, for the masque, danced by madmen and culminating in attempted murder, would have achieved a dovetailing of main and subplots which was both narrative and thematic, as Beatrice watched an image of the moral madness to which she has herself succumbed.[26]

These snags have not stopped *The Changeling* from being Middleton's most performed play, though they may explain why the subplot is sometimes dropped altogether. Having seen some dozen productions, I have observed various interpretative trends. De Flores is usually made the dominating figure, with the accent on his malevolence and erotic mania. This can, however, make the view of him as 'honest De Flores' which several characters share seem odd if not incredible, as well as suppressing the idea, which the text explicitly encourages at v iii 112–13, that he is Beatrice's 'prey' as well as she his. Similarly, if the commonest rendering of Beatrice as a spoiled child is overdone it can fail to explain why three men find her so fascinating, and if she is later shown as simply emboldened by sin the sense of her continuing isolation and vulnerability, evident in such floundering admissions as 'I must trust somebody', can be lost. Most productions treat the main plot's secondary characters neutrally, to give prominence to the two principals. Some, however, exploit the arranged marriage, Vermandero's determination to have his 'will', and Alsemero's virginity-test to present Beatrice's father and husband as representatives of patriarchal oppression, through which a sense of her as victim as well as criminal can emerge.

The subplot is more freely handled. Inevitably, in view of critics' emphasis on their importance, the madmen tend to make non-textual appearances, often lurking in the wings during the main-plot scenes. Less defensibly, I have seen several Isabellas whose flirtatiousness undermined the intended contrast with Beatrice. (In Elia Kazan's production at the Lincoln Center, New York in 1964, Antonio actually seduced her.) Most directors strive to make the subplot more intelligible, at least by having Antonio and Franciscus reveal their imposture to the audience when they first appear. A much bolder intervention occurred in the Contact Theatre production in Manchester in 1985. Diaphanta replaced Pedro as Antonio's escort, to tie him in with the castle. As the conclusion, the declarations of forgiveness between Isabella and Alibius in v iii were tacked onto the end of Act iv, after a veiled Isabella, dressed as a bride to resemble Beatrice, danced in turn with Antonio and Franciscus, and then unmasked them and herself while her husband looked on. The business of the mistaken arrests and the subplot characters' contribution to the final recitation of 'changes' were therefore lost, but there was a gain in coherence.[27]

SOURCE: first published in this Casebook.

NOTES

1. David L. Frost (ed.), *The Selected Plays of Thomas Middleton* (1978), p. xiii.

2. Jackson I. Cope, 'The Date of *Women Beware Women*', *Modern Language Notes*, LXXVI (1961), pp. 295–300.

3. Cf. *The Black Book*, p. 20; *Timon of Athens*, III ii 38; *The Revenger's Tragedy*, IV ii 55; *Your Five Gallants*, I i 12; and *The Old Law*, I i 269 (also referring to a character's age). Note also *A Trick to Catch the Old One*, II i 134–42: 'fifty-four . . . a man of wisdom'.

4. See Dorothy M. Farr, *Thomas Middleton and the Drama of Realism* (Edinburgh, 1973), pp. 126–7, and N. W. Bawcutt's notes in his edition of *The Changeling* (1958), I i 8, III iv 167, and v ii 54–5.

5. The spoken text of *Women Beware Women* is 25 151 words long, shorter only than *No Wit, No Help Like a Woman's* (25 465). The average length of Middleton's unaided plays, excluding the abnormally short *A Yorkshire Tragedy*, is 19 133 words.

6. See Marjorie S. Lancaster, 'Middleton's Use of the Upper Stage in *Women Beware Women*', *Tulane Studies in English*, XXII (1977), pp. 73–5.

7. For further couplings of windows and whoredom in Middleton, see *A Chaste Maid in Cheapside*, v i 161; *Hengist, King of Kent*, III i 143; and *More Dissemblers Besides Women*, v i 134.

8. Middleton also puns on 'aunt' 'uncle', and 'niece' in these senses in *A Mad World, My Masters*, III ii 237–8, *A Trick to Catch the Old One*, II i 11–13, 257, and *A Chaste Maid in Cheapside*, where Sir Walter Whorehound and his whore the Welsh Gentlewoman pose as uncle and niece.

9. I ii 65–7. Hippolito and Isabella as thus already sealed in 'the dead sleep of adultery' (*The Second Maiden's Tragedy*, I ii 226).

10. G. B. Shand, 'The Stagecraft of *Women Beware Women*', *Research Opportunities in Renaissance Drama*, XXVIII (1985), pp. 29–36. In view of this stress on apartness, the Revels edition is probably wrong to make the Mother exit at III i 81 and re-enter with Bianca at III ii 27. In the original text she remains on stage and Leantio's speech on his return is an aside, leaving Bianca to enter alone. This staging creates a more powerful image of the disunion attendant on Bianca's corruption.

11. See Neil Taylor and Bryan Loughrey, 'Middleton's Chess Strategies in *Women Beware Women*', *Studies in English Literature 1500–1900*, XXIV (1984), pp. 341–54.

12. Note too that Hippolito's cry that the poison 'runs through my blood, in a wild flame' (v ii 139) connects ironically with his earlier declaration that the prospect of killing Leantio, in order to save Livia from the 'poison' of a base match, 'Puts fire into my blood' (IV ii 14–16).

13. '"Enter Above": The Staging of *Women Beware Women*', *Studies in English Literature 1500–1900*, XXVI (1986), pp. 338–9.

14. 'The Stagecraft of *Women Beware Women*', pp. 33–4.

15. '"Enter Above": The Staging of *Women Beware Women*', pp. 331–43.

16. Marilyn Roberts, 'A Preliminary Check-List of Productions of Thomas Middleton's Plays', *Research Opportunities in Renaissance Drama*, XXVIII (1985), pp. 37–61. Most of the productions are by student groups.

17. For more details of these and other productions, see Shand, 'The Stagecraft of *Women Beware Women*', pp. 29–36; J. R. Mulryne, ed., *Women Beware Women* (1975), pp. lxxvi–lxxix; and Angel Luis Pujante, 'Leantio as an Outsider in Middleton's *Women Beware Women*: Text and Performance', *Atlantis*, VII (1985), pp. 9–17. For reviews of later productions, see *Research Opportunities in Renaissance Drama*, XXII (1979), p. 81; *Renaissance Drama Newsletter*, VI, no. 2 (1985), pp. 6–8; no. 3 (1986), pp. 12–14; and *The Times*, 6 and 7 February 1986.

18. See Dale B. J. Randall, 'Some Observations on the Theme of Chastity in *The Changeling*', *English Literary Renaissance*, XIV (1984), pp. 347–66. The tests which Randall cites are from the previous century or earlier, and derive from Pliny or gipsy lore.

19. See R. V. Holdsworth, 'Sexual Puns in Middleton, Chapman, and Dekker', *Notes and Queries*, CCXXIX (1984), pp. 242–7.

20. For a perceptive discussion of the alternatives, see M. Kelsall, *Studying Drama: An Introduction* (1985), pp. 4–6.

21. Middleton had previously used sexual ring-and-finger allusions in *A Chaste Maid in Cheapside*, I i 175 and III i 14–18; see the notes in R. B. Parker's edition (1969). For further discussion of the idea in *The Changeling*, see J. Chesley Taylor, 'Metaphors of the Moral World: Structure in *The Changeling*', *Tulane Studies in English*, XX (1972), pp. 41–56, and Penelope B.

R. Doob, 'A Reading of *The Changeling*', *English Literary Renaissance*, III (1973), pp. 183–206.

22. Quoted by G. R. Owst, *Literature and Pulpit in Medieval England* (Cambridge, 1933), pp. 80–1.

23. Anne Lancashire, 'The Emblematic Castle in Shakespeare and Middleton', in *Mirror up to Shakespeare*, ed. J.C. Gray (1984), p. 232.

24. Middleton had already invoked this parallel in *A Yorkshire Tragedy*, where the Husband is a 'serpent' destined for 'that pit bottomless' (ix 7, x 22).

25. Ann Pasternak Slater, 'Hypallage, Barley-Break, and *The Changeling*', *Review of English Studies*, XXXIV (1983), pp. 438–9, notes that the audience cannot be sure, until Beatrice and De Flores emerge bleeding, whether her cries are cries of orgasm or of anguish. Compare *A Mad World*, III ii, where Harebrain, who is being cuckolded, interprets his wife's offstage cries as weeping.

26. A further sign of compression in the finale is the surprising absence of Lollio and Jasperino, which may be the result of doubling of parts in the production from which the printed text derives. For a defence of the subplot as it stands, see Sarah P. Sutherland, *Masques in Jacobean Tragedy* (1983), pp. 103–11.

27. For reviews of major recent productions, see *Research Opportunities in Renaissance Drama*, XVII (1974), p. 63; XXI (1978), pp. 68–70; XXVII (1984), pp. 136–8; XXIX (1986), pp. 64-5; *Plays and Players*, XXVI, no. 4 (1979), p. 13; *The Observer*, 22 October 1978, p. 33; *The Times*, 6 September 1978; p. 17; *Country Life*, 30 June 1988, p. 225; and Michael Scott, *Renaissance Drama and a Modern Audience* (1982), pp. 86–8.

APPENDIX:
THE CANON OF MIDDLETON'S PLAYS

Dates of performance and order of composition are often uncertain; * = lost;
c = comedy; tc = tragicomedy; t = tragedy.

	Date	Type	Theatre Company
Caesar's Fall (with Dekker, Drayton, Munday and Webster)	1602	t	Admiral's
*Unnamed play	1602	?	Worcester's
Randal, Earl of Chester	1602	t	Admiral's
The Family of Love (with Dekker)	1602–3	c	Admiral's?
The Phoenix	1603–4	c	Paul's
The Honest Whore Part One (with Dekker)	1604	c	Prince Henry's
A Mad World, My Masters	1604–6	c	Paul's
A Trick to Catch the Old One	1604–6	c	Paul's
Michaelmas Term	1605–6	c	Paul's
A Yorkshire Tragedy	1605–8	t	King's
Timon of Athens (with Shakespeare)	1605–8	t	King's
The Revenger's Tragedy	1606	t	King's?
*The Viper and Her Brood	1606	t	Queen's Revels
The Puritan	1606	c	Paul's
Your Five Gallants	1606–7	c	Queen's Revels
The Roaring Girl (with Dekker)	1611	c	Prince Henry's
The Second Maiden's Tragedy	1611	t	King's
No Wit, No Help Like a Woman's	1611	c	Lady Elizabeth's?
A Chaste Maid in Cheapside	1613	c	Lady Elizabeth's
Wit at Several Weapons (with Rowley)	1613	c	?
The Witch	1614–16	tc	King's
A Fair Quarrel (with Rowley)	1615–16	tc	Prince Charles'
The Nice Valour	1615–16	tc	?
The Widow	c.1616	c	King's
Hengist, King of Kent	c.1616–20	t	?

The Old Law (with Rowley)	c.1618	tc	?
More Dissemblers Besides Women	c.1619	tc	King's
Women Beware Women	c.1621	t	?
Anything for a Quiet Life (with Webster)	1621	c	King's
The Changeling (with Rowley)	1622	t	Lady Elizabeth's
A Game at Chess	1624	c	King's

In addition there are passages by Middleton, the number and extent of which are hard to define, in the extant text of *Macbeth* (King's Men, 1606); they include two songs which appear in full in *The Witch*. Two lost and undatable plays – *The Conqueror's Custom, or The Fair Prisoner* and *The Puritan Maid, the Modest Wife, and the Wanton Widow* – were attributed to Middleton some thirty years after his death.

SELECT BIBLIOGRAPHY

EDITIONS

The current standard edition of Middleton by A. H. Bullen (8 vols, 1885–86) is highly unsatisfactory, not least because it contains two plays which are not by Middleton and omits eight, one of them *The Revenger's Tragedy*, which are. A new *Complete Dramatic Works*, to be published by the Clarendon Press in the 1990s, will remedy these deficiencies. Meanwhile, *The Revenger's Tragedy*, *Women Beware Women* and *The Changeling* are edited together by B. Loughrey and N. Taylor in *Thomas Middleton: Five Plays* (Harmondsworth, 1988), and the last two are included in *The Selected Plays of Thomas Middleton*, edited by David L. Frost (1978).

A facsimile of the first quarto of *The Revenger's Tragedy* has been edited, with an excellent introduction, by MacDonald P. Jackson (1983). The fullest modern-spelling edition is by R. A. Foakes (1966). However, its introduction, text and commentary contain errors and oversights caused by the editor's failure to treat the play as by Middleton; a few of these are corrected by D. J. Lake, *Notes and Queries*, ccxvi (1971), pp. 455–6. The best edition of *Women Beware Women*, by J. R. Mulryne (1975), is also not wholly trustworthy; for a detailed review see *Review of English Studies*, xxix (1978), pp. 88–93. N. W. Bawcutt's edition of *The Changeling* (1958) can be less reservedly recommended; corrections are offered by T. W. Craik, *Notes and Queries*, ccxxii (1977), pp. 120–2, and ccxxv (1980), pp. 324–7, and R. V. Holdsworth, *Notes and Queries*, ccxxxiv (1989), pp. 344–6.

CRITICAL STUDIES

1. The following contain useful studies of all three plays

R. H. Barker, *Thomas Middleton* (1958).

M. C. Bradbrook, *Themes and Conventions of Elizabethan Tragedy* (Cambridge, 1935).

Nicholas Brooke, *Horrid Laughter in Jacobean Tragedy* (1979).

David L. Frost, *The School of Shakespeare* (Cambridge, 1968).

Irving Ribner, *Jacobean Tragedy: The Quest for Moral Order* (1962).

Christopher Ricks, 'The Tragedies of Webster, Tourneur and Middleton: Symbols, Imagery and Conventions', in *English Drama to 1710*, ed. Christopher Ricks, Sphere History of Literature in the English Language, vol. iii (1971).

Samuel Schoenbaum, *Middleton's Tragedies* (New York, 1955).

2. *The Revenger's Tragedy*

Philip J. Ayres, *Tourneur: 'The Revenger's Tragedy'* (1977).

Larry S. Champion, 'Tourneur's *The Revenger's Tragedy* and the Jacobean Tragic Perspective', *Studies in Philology*, LXXII (1975), pp. 299–321.

Daniel J. Jacobson, *The Language of 'The Revenger's Tragedy'* (Salzburg, 1974).

Alvin Kernan, *The Cankered Muse* (New Haven, 1959).

B. J. Layman, 'Tourneur's Artificial Noon: The Design of *The Revenger's Tragedy*', *Modern Language Quarterly*, XXXIV (1973), pp. 20–35.

Peter Lisca, '*The Revenger's Tragedy:* A Study in Irony', *Philological Quarterly*, XXXVIII (1959), pp. 242–51.

Michael E. Mooney, '"This Luxurious Circle": Figurenposition in *The Revenger's Tragedy*', *English Literary Renaissance*, XIII (1983), pp. 162–81.

Samuel Schoenbaum, '*The Revenger's Tragedy:* Jacobean Dance of Death', *Modern Language Quarterly*, XV (1954), pp. 201–7.

J. L. Simmons, 'The Tongue and Its Office in *The Revenger's Tragedy*', *PMLA*, XCII (1977), pp. 56–68.

3. *Women Beware Women* and *The Changeling*

A. A. Bromham, 'Political Meaning in *Women Beware Women*', *Studies in English Literature 1500–1900*, XXVI (1986), pp. 309–29.

Lois E. Bueler, 'The Rhetoric of Change in *The Changeling*', *English Literary Renaissance*, XIV (1984), pp. 95–113.

Anthony Dawson, '*Women Beware Women* and the Economy of Rape', *Studies in English Literature 1500–1900*, XXVII (1987), pp. 303–20.

Penelope B. R. Doob, 'A Reading of *The Changeling*', *English Literary Renaissance*, III (1973), pp. 183–206.

Douglas Duncan, 'Virginity in *The Changeling*', *English Studies in Canada*, IX (1983), pp. 25–35.

Helen Gardner, 'Milton's "Satan" and the Theme of Damnation in Elizabethan Tragedy', *Essays and Studies*, I (1948), pp. 46–66.

G. R. Hibbard, 'The Tragedies of Thomas Middleton and the Decadence of the Drama', *Renaissance and Modern Studies*, I (1957), pp. 35–64.

Paula Johnson, 'Dissimulation Anatomized: *The Changeling*', *Philological Quarterly*, LVI (1977), pp. 329–38.

Dorothea Krook, *Elements of Tragedy* (1969).

Richard Levin, *The Multiple Plot in English Renaissance Drama* (1971).

R. B. Parker, 'Middleton's Experiments with Comedy and Judgement', in *Jacobean Theatre*, ed. J. R. Brown and B. Harris, *Stratford-upon-Avon Studies*, vol. I (1960).

John Potter, '"In Time of Sports": Masques and Masking in Middleton's *Women Beware Women*', *Papers on Language and Literature*, XVIII (1982), pp. 368–83.

L. G. Salingar, '*The Changeling* and the Drama of Domestic Life', *Essays and Studies*, XXXII (1979), pp. 80–96.

J. L. Simmons, 'Diabolical Realism in Middleton and Rowley's *The Changeling*', *Renaissance Drama*, XI (1980), pp. 135–70.

Ann Pasternak Slater, 'Hypallage, Barley-Break, and *The Changeling*', *Review of English Studies*, XXXIV (1983), pp. 429–40.

NOTES ON CONTRIBUTORS

WILLIAM ARCHER (1856–1924): Critic, editor and journalist, translator of Ibsen and evangeliser of his theatrical gospel and works. Archer was drama critic of the *London Figaro* (1879–81), *World* (1884–1905), *Tribune* (1905–8) and *Nation* (1908–10).

J. B. BATCHELOR: Fellow of New College, Oxford; his publications include *The Edwardian Novelists* and a study of H. G. Wells.

N. W. BAWCUTT: Reader in English Literature in the University of Liverpool; he has edited plays by Ford, Marlowe and Shakespeare.

FREDSON BOWERS (born 1905): distinguished bibliographer and textual critic, formerly Professor of English in the University of Virginia; his work in Renaissance drama includes major editions of Dekker and Marlowe.

JOHN CHURTON COLLINS (1848–1908): literary critic and Professor of English in the University of Birmingham (1904–08); a vigorous antagonist of the 'belle-lettriste' approach to literary criticism, he worked hard in his teaching and many writings to establish English literature as an academic discipline.

T. S. ELIOT (1888–1965): poet, dramatist and critic.

UNA ELLIS-FERMOR (1894–1958): Professor of English at Bedford College, University of London; she published many works of drama criticism, editions of plays by Marlowe and Greville, and translations of plays by Ibsen.

WILLIAM EMPSON (1906–84): distinguished critic and poet, working initially at Cambridge and subsequently in universities overseas, then Professor of English in the University of Sheffield (1953–71). His critical works include *Seven Types of Ambiguity*, *The Structure of Complex Words* and *Milton's God*.

EDWARD ENGELBERG: Professor of Comparative Literature, Brandeis University; his publications include studies on Yeats and on literary consciousness (*The Unknown Distance*).

INGA-STINA EWBANK (EKEBLAD): Professor of English in the University of Leeds; she has published many essays on Renaissance drama and a study of the Brontës.

DAVID L. FROST: Professor of English in the University of Newcastle, New South Wales; his publications include *The School of Shakespeare*.

WILLIAM HAZLITT (1778–1836): essayist, critic and political publicist; his critical writings on the Elizabethans had an important influence on literary appreciation in the nineteenth century.

R. V. HOLDSWORTH: Lecturer in English in the University of Manchester; his publications on Middleton include the 'New Mermaid' edition of *A Fair Quarrel*, and he is the editor of the Casebooks on Webster: *'The White Devil' & 'The Duchess of Malfi'* and Jonson: *'Every Man in his Humour' & 'The Alchemist'*.

JAMES RUSSELL LOWELL (1819–91): American writer, editor and diplomatist; best known for his satirical *Biglow Papers*, he was the first editor of the *Atlantic Monthly* (1857–61) and Longfellow's successor as Professor of Modern Languages at Harvard.

PETER B. MURRAY: Professor of English at Macalester College, Minnesota; author of *A Study of John Webster* and *Thomas Kyd*.

NATHANIEL RICHARDS (fl. 1630–60): poet and dramatist, author of *The Tragedy of Messalina*.

CHRISTOPHER RICKS: King Edward VII Professor of English Literature in Cambridge (1975–85) and currently Professor of English in the University of Boston, Massachusetts; his publications include major studies of Milton, Keats, Tennyson and T. S. Eliot.

L. G. SALINGAR: Fellow of Trinity College, Cambridge; his works include *Shakespeare and the Tradition of Comedy* and *Dramatic Form in Shakespeare and the Jacobeans*.

JOHN STACHNIEWSKI: Lecturer in English in the University of Manchester; his publications include essays on Burton, Donne and Shakespeare.

A. C. SWINBURNE (1837–1909): poet and critic; his writings in criticism include essays and monographs on Shakespeare and other dramatists, and articles on poets and playwrights in contemporary editions of the *Encyclopaedia Britannica*.

JOHN ADDINGTON SYMONDS (1840–93): man of letters; he wrote extensively on the Italian renaissance, translated Benvenuto Cellini's autobiography, and published books on Shelley and Whitman.

HERMANN ULRICI (1806–84): German scholar; professor of philosophy at the University of Halle, he wrote studies on Greek poetry and on Shakespeare.

ACKNOWLEDGEMENTS

The editor and publishers wish to thank the following for permission to use copyright material: John B. Batchelor, extract from essay on 'The Pattern of *Women Beware Women*' in *Yearbook of English Studies*, 2 (1972), by permission of Modern Humanities Research Association and the Editor; N. W. Bawcutt, extract from the Introduction to *The Changeling* (Revels Plays), (1958), by permission of Manchester University Press; Fredson Bowers, extract from *Elizabethan Revenge Tragedy, 1587–1642* (1940), by permission of Princeton University Press, Copyright © 1940 renewed 1968 by Princeton University Press; T. S. Eliot, extracts from *Selected Essays* (1932), by permission of Faber and Faber Ltd.; Una Ellis-Fermor, extracts from *The Jacobean Drama* (1936), revised edition, Methuen & Co. (1958), by permission of Associated Book Publishers (UK) Ltd.; William Empson, extract from *Some Versions of Pastoral* (1935), by permission of Chatto and Windus Ltd. and Lady Empson; Edward Engelberg, essay on 'Tragic Blindness in *The Changeling* and *Women Beware Women*' in *Modern Language Quarterly*, 23 (1962), by permission of Modern Language Quarterly; Inga-Stina Ewbank, extract from essay on 'On the Authorship of *The Revenger's Tragedy*', writing as I.–S. Ekeblad, in *English Studies*, 41 (1960) by permission of Swets & Zeitlinger B.V., and essay on 'Realism and Morality in *Women Beware Women*' in *Essays and Studies*, 22 (1969) by permission of John Murray Publishers Ltd. and the English Association; David L. Frost, extracts from editorial commentary in *The Selected Plays of Thomas Middleton* (1978), by permission of Cambridge University Press; Peter B. Murray, extracts from *A Study of Cyril Tourneur* (1964), by permission of University of Pennsylvania Press; Christopher Ricks, essay on 'The Moral and Poetic Structure of *The Changeling*' in *Essays in Criticism*, 10 (1960), by permission of Essays in Criticism, and essay on 'Word-play in *Women Beware Women*' in *Review of English Studies*, 12 (1961), by permission of Oxford University Press; L. G. Salingar, essay on '*The Revenger's Tragedy* and the Morality Tradition' in *Scrutiny*, 6 (1937–38), by permission of Cambridge University Press; John Stachniewski, essay on 'Calvinist Psychology in the Tragedies of Middleton', by permission of the author.

Every effort has been made to trace all the copyright holders but if any have been inadvertently overlooked the publishers will be pleased to make the necessary arrangement at the first opportunity.

INDEX

Note. Since discussion of *The Revenger's Tragedy*, *The Changeling* and *Women Beware Women* also occurs outside the sections of this Casebook nominally devoted to them, references to the plays themselves, as well as to their characters, are included in the index.